How you can make

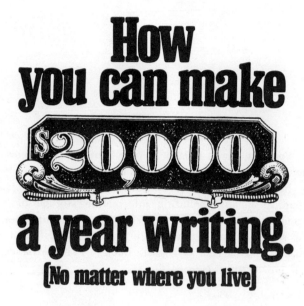

$20,000

a year writing.
(No matter where you live)

Cincinnati, Ohio

Prices and rates quoted in this book were current at the time of its first printing; they are subject to change due to changing economic conditions.

First printing, 1980
Second printing, 1981
Third printing, 1982

Library of Congress Cataloging in Publication Data
Hanson, Nancy Edmonds, 1949-
    How you can make $20,000 a year writing (no matter where you live)
    Includes index.
    1. Authorship. I. Title
PN147.H313   808'.025   79-22725
ISBN 0-89879-011-5 (cloth)
ISBN 0-89879-025-5 (paper)

Book design by Barron Krody

To Cal Olson, Howard Binford, and Bill Miller—who've
taught me writing is a joyful pursuit,
and Russ, who cheers me on.

Contents

Introduction: **1**
To Hell With Manhattan

1   9

You're About to Become an Entrepreneur: The Creative Approach to Hometown Freelancing

The myth of the starving freelancer/Fear of freelancing (only normal)/Negative thoughts and positive answers/The traditional approach is not enough/How to make your dream work: creative freelancing.

2

21

Getting Down to Business

The right time to go freelance/Cutting your risks and improving the odds/Scouting out your prospects/The best and the brightest opportunities/Start-up insurance: a financial cushion/Building your experience bank.

3

38

Nuts and Bolts Beginnings

Setting up/Ins and outs of offices/Controlling your overhead/The Ma Bell connection/Working furniture/ Equipment/Supplies/Stationery/Your friend, the mailman (and when to phone instead)/A boonie-writer's guide to T & E/Deductive reasoning—get an accountant.

4

55

Make Them an Offer
They Can't Refuse

The (nearly irresistible) appeal of freelancers—how to put it to work for you/Raising the freelance consciousness of your chosen place/Setting your income goal/Your hourly income guideline/Making assignments measure up/Should you *ever* write for free?

5

69

Magazine Writing
for the Nonmetropolitan

The truth about magazine writing today/Psyching out the markets from your special perspective/How your address affects your salability—making it work for you/Bad bets/Even bets/The six best magazine stories for writers anywhere.

6 104

Easy Access Markets: No Matter Where You Live

Regionals: your closest and best article markets/Why they can do more for you than meets the eye/How to approach regionals/Their varying styles and their favorite stories/Newspaper pitfalls and pay-offs/How to make good markets out of marginals/Finding gaps you can fill/Stringing along with all kinds of clients.

7 127

Photography (Picture the Possibilities)

Getting good photos when and where you need them—it's up to you/How photography fits in/How photos can brighten the picture for boonie writers/Finding a photo collaborator/Managing it yourself/Cameras and films and how to focus/Learn by doing/Learning more.

8 143

Book Writing in the Boonies

The hard-headed advantages of book writing/Why you should do your first book *now*/The odds are better than you think/Finding a national publisher/The realities of regional pubishing/Do-it-all-yourself publishing/Sponsored books and premiums/A checklist for weighing your options.

9

168

Editing, Copy Editing, and the Ghost

Editing jobs are everywhere—how to find them/A short course in hometown editing/The peculiar skills of copy editors and freelance editors/How to locate copy to edit/Ghostwriting in your own hometown/Business tips on speechwriting and ghostwriting.

10

190

Writing for Voice and Visuals: A-V Markets

Making the switch from print to A-V/The varieties of A-V writing prospects/A technical primer for the novice/How to find potential clients/Creating filmscripts/Freelancing for radio and television/How to develop and sell your ideas.

11

211

Bread and Butter Writing

A word from your sponsors/Commercial writing—respectable jobs that pay off big and keep on coming/How to sell your services to clients/Brochures and reports/Production pointers: a graphic introduction.

12

224

PR Prospects

Why writers are ideal sources of local PR expertise/Dealing with newsmakers and newsgatherers/Working with your clients/The media need you, too/A guide to professional media releases/Using photos/News conferences/Public service announcements.

13 238
Great Grant Writing
A means to your ends and an end in itself/Reaching the people who hand out money/How to find potential clients/The basics of great grant writing/How to build yourself into your proposal/Writing a final report that insures new assignments.

14 245
Writers Out Loud: Working With Students and Strangers
Public speaking possibilities/Coming out of the woodwork can pay off in more ways than one/Lectures/The convention circuit/Freelance advice-giving/Teaching options/A meeting-planner's survival guide.

15 259
Epilogue
The $20,000 perspective/Rhythms and rewards of the freelance life/Take stock, take note, take heart.

Introduction:
To Hell With Manhattan

Geography giveth, but geography also taketh away.

One of the things it taketh the quickest is the dream of life as a freelance writer. Not just life—making a decent living with your own words, your own ingenuity, your own particular gift for communicating in print.

Oh, geography doesn't take away the whole cake. Wherever fate or fortune has planted you, it leaves you tantalizing tastes of what freelancing might be like. It allows you to savor the half dozen natural stories that sprout within easy reach of your corner of the world and to sell them to minor or middle markets. It permits you to chortle over checks from publishers now and then.

But while you mine this apparently shallow vein, you're never for a minute allowed to forget that such sales are only occasional nuggets—hardly the Mother Lode. Your working friends, as brainwashed as you may be, echo the same creed: You can't succeed in freelancing no matter where you live, unless it's in New York.

The writers' magazines whet your appetite but feed it mostly undersized portions, along with enthusiastic lessons on how to succeed through hard work and rejection-proof optimism in selling stories for three-fourths of a cent per word. That's $7.50 for an article which takes a couple of hours or days (plus $1.25 in postage, $6.00 in photo supplies, and the price of several paper clips) to complete.

Obviously people do live by freelancing, but they certainly have assets geography has denied you. New York writers, living around the corner from Condé Nast, Harper & Row, Time/Life, and the thousand big and little houses on Publishers' Row—their advantages seem undeniable. Editors and other freelancers with whom to confer and commiserate. Monthly dinner meetings of professional writers. Agents' offices, and handy access to all those big eastern experts quoted in article after article. Same-day delivery of the *New York Times*. It all surely adds up to an ineluctable something that makes their work right and yours just off the mark.

Whatever it is, writers all over the rest of the country doubt that it grows in their own local climates. Yet they keep trying, keep hoping. . . and keep going to salaried jobs where they chat over coffee about making the big break to become freelancers themselves (privately called the Impossible Dream).

Poor old geography gets the blame.

And yet I have discovered the ideal place from which to launch a successful writing career.

It must be Bismarck. That's North Dakota, land of wide-open spaces, tumbleweeds, gophers, Herefords, wheat fields and badlands, a state blessed with the very fewest of native publication markets and perhaps the very least of the editorial world's curiosity and concern.

I've made a comfortable living here for years as a freelance writer, all the while enjoying the easy hometown atmosphere the "experts" on freelancing swore I'd have to give up to follow my dream full-time.

In Bismarck, I have happily discovered that where you live matters only if you're miserable there. I have become convinced that you can carve out a successful freelance career virtually anywhere you live or want to live.

You think, perhaps, that stories don't leap out at you in a place like North Dakota? True. A few do tumble past on their own, but if you don't search for most of them, they sit right where they are and await a hungrier writer, maybe from New York, to spot them.

Good assignments never wing their way Dakotaward?

Partly right; many start their lives right here on the prairie in the first place. Others make their dates with destiny in the same editorial offices in the same metropoli where Nora Ephron, Truman Capote, and all the major-market writers whose names inspire your envy sell their own proposals, and then get taken out to lunch.

The real money, though, isn't made by freelancers in states like North Dakota? Don't you believe it. But don't move to North Dakota. Stay right where you are and make your ambitions work in your own locale, in your own way.

North Dakota is mine.

What struggling New York writers have always had going for them is the certainty that they've come to the absolutely right place to launch their careers, the planetary capital of the publishing industry, where hundreds of others have come and succeeded before them. (Whether all those dreams actually come true is another story.)

What struggling North Dakota writers—and Georgians, Minnesotans, Utahans, West Virginians and all the rest—do not have going for us is the kind of tradition and camaraderie that New York writers possess.

And yet I have a hunch that my prospects in Bismarck were always better than those of the average uninitiated writer in New York. For when I stopped shivering at the cold, hard challenges I expected to face, there they were, waiting to be picked.

The same kinds of opportunities abound in your own backyard. That's what this book is all about. If I can live the comfortable, satisfying, exciting freelance life in North Dakota, it's a foregone conclusion that you can do it too—wherever you live right now, or wherever you want to live in the future.

You *can* overcome your terror of abject poverty as a freelancer of unconventional address and high-numbered zip code.

You *can* support a family as a full-time freelancer, even if it's never been done by anyone within your sight before.

You *can* live as you want to live, and earn the income you desire, without selling yourself to a corporate or governmental bidder. You can equal the income you receive on a regular job. And double the emotional rewards. You can even get all the satisfactions expected by the city folks who are rushing to move back to the land: You reap what grows from the freelance seeds you've sown and cultivated, and honestly do live by the work of your hands and mind.

And you *can* sleep until 10 a.m. if you feel like it.

The prerequisites include no mysteries. You take the risk and display the confidence you'll need to really explore its possibilities. You develop your skills as a writer. And you resolve to stay flexible so that you can enjoy and change with the challenging, shifting markets for your work.

There are two principles you'll have to adhere to like the True Faith, two keys that make the freelance life possible anywhere in the country.

One is that you must be as creative in the kinds of jobs you'll search out and tackle as you are in the "serious" creative writing you've produced in the past. I don't mean jobs driving street sweepers or rustling cattle. I do mean the enormous range of assignments that require solid research and writing, that challenge you perhaps as dramatically as a major magazine article or book, but which are unconventional enough to remain fallow and overlooked until you set out to invent or uncover them.

The second is that freelance writing is a business. Not a calling. Not a gift of the Muse. Not some kind of pure and sacred quest that's somehow cleaner and more noble than jobs you've held in the past. Nor is it an escape from all the pressures of employment which you lament as roadblocks to your creative flow.

It is a business. The bottom line can be survival, if you habitually set your sights on easy targets, or considerably more than survival, when you're ready for the challenge.

It is a business. You are selling your time, the unique background that makes your writing valuable and, yes, your daily ration of inspiration in return for a living and lifestyle that offers rewards like no other. You're selling those same natural resources no matter what kinds of assignments you tackle: major magazine articles, books, public relations-oriented publications, audio-visual writing, or whatever you come up with.

If you're ready to get out and hustle, if you're serious about freelancing in your community—well, then, I have some proven ideas for you to apply to your own setting.

Every word in this book is based on the experiences of your counterparts who've taken up the challenge and made it work for them. I have personally taken on every kind of writing assignment detailed here, some of them with prior training or experience, others with only the will to learn how to do them. Some methods I've invented (or thought I had, until I began talking to other successful freelancers in isolated areas who are convinced they invented them themselves). Others I've learned from books and magazines—books on writing, books on small business, books on a whole curious mishmash of subjects. But I have managed each of them sooner or later by hands-on practice.

So that you won't suspect that my freelancing in North Dakota is a lucky aberration, I've rounded up the experiences of old friends and new acquaintances who've also created exuberant freelance lives in the oddest locations.

To hell with Manhattan. We're engaged in demonstrating that the myths about how to make it as a freelancer are out of date.

You can make a good living as a freelance writer in the boonies, in the towns and suburbs, in the great American cities that do not happen to be New York. Like all of life's best dreams, you have to forge ahead on your own to make it happen.

I didn't start out as such a Norman Vincent Peale of freelance writing.

Like you, perhaps, I grew up in a town where there were three role models for daughters and roughly the same for sons. Girls: teachers, clerks, and mommies. (Even for nurses, you'd have to go to the nearest hospital, fifty miles northeast.) For boys, the choices were farming, owning a general store, and driving the Coke truck that called weekly.

But I had "Aunt Helen." I don't know if she ever lived and breathed, but she really did introduce kids in the Dakotas to freelancing through her children's page in the *Dakota Farmer*. I sent in four-line poems about my mother's brownies and one-paragraph essays on leopards and other important subjects, and savored the surprising pleasure of my first by-lines.

The pay wasn't so hot. When I was a third grader, it was

thirty-five cents per six acceptances (about the same as some of the minor markets still pay today). But I learned to bless geography for its special gifts. For of all the world's children, only we in the two Dakotas could earn this bounty.

Thus a seed was planted that sprouted over the years and grew into a vague idea of what I wanted to do—something so impossible that I never dared unveil it when we were assigned those high school essays on our career goals.

I continued to learn a bit here and there. I sold a story to a teen magazine at 14, and got a lesson in depending on magazine checks. It took two years to get paid (an experience that's been duplicated a time or two since, and dims that first proud flush at seeing your by-line). I succeeded only after sending the editor a second-anniversary card spotted with red Kool-Aid tears, a method I've held in reserve as my ultimate secret weapon ever since.

A freelance submission purchased by the state's largest daily newspaper got me a job offer at 17, back in the days before I knew newspapers never bought freelance submissions. And there I learned that reasonable people really did share my freelance writing dreams.

Approximately ninety-five percent of my colleagues saw that vision when they closed their eyes. We talked endlessly, over my eight years, of the two futures that tantalized us: breaking away to start the world's only truly ethical and victorious newspaper, or becoming freelance writers.

The world of victorious newspapering was left neither better nor worse for lack of me when I finally departed to take a position in government. I looked longingly at freelancing, but set it aside as unrealistic. I'd been a stringer for *New Times* and sold a dozen or so articles to regional and minor national markets, but had reluctantly concluded that it takes a whole lot of twenty-five-dollar checks to add up to the rent.

At that moment, I was totally taken in by the myth that freelancing can't work here—as brainwashed, under guise of realism, as you might be today.

I was wrong.

My two-plus years as assistant travel director for the

state taught me a great many things, among them hatred of eight-to-five jobs and long, intransigent chains of command. But more important, that job gave me a vantage point that most writers, isolated by geography and resignation to their fate, never get to share.

I began to see full-time freelancers. Real ones. And as they corresponded with me about tourism in North Dakota, I got a chance to observe their addresses.

Des Moines.

Charlotte.

Upper Michigan.

Utah.

Jackson, Wyoming.

Wyoming? That's the only state that makes us North Dakotans feel metropolitan. While some of the travel writers we worked with were retired, or freelanced on the side, a few—an *inspiring* few—really wrote nonfiction for a living and showed none of the normal signs of starvation.

This was the confirmation that everyone with impossible dreams longs for . . . and dreads. So it really could be done. I was enthralled.

I considered and dawdled, considered and retreated . . . coping as everyone does when the dream of freelancing suddenly seems both remotely possible and impossibly remote. I spent days making lists of ideas for stories and markets, and nights having hollow nightmares of humiliation and defeat. I studied every form of the printed word that I could find and noted that my skills were certainly good enough for cereal boxes, which have wider readership than any of the magazines I hoped to reach.

I took long coffee breaks and asked my friends' advice. They knew no more than I about the real odds, but were quick to advise that a writer could never make an independent living in our part of the country.

"You could do great. I just know it," one of the most loyal told me again and again. "But you'll have to get out of here."

Only one, a wildlife writer with some considerable national success, suggested I cut out the chitchat and give full-time freelancing a try. I valued his advice. But I'm allergic to half the grasses that grow on the prairie, and nearsighted, and though wildlife is one thing North Dakota has in abundance, I figured all that sneezing and squinting would scare the critters away.

My husband hates indecision. Finally he announced, "I can't stand any more of this whining. You have to try it. If you can't manage freelancing, you can always get another job."

My mother was horrified. I'd given up a secure job in government for this nonsense.

Relatives suggested that it was about time I realized a woman's place was in the home.

My writing friends envied me, and gave me six months.

Other acquaintances concluded I must be pregnant. For all I know, they're still waiting.

I was as scared as I'd ever been in my whole timid life, and as thrilled as the first time Aunt Helen said yes.

The fear goes away.

The delight doesn't.

I've learned to know my share of the country very, very well. More, I've learned to respect it for the many opportunities it offers me—some subtle, some so obvious that I'm truly amazed they were still here waiting for me when I finally was ready for them.

Freelancing may be a very exclusive career in this part of the world. But that only makes it better.

1

You're About to Become an Entrepreneur: The Creative Approach to Hometown Freelancing

Like yours, my attitudes toward freelancing were stunted in my youth (and for years thereafter) by the "realistic" assessment of its financial potential. While hope may spring eternal, depressing pronouncements by those in the know have proven just as perennial and a great deal less uplifting.

"Can you make a living at freelance writing? The best answer is 'no.'" —Nora Sayre. "How Free Is the Free-lance Writer?" *Mademoiselle*, March 1968.

"The average professional author earns insufficient income to live on." —William Jackson Lord, *How Authors Make a Living*, Scarecrow Press, 1962. (He concludes full-time freelancers he surveyed had an annual income of $3,055—in the mid-1950s, mind you, but still low when adjusted for inflation.)

"For most freelancers, magazine writing today has become the slum of journalism—overcrowded, underpaid, littered with rejection slips—and the denizens are growing restless."—"Grub Street Revisited," *Time*, April 10, 1978.

"Let's face it. If I were going to say anything at all about potential earnings in the magazine field, I'd have started . . . with You Too Can Earn Less Than a Trappist Monk in Your Spare Time—and Have More Aggravation

Than You Get in Your 40-Hour-a-Week Job. Most freelance magazine writers—were you to divide the number of hours they work into the number of dollars they earn—probably don't make the minimum wage." —Art Spikol, *Magazine Writing: The Inside Angle*, 1979.

There is not a great deal of hard, current data to rely on for realistic figures of what freelancers are making. The most reliable, a 1977 income survey by the American Society of Journalists and Authors, showed the median annual earnings of five hundred established writers polled to be ten thousand dollars.

And though every potential freelancer thinks of income first, that's not the only question that troubles those trying to decide whether to follow such a poorly-propheted career.

Do I have what it takes to be self-employed as a writer?

Will I find enough work to keep going?

Will my backlog of ideas run out?

Will I be up to managing all that unscheduled freedom and working without a boss hanging over my shoulder?

Am I talented enough?

Will my writing measure up?

Can I get others to believe in my talent and my ideas?

Will people laugh at me if it doesn't work out? If I fall on my face as a freelancer, will I have to leave town?

Can I risk my family's security and my own peace of mind on this silly writing dream? Really, now?

These are not doubts unique to writers. Anyone who's ever left employment to follow his own dream has been beset by the same worries, nagged by the same concerns. I know that I considered each and every one in labored detail.

Your doubts aren't just figments of a paranoid mind. They're a good counterweight to the adrenalized enthusiasm you feel when it first seems that freelancing is within your reach right where you are, whether under the bright lights of New York or the northern lights of Fairbanks, Alaska. Those who've been intimidated by those questions and backed out may have been saved a great deal of trouble, for I must concede that your prospects are glowing only if you pursue them to their utmost limits.

It does take more than a talent for words to make a living as a freelancer. A lot more. As a writer, you're joining the ranks of the self-employed, entrepreneurs who've tested themselves by more than a single standard—not just literary quality, but business sense; not just creative thinking, but the tenacity to overcome doubts and obstacles to success.

The U.S. Department of Commerce has sketched out a list of qualities they say are advantageous for anyone considering self-employment. They include getting a kick out of independence; genuinely liking people; thriving on responsibility; taking good and bad breaks in stride; learning from mistakes; juggling myriad details at once; and being businesslike in the use of time. "In other words," the booklet concludes, "he keeps his eyes wide open, is smart enough to seize a good bargain and honest enough not to take unfair advantage of anyone."

Perhaps you can round those qualities off as enjoying your work, enjoying people, and being willing to give the best of yourself to both.

Will you get enough assignments as you go along? If you must, I think you will. That's why self-supporting freelancers learn to be so flexible about the kinds of writing they tackle. Perhaps that's also why there seems to be a disproportionate share of male breadwinners among serious full-time freelancers, and more housewives or retired persons writing only occasional pieces on favored topics or for a few select minor markets.

To a large extent, you create your own work flow—through the volume of queries you produce, through the zeal with which you approach editors, through the numbers and kinds of proposals you make to commercial clients, and generally through the heightened enthusiasm you bring to the catalog of assignments and subjects that challenge you.

Will you run dry? Not likely. Ideas breed more ideas. The only time in my own life when I was in danger of running dry was when, as an employee of multiple bureaucratic hierarchies, I didn't really have to perform with increasing quality to hang on to my job. Too much security dries you up. The challenge of making a new living every month is going to keep those creative and curious juices flowing.

Will you have the self-discipline to manage the uncharted hours ahead of you? That's a universal question. It inspired all kinds of admiration among my friends on the eve of my own departure. "I'd never have the self-discipline to keep working," more than one whispered to me. (I suspect they eyed me speculatively as well, noting my record of unfinished Christmas projects, broken diets, and promises to write letters.)

Will you, then, be self-disciplined? I found I could be. You may find the same, but it depends. If you don't really need the income from your writing to survive, you will have to struggle against a million temptations, from researching a story endlessly and beyond reason to sneaking off to watch the soaps after lunch or taking off with fishing rod on a balmy afternoon.

But if you threw away your only visible means of support when you quit your job, and if you're stubborn enough to refuse to sabotage your own decision to go it on your own, you'll probably do just fine. Self-discipline as a freelancer is quite different from the kind you've struggled with on a job that leaves you listless, or a New Year's resolution that gives you mixed feelings on January 2. Self-discipline thrives in the atmosphere of intense interest in your income generated by the bank that holds your mortgage and your local utility company. In other words, when you have to work to live, the choice of whether or not to work is easier to make.

Are you talented enough? Is your writing stylistically dazzling? Listen. It truly is a myth that only those who write like angels can freelance successfully. More to the point, you've got to work like *hell*. My experience as a member of a couple of national writers' organizations has shown me, time and again, that the best writers don't necessarily make the best livings. The successful members are usually the solid (but sometimes unsensational) craftsmen who apply the most dedication to their trade.

Can you make others believe in you? Of all your fears, this is probably the most crucial. You can only answer the question for yourself, and often only after trial and error. You have to have something of a salesman's flair for convincing an editor who's never seen you that you can come through with a manuscript he's willing to buy, or for making an executive at the State Association for Midgets believe that, at five feet ten inches, you can empathize and research adequately to edit their organizational newsletter.

Unless you're one of the few who are genuinely reluctant to talk about your good points to total strangers (and not just patiently waiting for your chance), I do think you can "sell" yourself. When I say "sell," I mean it in its gentler but just as persuasive forms: demonstrating your qualities shamelessly rather than modestly shuffling your feet. Instilling trust among those you've never met. Appearing to be the kind of person who ought to be given a chance.

It's nothing like hawking those packets of overpriced garden seeds around your neighborhood as a kid, or peddling raffle tickets for the church men's group, or strong-arming political contributions from reluctant acquaintances. This is real life. This is you. Rather than fearing this aspect of freelancing, at times I've noticed myself beginning to enjoy it. After all, who else gets to reel off her accomplishments and background without the slightest blush of shame?

Your real problem is whether you're willing to promote yourself to editors and clients, not whether you have some brash, innate ability to do so. I'd never sold so much as a glass of nickel lemonade when I began. Now, on good days, I approach the promotional side of my business with as much enthusiasm as I bring to the writing of a story that entrances me; sometimes I have to fight myself to settle back down to the typewriter, in fact, instead of endlessly promoting new projects while leaving current assignments waiting.

Marketing yourself and your abilities is going to be as important to your survival as a freelancer in the boonies as your polished interviews, your clever turns of phrase and your self-correcting typewriter. You can learn it through any number of self-help books, through evening or college courses on salesmanship, through experience. But not everyone can learn to like it. If you cannot or will not sell your ideas on the open market, freelancing is as unlikely a career for you as real estate.

Will you have to leave town in humiliation if you try freelancing and fail? Every small business owner in the world has wondered that as he or she followed a dream and risked money and reputation on a new idea. Some of those ideas turned into IBM and Standard Oil. Others turned into statistical fodder; the Small Business Administration estimates that 90 percent of the new small businesses launched in your community this year won't be around in the same form five years from today. (Freelance writing, incidentally, is one of the categories of small business for which the SBA won't lend money.)

If all those people can try and fail, you can, too. But the odds that you'll really fail and give up are slim, if you bring your own enthusiasm and energy to a well-researched plan for freelancing. Some avenues will certainly turn out to be less lucrative or rewarding than others. The range of choices before you, however, is limited only by your own ambition and imagination.

You should really intend to succeed if you're going to give freelancing an honest try. You'll make mistakes almost surely, and you'll learn from them. The only really humiliating defeat for the freelancer is giving up too soon and later finding you were on the brink of success.

And you can succeed, no matter what the experts would have you believe. Freelance writers do make a living—a good living—in every part of the country. That ASJA median of ten thousand dollars a year is only part of the story. I've easily doubled that figure for years, and I've met dozens of counterparts with addresses as unlikely as mine who can say as much or quite a bit more.

Why, I wondered, were we different—living in what the freelancers Time quoted would consider No Man's Land?

The answers were buried in the same article that puzzled me.

Gay Talese: "There is no way you can prosper writing for magazines alone."

A few paragraphs later: "Says Literary Agent Scott Meredith, 'There are no writers left who can make a living just by articles.'"

That's just about what I'd figured out all by myself here in Bismarck, while my friends had been discovering it individually in the mountains, woods, lakeshores, and prairies of the land. Only we had had an initial advantage over the poor, disillusioned city writers: We'd sort of suspected it all along.

Flexibility. If you're going to write to eat, you can never, never afford to limit yourself to only one kind of writing. Not just major markets, though their fee scales look so tempting from a distance. Not just travel or women's or sports magazines. Not just newspapers, or regional publications, or even just one facet of the many commercial freelance assignments open to you in your own locale.

When you live in a place where no freelance writer's lived before, you carry fewer preconceptions about what freelancing means. We struggle and scheme simply to make our mark as writers, not as "writers for the top dozen major magazine markets" or bust.

If the only writing you think can give you pleasure is that packed between slick, full-color covers of magazines stocked in even the tiniest drugstore, you're not ready to burn your salaried bridges and become a freelancer where you live today.

The same's true if you harbor a little hierarchy of markets: all-out effort for Class A, half-hearted effort for Class B, and, for Class C, work that's slapped out on a hot, uninspired afternoon between cold cans of Coors.

If you're ready to meet the challenges of freelancing, you accept that every assignment is worth your best efforts. You accept that your classiest work is never "too good" for the clients who'll enable you to pay your rent. You acknowledge that Betty Friedan and Norman Mailer might not be impressed by some of the jobs you invite: the annual reports, the brochures, the monthly Elks Club newsletter. You also get used to the fact that they're not even looking.

One more thing. If you're serious about making a living by your writing in the community where you live, you seldom can afford to nurture the old news media prejudice that only work for magazine and book publishers "counts." You need to be willing to look at a client as a client, whether editor or association director or marketing manager for a local bank.

That doesn't mean you'll have to compromise your ethics by accepting assignments that involve lies or deception, or undermine and negate every value you hold dear. As a freelancer, you're in the best position of all to turn down those requests. You simply explain why you won't take them on in a civil tone of voice, and walk away.

But you may discover that commercial assignments are no more compromising per se than those given out by newspapers or magazines, who for equally commercial reasons you may never know find a certain query or manuscript exactly right for their readers . . . and their advertisers.

This may not sound like the kind of freelancing you expected to read about. There's a reason for that. Most freelancers I've met share a quirk that I think explains the contradiction.

Asked about our work, we first tell about the top magazines we've sold to. Then the best medium markets. Then every other that's ever carried our by-lines—right down to the time we were quoted in the *Reader's Digest*'s "Toward More Picturesque Speech" column. Only if pressed do we volunteer the other half of the story—which is that survival on these apparent triumphs alone can be a mite thin at times, no matter what address we call home.

Most freelancers who write magazine nonfiction have greatly expanded from their preconceptions about writing markets. I don't know one who'd turn down an invitation to write a lucrative, honest but anonymous annual report. Or sell reprint rights to a minor, minor publication market. Or who'd say no to the chance to edit the right newsletter, write for a good house organ, or develop publicity plans for a new civic group that the writer believes in.

To flourish, they've explored all the possibilities of the written word. They write books, sometimes for trade publishers, sometimes self-published, sometimes for commercial clients. They make minor markets pay, selling the same story to several publications, or perhaps through self-syndication to low-paying newspaper buyers. They create opportunities to use their expertise in other media—radio and TV, maybe, or by teaching and putting together seminars. They sample the smorgasbord of commercial opportunities that lie just beneath the surface in the average community.

They are open to new assignments, whether they're jacks-of-all-trades or specialists in a few subject areas. Basically they found their careers on the principle that freelance writers in the wilds of America need to be as creative in their marketing and media as they are in the articles they write.

And you should be, too.

I've learned firsthand to stay open to new opportunities.

But that wisdom came the hard way. Initially I set out to discover freelancing armed only with my tremulous confidence, lists of bright ideas to be pursued, and a secret fallback resolution (that come total disaster, I'd hunt up another job in six months).

Phase One of my freelance life was a heady time of endless cups of coffee beside my desk, carefully putting the dust cover back on the typewriter when I turned it off for the night, and fending off questions about whether I was pregnant.

I applied the principles that had worked for me in the past and helped sell my quarterly freelance manuscripts. I wrote brilliant query letters to the best and brightest markets. I took rejection in stride, and rejoiced over editorial go-aheads issued "on spec," with no guaranteed sale or kill fees.

No writer's block. No drought in the idea department, either. I wrote and polished half a dozen articles which editors had agreed to see. Typed error-free in perfect manuscript form (adopted from *Writer's Market*, for where else would I see a real manuscript in North Dakota?) and accompanied by immaculate self-addressed stamped envelopes, they fairly reeked of a newly minted freelancer's high hopes. I sent them away.

I waited.

And waited.

And.waited. There's nothing more pitiful than a grown woman waiting on the sidewalk for the mailman in January in Bismarck, North Dakota.

It began to dawn on me that following the rules I'd memorized from writers' magazines was not going to, of itself, insure my half of the household budget. While I was still gaily receiving the congratulations of colleagues and basking in compliments about my courageous and industrious nature, I was noticing that something was lacking in this perfect life.

It was cash.

I reconsidered my approach.

During Phase Two of my freelance career, I began to do what I should have done while my daydreaming was still underwritten by someone else's salary budget. I took stock of my local assets, personal and professional. I began to seriously study every permutation of the printed word around me. I multiplied my potential skills, and divided my monomaniacal attention to national markets, and came up with the conclusion that writers are as necessary here as they are in New York. Better yet, there were demonstrably fewer writers to fill those needs in North Dakota.

One major item on my inventory was my telephone file. I'd always thought of those men and women as friends or business acquaintances or highly placed sources. Now, as an independent, I knew they'd become something new and priceless: contacts.

They had for me an advantage not shared by the anonymous editors with whom I'd been corresponding. They already knew me, knew my work, and were accustomed to the far-out home addresses we generally had in common. They would know what I could do without query letters. All I had to do (all!) was convince them that they had an unrecognized need for outside writing help, and that I was conveniently available for their aid and comfort.

Also on my inventory were the local and regional publications and buyers of the written word most easily reachable from my home base. Like most casual freelancers-on-the-side, I'd disdained these easy markets in my attempts to crack *Redbook* and *Saturday Review*. I'd only occasionally looked at the handful of North Dakota magazines (two, actually) that buy the kind of writing I do best. I'd even less often stopped to reflect on how many nonwriters in business and government put words on paper every day, not because they want to, but because they have no facile writer to do it for them. Poor folks, they often loathe the whole idea of writing and would gladly turn it over to more willing and experienced hands.

While gazing at the top of the magazine mountain, that most remote of beginners' challenges, I seemed to have overlooked richer, sunnier valleys right here in the foothills.

During Phase Two, I mapped out that territory. Almost immediately I realized that here at home I could build a foundation that would support whatever writing challenges I'd eventually conquer.

In the words of the three-martini-lunchers, I began to send out feelers. I listened to the grapevine's news of who was doing what and needed help. I made no straightforward pitches to gain assignments during this period . . . but only because I wasn't to have enough time to get started before work began heading my way.

My telephone, which I'd previously had to dust to keep presentable, began to ring of its own volition. I was invited to offices for cups of coffee and casually loaded conversations. I bought a few coffees myself and had business cards designed to drop off as an afterthought.

The results? In six months my billings added up to exactly 150 percent of the salary—and it was respectable—I'd have received if I'd stayed employed. Most heartwarming of all was the speed with which my business was picking up; soon I didn't have time to count the minutes until the mailman's daily call.

Those six months included some assignments similar to ones I'd done on both my previous jobs, others I'd handled casually as a freelancer or sometime-volunteer, and a couple that had never before occurred to me. At the end of the first year, my tally included the following undertakings:

■ A continuing assignment as a humor columnist and book reviewer for *North Dakota Horizons*, the quarterly image magazine published by the state chamber of commerce.

■ Stories on energy development for the *North Dakota REC Magazine*, the other statewide magazine for a general audience, sponsored by an association of rural electric cooperatives.

■ A two-hundred page final report published in book form by the state bicentennial commission. By then their term was over and the staff dispersed, with no one but a freelancer to edit the bits and pieces of hundreds of local reports.

■ The first of many slide/tape productions, this one for the state's emergency radio network. It was accompanied by an illustrated booklet covering the same facts about a then-unique law enforcement communication system.

■ Planning and promotion of North Dakota's International Women's Year conference, a strictly part-time position including publications, publicity, and physical arrangements.

■ Several ghostwritten speeches for a highly placed state official whose office was too busy and too understaffed to handle them in-house.

■And all the queries and articles I could keep up with. Between these other projects, which captured more and more of my interest, they were beginning to reward me with both encouraging successes and the foundations of my magnificent rejection slip collection.

Now, even as I was cashing checks and improving my outlook day by day, I felt an uneasy tingling. Something had to be wrong. Freelancing couldn't be this rewarding in Bismarck, North Dakota . . . that's not how the books and articles said it would be. It wasn't bounded by sacrifice and desperate struggle.

In fact, it was fun.

2

Getting Down to Business

Only one person can tell you when the time is right to launch your freelance adventure.

That person is you.

Big help, isn't it? Especially when those around you—who depend on your income, say, or share your dream but haven't the courage to follow it themselves—are likely to have fixed notions about what constitutes the right time: When you've just inherited a secure income for life and want to avoid the stigma of becoming one of the idle rich. When you've just won the Publisher's Clearing House $100,000 giveaway.

■ When you've just inherited a secure income for life and want to avoid the stigma of becoming one of the idle rich.

■ When you've just won the Publisher's Clearing House $100,000 giveaway.

■ When you're ready to admit to the world you were a secret paramour of Richard Nixon's.

■ When *National Geographic* is begging for the story of your solo swim across the Great Slave Lake.

Most of those writers have found their own "right times" by instinct rather than calculation. Yet our experiences demonstrate that there actually can be a certain moment when the time is right for you to take the big step.

It's when you've finished your homework.

By delving into your market potential *before* you take the plunge into self-employed writerdom, you can allay your fears. You can afford to risk your family's financial security and a bit of your peace of mind to follow the freelance dream. But there are logical ways to take a chance like this one, and then there is the other way, akin to stepping off a cliff and expecting the Lord to catch you.

You can minimize the drop-off considerably when slipping into the freelance life by researching exactly what you're getting into before you expose yourself to the first breath of the winds of fortune.

Essentially, that means a realistic picture of how your location affects your freelance potential. Only a fool would leave a good job instantly to try freelancing in an untried location simply because I say it can work in North Dakota. You must begin your writing program forearmed with the knowledge of your strong points, your weak points, and the many matters in which geography is simply a neutral factor.

With that background, you can make a choice from a well-informed point of view. Hopes and fears aside, you'll be able to decide: (*a*) you can make it as a freelancer right now, right where you live; (*b*) you can freelance there someday, but will require more time to build up your skills and your credentials as a writer; or (*c*) freelancing will make a lovely hobby.

The difference between the first two choices and (*c*) lies in the results of a scouting expedition you can conduct around your own community, state, and region before you ever step out to take advantage of what you turn up. You chronicle the ready buyers of the written word by locating all the publications that may be open to your work. You begin to identify the local subjects and resources that have good prospects of interesting some national editors. You get started making contacts that can turn into articles by knowing the expertise (sometimes slightly offbeat) that resides in the town where you live.

As for commercial clients, you can scout them, too, during the months when you're getting ready to begin freelancing. Find out who already hires freelance writing assistance; who needs help and might be open to your new service; and where to find ongoing currents of this information you can tap.

There are three methods you'll use to chalk up all this abstract and concrete information:

■ The library—where you'll read every kind of publication that might use your work, dig through periodical indexes, and enlist the reference librarian for his own excellent background in books and publications.

■ Other writing professionals, who are your allies and sources of valuable information on the writing business in your area.

■ The buyers of writing themselves—nearby editors and potential commercial clients who can tell you firsthand what your prospects for selling are in their own offices.

Libraries are the logical first step in your scouting expedition. Their periodical collections can take up where *Writer's Market* leaves off. Most include the broad spectrum of magazines and newspapers published in their own areas. While these are smaller markets, they're often your best bets and those whose assignments you can fill most conveniently. A look at these racks should convince you that even *Writer's Market*, with its thousands of listings, is only the tip of the iceberg; not one of the state and regional magazines I've written for is listed in the most current edition.

The periodical indexes, of which the *Readers' Guide to Periodical Literature* is best known, hold clues of another nature. They can help you pinpoint some of the subjects for queries that may sell most easily to markets outside your own region.

Let me explain. One of the handicaps of writing from an odd corner of the country is that it's almost impossible to envision how the nation sees you. How would a fish describe water? But you can hop outside your local fishbowl with a few minutes' research on what local topics have in the past appeared in national publications—almost always the context in which outsiders are likely to think of the geographical territory at your command.

Under my own state, for example, you'd see stories about farming and farmers, stories about severe weather, stories about the energy industry, and topics that range from controversial western water projects to oddball politicians.

Farming, the energy industry, and rotten winters are all part of the scenery for those of us who live here. We take them for granted. The stories that seem to us to be worthy of coverage are those that are unusual, atypical—not farming, power, and blizzards.

What do you take for granted? In Utah, perhaps it's the Mormon Church or the preponderance of underpopulated national parks. In Hershey, Pennsylvania, it's chocolate; in Milwaukee, beer; in Missouri, the Ozarks. In every case, it's so much a part of local life that you think it's been done to death.

Yet familiarity makes the national editor's pencil tap. Totally new subjects are destined for the newspapers. Magazines prefer to examine the relatively familiar for new facets and in new depth. Those standard topics they already associate with your address may be exactly the ones on which they presume you to be most authoritative. They just make sense when considered in the shadow of your poor, maligned address.

While you won't, as a rule, concentrate on stories specifically about or limited to your own region, this kind of research provides some free insight into the image your geography imparts to you. It's somewhere to start, suggesting subject areas where you'll be moving with the current rather than battling your way upstream against outsiders' preconceptions and geographical prejudices.

While you're at the library performing these two pleasant exercises, introduce yourself to the reference librarian (or, in very small libraries, the head librarian). Share your intentions. Ask advice on publications, specialized local libraries for certain industries, or just about anything else on your scouting agenda which has been giving you trouble. Besides being generally great people, librarians can be as close to all-knowing about your community as anyone you're likely to find.

Your next step in this scout-out is right through the door into the territory where you plan to freelance. If you're in place already, it's as easy as making appointments to visit those who can fill you in on various facets of the writing outlook.

On the other hand, your chosen freelance location may be a region to which you hope to move. Scouting at a distance is far less effective than facing your sources across a desk or table in a coffee shop. What kind of excuse can you make to spend some time in your future locale before you lead moving vans there? You might combine your next vacation with a research trip. Besides the pleasure of exploring the destination's personality, you can spend weekday working hours calling on editors and potential clients. (Traveling to talk with them may even carry hidden benefits, since many people tend to be more candid with visiting strangers than with more familiar faces.)

Editors of nearby publications deserve a personal visit during your scouting days. More than any other group in your selected locale, they know about freelancing where you plan to live, at least as it's now being performed. They'll tell you far more in person about your genuine prospects of writing for them than they're likely to mention over the telephone or by letter. A visit is guaranteed to be a dozen times more helpful to you than even the best market listing. The editor will tell you outright what your chances for sales are and what he thinks he's looking for, and may even suggest some specific stories he's had in mind to try out your work.

Don't let your reticence prevent you from "bothering" these presumably busy individuals. For one thing, editors of local and state publications deal with far fewer freelancers than those whose circulation covers a larger part of the country. Many of those who write for them may not be professional writers at all, but hobbyists and spare-timers to whom deadlines and heavy research are a burden they don't care to shoulder.

For another, you can save both your own time and theirs by weeding out sure misses in person rather than sending in long-shot queries that require a written response. The protocol of dealing with editors on Publishers' Row, as described in books and articles on magazine writing, is often suspended or greatly condensed when the office is in downtown Fargo.

Editors aren't the only sources of valuable writing insights, however. Professionals in advertising, public relations, and the printing industry are close to what's being written and by whom in your community.

Public relations and advertising agencies are a special

case. To some small extent the freelancing writer competes with them on some kinds of commercial jobs, such as annual reports or publicity campaigns. In general, though, you're going to be allies and even coworkers. The competition angle need not sour the relationship, for most jobs that I've seen contracted out to freelancers (including me) are smaller or more specialized than the work that agencies excel in.

Agencies can be among your best local clients someday, once you get past the competition bugaboo. They often have writing overloads that back their own staff against imminent deadlines, and are generally accustomed to farming out assignments to independent contractors in other creative fields (notably photography). Once they've learned you're available, they may be interested in subcontracting writing jobs to you as well.

Advertising being the business it is, your own contacts may be sources of information on their competitors' clients as well. It's a small professional world, and word travels fast; one or two contacts can keep you up-to-date on possible assignments in most of your community.

Men and women employed full-time as writers for business, government, and industry also may prove to be useful allies. With information the core of their own business, is it any wonder they're so good at keeping up on developments in the public relations field? They can let you know whether their own employers are prospects for freelance writing as well as fill you in on leads in related offices.

But commercial writing isn't the only part of your freelance outlook that they can help improve. Getting coverage of consumer or trade stories for their companies or agencies is part of their own assignments; as a freelancer, you may be interested in developing their suggestions into salable, readable magazine articles. These same friends on the inside can help you line up interviews and background information for projects that touch their fields.

As if this weren't enough, there's a third area for cooperation. Many employers do not permit their own writers to moonlight. Yet these writers are sometimes asked by business associates if they'd be interested in taking on freelance work. If they know you're available, they may be able to refer some of these potential clients to you. The reference of a known professional can be a valuable foot-in-the-door, especially for beginners.

Printers provide a special category of scouting information. If you're serious about investigating all the kinds of potential writing jobs in your area—as I think you should be—they're among your very best allies.

I've suggested that editors and those who work in advertising and public relations have a strong grasp on the local writing grapevine. In my experience, printers have proven to know even more about what's going on—who's producing what, who needs editorial or writing help, who has a good budget for the printed word but lacks expertise in writing it.

Printers have a stake in the written word. They need words, after all, to set type, lay out publications, and print them up. The enormous range of customers who seek out their services includes nearly everyone who might be a potential client for your freelance writing. Their customers, too, sometimes mention the need for assistance. If the printers know you're available, they can pass the word on.

The third group your scouting expedition should introduce to you are the potential commercial clients themselves—the local government agencies, businesses, and associations who may contract with you for editorial and writing services.

Many of the best freelance commercial clients are far less than obvious to you as you begin your search. Some of my clients not only had never worked with a freelance writer themselves; they'd never even seen one. My availability in some cases changed their plans for spreading the work among reluctant in-house staffers. In other cases it's allowed them to take on projects their regular staff was too busy to handle. In nearly every case, I was worked into their normal information plans after they learned I was available. At the time I began freelancing, there was almost no one else locally who took on the kinds of assignments I've sometimes handled.

Who are your potential clients? Now, there's a good question. At one time I would have pinpointed the company or agency whose staff was too small to include a full-time public information person, for some that fit this description have been among my best clients. But in other instances, those who can't afford to add staffers also can't afford to hire outside help (unless you're working on grants or cooperative projects, which are another story).

Very large agencies and businesses at first seem to present just the opposite picture: Most have staff assigned full-time to writing duties. Again, first appearances can be deceptive. If they value the written word highly enough to hire their own writers, they often also value the variety and fresh viewpoint an outside contractor can bring to their projects. They're used to working with writers, and can be less surprised by the amount of time required to perform a "simple" assignment that demands extensive research and rechecking.

Nor is the vast middle ground a wasteland for freelancers. In a medium-sized community, they're the great majority of the clients you'll work for. Some have writers of their own; some don't, relying on ad agencies or reluctant executives to put together what few words normally need to be written.

But they have special projects. They have expansions and changes of direction. They have one-time or infrequent needs to reach the public with specific information. They sometimes long for fill-in help, due to staff changes or reassignments, and sometimes just need someone with different or more polished skills than their own staffers possess.

At any level, the best approach to finding out your prospects is to make an appointment and talk with the highest executive you can reach—the one who can decide to depart from tradition by engaging freelance help. During these scouting stages, you won't be really looking for assignments. You'll be testing the climate . . . and planting the seed of an idea that may come to fruition after you've actually quit your job and moved into your freelance career.

Those contacts may potentially be as good as money in the bank. But during the first months while you're turning the ideas you've scouted out into cash, you need a reserve to live on. Your scouting period is the ideal time to begin to cover your start-up financial obligations. You have two ways to do this: amass enough capital to pay your bills for several months (possibly through test freelance assignments handled by moonlight), and reduce your regular obligations to the absolute minimum you find feasible.

The need for savings doesn't indicate a lack of confidence on your part. No matter how wildly successful your first freelance efforts, you still need to plan for the worst: magazines that pay slowly or fold before they get your check made out; government clients for whom payment is an excruciating procession through one office after another; business clients who try to delay paying their bills for sixty days or longer to use your money interest-free as long as they can. And for that matter, typewriters that break down, bouts with the flu, and sudden midwinter crises of spirit that desperately demand a vacation.

Some experts advise all workers to keep three to six months' income on hand where it can be reached easily in case of emergency, recession, or sudden de-employment. I don't think their advice is too conservative for novice freelancers to follow. Six months' reserve will get you over the worrisome moments of starting your new venture; it'll relieve you of money anxieties long enough to concentrate on more important things, like writing.

I believe you need to try freelancing for at least a year before you can make a fair assessment of whether it's working for you. Six months' reserve should guarantee that, since even in the beginning you should be able to bring in at least half as much income as you want to make.

Even after you've pared down your monthly expenses, the sum of six months' paychecks may seem like a lot. Your answer to how to acquire that financial stake must be as individual as your own writing dreams.

If you have investments that can be turned into cash, consider your writing a better investment and cash them in. A cache of solid stocks, a little real estate, the savings bonds your grandma has given you for every birthday—all can mean the cash security you need. A bonus is that since your initial freelance income may be lower than your salary for a time, your tax bracket will shrink and you'll minimize the capital gains tax to be paid on your profits.

If you have no such cashable cushions, you'll just have to find a way to save. Cut down your obligations now and continue on your job for another year. Test the waters by freelancing in your spare time, saving every cent toward the day you make your break. Cut back a little (or a lot). Take a temporary second job.

Building up your financial foundation is a necessary step toward freelancing. It may postpone your escape from your job or represent unwelcome belt-tightening for awhile. But it's worth the sacrifice for a shot at your dream.

You can limit the size of financial reserve you need by cutting down your regular bills. I was able to securely start with much less money in the bank because over a period of three months my husband and I applied extraordinary effort to paying off every credit card, every store charge account, and every other obligation due to come up during my first freelance months—regular insurance premiums, college loan repayments, and the like.

If you're already living the middle-class life, you may find—as I did—that it's virtually impossible to cut your obligations to zero. Home mortgage payments roll around like phases of the moon. Car payments continue. Utility and telephone bills can be counted on, and the expenses of freelancing require accounts at office supply stores, camera shops, and travel agencies.

A working spouse simplifies. Your cash reserve has to take care of the rest. It's up to you to find the level of financial backup, coupled with reduced expenses, that will free your mind to turn creative thought to your new career. If you feel real confusion about how much money you need to get started, talk with a good accountant accustomed to working with small businesses; his expertise will provide you with good guidelines and great peace of mind. (Warning: Accountants tend to err on the side of conservatism. Don't let a gloomy one talk you out of your freelance plans, because he probably doesn't know one thing about it.)

I don't think you'll really need the financial contingency plans you're laying out during this start-up period. Nor do I think it's necessary, or even prudent, to prune your expenses (and lifestyle) to the nub. If you've done your homework thoroughly and mastered your craft, you should see results much sooner than six months from when you start. I was out flexing my Master Charge within a month of cautiously resolving to pay cash forevermore.

Yet no matter how promising your prospects, it can never hurt to establish a financial course of action for your first days of freelancing. It eases your predictable doubts about the wisdom of your decision, the visions of your children going hungry or with cavities unfilled. And others who depend on your monthly paycheck won't agitate quite so vigorously on behalf of regular income instead of adventure.

You'll be freed to spend your hours, instead, weighing the options your scouting has shown are available for your initial freelance assignments. The issue of money will fall into place. But first you ought to examine all the background you've built up, and take a long, honest look at how this research has affected your own attitude toward freelancing.

There's some chance that your scouting project has already dampened your hopes. Oh, I don't mean that the leads you turned up aren't promising. They're almost certainly better than you—doubting Thomas that you are—really expected.

But this has been a blessed lot of work. It can be exhausting. It wears out shoes (and this has been only a foretaste). During at least your first few months on your own, you'll be spending as much time searching and selling as you will at your typewriter.

Which brings up another good point to consider now, while you still have time. Do you have the enthusiasm and vitality to dedicate yourself to digging up every opportunity your area can offer—not just now, but on a continuing, month-after-month basis? Freelancing is something you keep doing anew in your chosen part of the country, though after you've gotten started its demands may ease up a bit on the promotional end.

To keep up that level of energy, you need inner resources to maintain your buoyancy. You need as much confidence as you've ever summoned to be able to walk out your employer's door for the last time and eagerly embrace the unknown (whose terrors, of course, you've already cut down to size through astute scouting). You need to launch your freelancing venture on a mental high. It's not wise to try to take off from a low point of your psychological reserves.

We've all heard the one about the guy who gets fired by an unjust, insensitive boss and turns immediately to writing—he's next heard from when his best-selling manuscript endows him with income for life. (The boss then comes on bended knee to get him back again; the erstwhile employee spurns him, and the boss never forgives himself.)

While I'm not particularly qualified to pass judgment on fiction, I do know this one's a dilly. The post-pink slip period is about as rotten a time as you can pick to start yourself as a freelancer in your neck of the woods.

Two reasons: Your eagerness and energy are bound to be at a lifetime low after you've had that kind of blow to your vocational self-confidence. You may not notice it at first, and surge ahead powered by sheer spite. But sooner or later the adrenalin level is going to return to a flaccid norm, and your vitality will slip seriously.

And you're not going to be prepared for the challenge of getting started freelancing if you've suddenly found yourself tossed out on your ear. You haven't had the time to do your homework. You haven't made the important low-pressure contacts with those who can help you. You haven't got your business matters in order. If that's not enough, in the close-knit community where you're likely to live, you'll be starting out not only weak on hard data but shadowed by a suspicious little cloud—for people really do believe that where there's smoke, there's fire. In other words, no matter how much your boss is generally conceded to resemble Simon Legree, he must have had some solid reason to fire you. (Don't explain it to me. Explain it to all those good acquaintances and former colleagues who are whispering about the scandalous turn of events.)

I do know one gifted and prominent writer who started in this way, of hard necessity, and has gone on to greater income, visibility, and admiration. He wouldn't recommend his route to freelancing, though. It's unnecessarily traumatic and horribly destructive to the confidence you need to get started.

Confidence is a funny thing. Its absence is a lot more obvious than its presence. My father always warned me that large, ominous dogs could somehow smell if you were afraid of them; I've noticed his advice applies to editors and commercial clients as well. They may not go straight for your jugular like a nice, straightforward killer Doberman, but they do go straight for the door—and that can cut off your circulation just as quickly.

So if you have even the slightest element of choice, start freelancing at a high point in your life. Turn down some alluring promotion and set out on your own. Accept your coworkers' best wishes and have a grand time at your going-away party. Resist the impulse to tell your employer exactly what you've thought of him for the past thirteen long years. Smile and shake his hand instead.

There is a reason for all this good humor.

Who do you think your first writing client should be? How about someone who knows your work well, needs immediate help to fill an open position, and dreads having to train some upstart still wet behind the ears in all the intricacies of your former job?

Your just-barely-former boss, that's who. Consider discussing whether you can carry on some or all of your former duties on a freelance basis. You may be surprised at how well your full-time job can be transposed into a part-time contract as a freelancer. The chances of this will be substantially dimmed, however, if you've informed your boss of his resemblance to a snake in the grass or the wrong end of an equine.

You'll notice I assume your last job is one that includes writing duties. If it isn't, hold onto your paycheck a little longer. You're not going to savor what comes next.

If you do not already have professional experience in some aspect of writing, you're taking a foolhardy chance to try freelancing before you do.

You can get that experience through many kinds of salaried positions. You need to work somewhere where you're required to write often, accurately, and preferably quickly.

That's exactly what you'll master on a newspaper. Any kind of newspaper. The *New York Times* has certain advantages over the *Sioux Falls Argus-Leader*, but both provide commensurate gifts to freelancers intent on freelancing where they've ended up. At the *Times* you may rub shoulders with the famous and acquire a bit of notoriety yourself . . . especially if your writing tends to the truly spectacular and you're tough enough to elbow your way to the top.

But at the *Argus-Leader* you can accomplish the same thing on the scale of the place where you've chosen to live. You'll learn to write—and meet the local movers and shakers. You'll have the fear of the Lord of Deadlines pounded into you—and develop a readership which recognizes your name and knows that you're a bona fide writer. You might not excite quite so much envy from your peers, but your prospects may be just as bright and ultimately satisfying as your counterpart the megalopolis marvel's.

There are other places to hone your craftsmanship, of course. Public information, public relations, and advertising jobs involving copywriting all offer the same basic lessons in writing style and precision. They provide some visibility which you can build upon after you go out on your own. And the casual contacts you make on your job every day can lead to potential freelance assignments in the future.

You can take college courses in writing, too—even courses specifically in freelancing. They may be great for helping polish your work or teaching the rudiments of manuscript marketing. (Or they can be lousy.) But by themselves, they almost certainly will not make a self-supporting freelancer out of you.

Why not? Those who teach, for one thing, have seldom earned a freelance living themselves. They may urge grammatical, philosophical, and creative perfection, but their idea of how to write to earn money can be pretty fuzzy.

The courses can't teach you to hustle. They can't teach you to get out and meet people, to sell yourself, to scramble in all the ways the self-supporting freelance life requires. In fact, some that I've known actually work against the kind of enterprise demanded by serious freelancing, giving students a taste instead for the smoking-jacketed, brandy-sniftering, literary-salonish, writers' lifestyle that exists only in dated movies and fifty-year-old short stories.

(And while courses in fiction and poetry may be an enlightening pastime, they're virtually worthless when it comes to preparing yourself for serious self-supporting freelancing. Your chances of living on income from fiction are slim indeed, unless you write erotic historical romances by the dozen; from poetry, they're virtually zero.)

Of course, there are classes that differ from this mold, notably those special few taught by real live working freelancers. Maybe you'll teach one yourself someday. In the meantime, they can be at best just one block in the working foundation that'll enable you to freelance successfully.

You must write to get jobs as a writer. The more visible that writing, the better your freelance prospects become. Far-off editors will want to see solid samples of published work. Commercial clients will want printed proof that you can tailor your work to their special requirements before they hand out assignments.

Newspaper writers have this item checked off early. If your writing experience is in less visible channels, there are still steps you can take before you leave your job to get your name recognized by the public in your part of the world.

One way to build up your reputation as a writer is to make use of the most closely read publications in your city, state, or region. In later chapters I'll preach to you about the cardinal rule of the freelance business: Get paid what your work is worth. But in this single case—the quest for reputation—we'll push that rule to the back burner and concentrate instead on how to use low-paying local publications as a source of inexpensive self-advertising.

Those who live in urban areas served by all kinds of publications will never know how seriously we who are less advantaged take the few publications which serve us. In North Dakota there's one general-circulation magazine that reaches the bulk of the decision makers, the socially prominent, and the just-plain-people in the state all at the same time. (It falters badly with the *Rolling Stone* crowd, but they don't hire writers often anyway.) *North Dakota Horizons* has contributed an utterly disproportionate share to my visibility here. Though it's published only a tiny fraction of my total work in any given year, and though its circulation is a small percentage of that of other magazines I've written for . . . still, it's the one that strangers mention when they say they've heard of me. Publication between its scenic covers is a good entrée to just about any kind of writing assignment in the state. (That name recognition is especially handy when you try to cash checks out of town.)

Every community has its version of *Horizons*: if not the county seat weekly, then a city magazine, a business publication, an entertainment guide, a magazine for outdoorsmen, or some other kind of periodical that finds its way into lots of homes and gets taken seriously.

These articles may not pay very well, but they're a good investment just the same. Writers are an unusual and interesting species over almost all of the country, New York publishing circles aside. In North Dakota and states like yours, perhaps, your vocation—once recognized by enough people—can make you genuinely memorable.

Writing, however, isn't the only good way to make yourself known in your community. Don't look at freelancing as your chance to escape all the pressures of dealing with people (as too many of us are likely to hope). Actually, it's an invitation to get more involved than you've ever been before.

As a freelancer in your part of the world, you need people. They're clients. Sources. Inspiration. They're your instant, handy antidote to the loneliness that comes with facing no one but your typewriter for days at a time.

Back when I was employed, I was never a joiner. I treasured every minute of time to myself—for writing, for reading, for watching soap operas, napping, whatever happened to recharge my batteries. So when I began saying yes to invitations to join groups or serve on committees, I was as surprised myself as the members I took by surprise.

People are partly recreation. But getting involved with as many as you can manage to meet is a good sound business decision as well—one a freelancer can't afford to avoid.

The contacts you make as part of a group or public project can be the very best kind. You have interests in common. You get to know one another in a tension-free atmosphere. You become *friends*—not just cordial business acquaintances. You see each other as allies.

If you're new in town, these groups can help you learn all you need to know about your new home. They're a source of introductions, of referrals, of writing leads. Whether your own tastes run to the Sierra Club or the Lions, the

Audubon Society or the Elks, Zonta or NOW, you'll almost certainly enhance both your social life and your freelance career by being an involved part of a group working toward a mutual goal, not merely a passive, anonymous observer.

You've scouted out your area (or the spot where you want to live) now and have some notion of the pluses and minuses it's endowed with. You've identified some potential clients to work on locally; you're getting your first batch of magazine queries in the mail. You're building your reputation, your file of contacts, your confidence . . .

So are you ready to freelance yet?

There's still a little groundwork left to lay. A creative approach to finding freelance assignments is only one of the two laws of successful freelancing.

You still have to go into business.

3

Nuts and Bolts Beginnings

Freelancing is reputed to be the kind of business you can engage in with little or no expense outside of what it takes to keep your body warm and your fingers moving over the typewriter keys. If not a jug of wine, a loaf of bread, and the will to write poesy, then it would seem to require a minimum of a yellow legal tablet, a couple of felt-tip pens, and your junker of a portable typewriter set up on the kitchen table.

The real cost of freelance writing—your overhead—is modest in the long run, but requires some up-front investment and planning. The kitchen might work for your moonlighting counterpart who cranks out one story per season; it won't work for you for long. Writing is a business and, to be conducted successfully, needs to be set up like one. You need to look like a minor contender for membership in the chamber of commerce. A card table in the rumpus room just won't do.

A full-time freelancer deserves an office. That office is symbolic, to be sure. It's a place you must go in the morning and leave at night, a place where local clients can picture you at work, a place that you can casually refer to in conversations with friends who think you're unemployed and editors who call. It's a sanctuary.

But it's also a visible convenience. Shoeboxes full of notes and a portable typewriter reached by sitting on a barstool are depressing and make your freelancing feel temporary. Trust me: I spent my first month as a freelancer at a card table in the spare bedroom pecking away at an ancient Royal standard that goofed up its m's and e's. I was reassured each night by the sound of pounding from below, however. As soon as my husband had finished remodeling enough of our lower level to get the heat piped in and the light fixtures functional, I packed up and moved in with heartfelt hallelujahs.

The question of whether to work at home or to rent some picturesque garret (or a suite in a downtown bank building) is a thorny one, especially, I think, for the woman freelancer. A male writer is generally conceded to be what he really is. The mental image of Daddy in his study typing away while Mom shoos kids from his closed door is too ingrained in our imaginations to be questioned.

For the female freelancer, whose plight I sympathize with a bit more fervently, the home office has its drawbacks. Even if child care is a nonworry, as it is at our house, the woman who's home all day bears a burden of suspicion: Are you really working down there, or do you sneak away to vacuum or nap in mid-afternoon? A woman who works at home, dress-for-success suit and all, still looks entirely too much like a housewife for some tastes.

Yet the rented office is, to me, a poor solution, unless you reach the point where you have employees of your own. Commuting becomes a consideration, compared with the twenty seconds it takes me to pour a cup of coffee and come downstairs. The out-of-the-home office is going to be left locked and unresponsive while you're out on interview and research trips, causing clients to wonder if you've skipped town. If you have a lot of employed friends (I do), you're convenient enough for frequent distractions and drop-in visitors.

Worst of all, you've immediately added to your dreaded overhead the minute you sign a lease. No matter what your interests or sales in any future month, you'll have that rent payment due, along with all the other hidden and obvious costs we'll go into.

Perhaps that doesn't bother you now because you know

exactly what kinds of work you plan to take on. It does bother me. I quit my last job for the freedom freelancing offers. I'd no sooner want to have to cover several hundred dollars of overhead, no matter what I'm working on, than I'd want to commit myself to keeping a secretary busy eight hours every day. During the summer, my production drops off as we build up our photo files and travel. Even during my hard-work season (all the rest of the year), I frequently get into projects where the monthly cash flow is nil, though the ultimate payment is plenty. Any worrisome level of fixed expense makes me feel just a little like a wage slave again, for you can't deny it ties you down.

So I work at home. And get all the United Parcel Service packages in the neighborhood because our nice deliveryman can't find anyone else to take them (all our neighbor mommies work). And get visits once a month from Jehovah's Witness and Mormon missionaries who are dying to spend some time with me. And get calls from club chairmen and political workers and the Heart Fund to take on sticky chores because I'm "the only one in your neighborhood who's at home and has time."

But I also can watch the noon TV news while I fix lunch upstairs, can count another several hundred dollars a month as my own (as opposed to rent payments), and—luxury of luxuries—can sip all day at the pot of coffee my husband fixes before he goes to work in the morning. And I never, never have to carry work home at night or find I left critical notes in the office over the weekend.

What would an office be without a telephone? (Heaven, that's what, but it's not practical.) Wherever you do decide to do your daily work, you'll add another hunk of overhead when you have a telephone installed.

Technically, a freelance writer is using his telephone for business, which means higher rates than you're used to paying at home. The telephone company uses little tests like: Is the number on your business card? Your stationery? Do you deduct part or all of it from your income tax as a business expense? The difference in calling yours a business or home number may seem inconsequential but for one thing: A business telephone line, in my part of the country, costs twelve dollars more per month than the monthly home service charge (currently about $24). That's just equal to the proceeds of one medium-market article sale per year.

You can save money by converting your existing home line into a business number and adding no other new number or service. While the telephone company would love to sell you a second number for your business, it's totally unnecessary under any circumstances I can imagine. It just means you'd pay monthly charges twice and have *two* phones to interrupt your train of thought.

The business conversion is valuable if you decide to buy the one kind of paid advertising that I think will bring you business. You cannot advertise in or even be listed in the Yellow Pages unless you have a business line. I survived very well indeed without this advertising for two years, but have since succumbed and ordered a tiny ad under "public relations counselors" in our directory. (You might also consider "advertising agencies and counselors," "audio-visual production services," or "photographers—commercial" if you can provide services in those areas, which we'll discuss in later chapters.)

A half-inch listing increases my phone bill by less than six dollars per month—a bargain, I think, for the privilege of getting occasional calls from people I've never met and reminding those who know me that I'm still around. It also adds an extra note of legitimacy to my freelance business; after all, if I were just a masquerading housewife, I wouldn't be in the Yellow Pages, would I?

My office is equipped with everything else you'd expect to find downtown, too—a big desk (mine's a non-antique roll top), files, bookcases crammed with reference books and miscellany, a back-supporting stenographer's chair and the only machine I've ever loved, my big blue IBM Selectric II with its endearing self-correcting ability.

None of those furnishings was an extravagance, though they're not Salvation Army bargains either. That includes the typewriter, at almost a thousand dollars, and the chair at several hundred.

There's as much range in price and quality among office furnishings as you encounter in furniture stores catering to home decor. The logical place to buy such equipment would seem to be an office supply store; though a reasonable starting point for making comparisons, you'll seldom get the best value for the least price there. The national catalog stores—like Sears—offer a good selection of basic office furniture at high-volume prices. Discount stores sometimes offer real bargains also, though the quality can be less appealing. Don't choose the cheapest desk and chair that you can find; you'll give them hard use, and better-built pieces stand up much more dependably.

A good chair for your typing and desk work is the most important single item you'll purchase. Forget the big black executive chairs that cushion you, swivel you, and envelop you in enough leather to saddle a cavalry's horses; they're made to impress visitors, not provide a pedestal for serious work. Instead, consider the chairs scientifically designed for those who spend their days at the typewriter—stenographer's chairs, whose height and backs can be adjusted to fit your unique posture and posterior.

Occasionally you might be able to pick up top-quality office furniture at bargain-basement prices by watching big organizations on the verge of remodeling their quarters. Sometimes they sell older equipment and furnishings outright. More often they're turned over to the decorating firm or the supplier of the new furniture and sold for a fraction of their value. In my state, the government auctions off excess property, including furniture, several times a year; private citizens are welcome to make bids. Inquire about the availability of secondhand furniture in your area if you need a bargain, and watch classified ads for clues on who's selling what you need.

You can pay anything from pocket money to thousands of dollars for your typewriter, depending on whether you struggle along with a used Model T or go in for the sleekest of space-age models. You'll spend eight hours a day with the result of this decision. Go for a good piece of equipment.

My typewriter was my big investment. I bought it for several reasons, including a growing loathing for the cranky old standard manual, which caused shooting pains in my wrists and forearms after a few days of solid writing.

Electric correcting typewriters create the best-looking letters and manuscripts you can manage. They look like you mean business. Weird little gnomes who write oddball manuscripts that editors dread finding in their daily mail don't have typewriters like mine (unless they're rich weird little gnomes).

My typewriter can save me the cost of a secretarial service or manuscript service for retyping manuscripts. I'm fast and sloppy at the keyboard. With the self-correcting feature, even I can turn out a readable manuscript three times out of four.

It also saves eyestrain, muscle strain, and the strain of having visiting acquaintances coo, "So this is where you write your little stories. How sweet." Housewives don't have IBMs either (unless, like the gnomes, they're loaded).

That is not to say that harboring such a good-looking monster as my typewriter is entirely without aggravation. Every IBM owner in the United States orders replacement ribbons from the same toll-free number, which is busy almost every minute of the day. It's up to you to find the other minute. I've also had intermittent service problems—not the fixing itself, for I maintain a sixty-dollar annual service contract that covers the cost of repairs and adjustments. No, the problem is competing for attention with large offices with twenty ailing machines all in a row and platoons of good-looking secretaries to attract the repairmen. Nevertheless, I've succeeded in being taken seriously by occasional noisy protests, and now get uniformly excellent service on the few occasions when I need it—even way out here on the prairie.

Outside of those special typewriter ribbons and tapes, obtaining supplies should present you with little difficulty. Most moderately bustling cities have at least one office supply store. If you're not within reach of one, you can order some basics—nine-by-twelve-inch manila envelopes, typing paper—at discount prices—from mail-order firms. (Look for their ads in the back of writers' magazines.) I've found, though, that my own best suppliers are often the dime stores and large discount drugstores, where the same items usually cost substantially less. Office materials are eminently storable, besides; you'll find you can save as much as a third of their retail cost by buying during back-to-school sales and other special events, then squirreling them away in your bottom drawer.

You don't want to be cheap, though, in one category of supplies. That's your business stationery—letterheads, business cards, and any other official stuff you conjure up, including personal mailing labels, billing statements, postcards, or whatnot.

You can dash down to your rapid-print shop and have them type out your name and address and run it off for ten or fifteen dollars. But I'd counsel against it. Instead, reconcile yourself to the one-time expense and find a creative graphic designer to develop a logo (symbol) or distinctive letterhead design that can be carried through on matching envelopes, business cards, and other supplies. Most communities have freelance artists; try calling your local community college or high school and asking someone in the art department for a recommendation. Others are set up in business for themselves. You'll find them in the Yellow Pages. Don't hire the first artist you meet; study their samples to find one whose style seems to click with your own.

Don't take your letterhead project to an ad agency unless it's your very last alternative. Small jobs like stationery design cost proportionately more when done by an agency accustomed to four- or five-figure sums. They'll turn it over to an artist anyway (usually a junior one) and then bill you his cost plus their own overhead.

What'll it cost you? Around here, a good graphic letterhead with accompanying applications starts at about a hundred dollars and runs up toward five hundred or more, depending on complexity and how long it takes to produce a design that satisfies you. It's money well spent, for your stationery is the exhibit of your taste first seen by editors and, often, other clients.

Don't scrimp by hiring a five-dollar-an-hour amateur artist. Your stationery will reflect exactly the penny-pinching importance you've assigned it; it's there before the world as a sample of something you've chosen and presumably approved.

A good design is simple. It avoids gimmicks and clichés (cartoons of typewriters have probably been done to death by now). It uses professional typography, not shaky hand-drawn letters, and carries no marginal embellishments irrelevant to the basic design or purpose. It looks like business, not a medium for chatty personal notes. Above all, you feel comfortable with it.

Your letterhead needn't involve four-color printing, gold embossing, or authentic imported papyrus to make an impression. You can achieve the professional look you want with one or two colors of ink on decent nonerasable stock, usually white or a barely tinted approximation. It may cost you around a hundred fifty dollars for a thousand sheets and envelopes, but it will pay you dividends every time you mail a query or business letter.

These are the basic costs of doing business—your office, your furniture and equipment, your supplies. But there are other expenses you'll run into as you carry on your work that should be predicted and controlled to keep overhead down.

One is postage. I'm not going to coach you in saving pennies here, either. Instead, you should become an informed consumer of the services the post office and its main competitor, United Parcel Service, provide.

First-class mail is the way to send your valuable manuscripts. Don't be tempted by that special fourth-class book rate. The speed of first-class delivery from your undistinguished address is so advantageous that a few extra dimes are fully warranted. But you can go even better—priority mail, registered mail, and other services for special needs. With these kinds of send-offs, I find it possible to mail from Bismarck to New York in two days or less. Since rates go up so quickly, there's no point in getting down to figures here; instead, have a heart-to-heart talk with the most congenial clerk in your own post office, who's likely to advise the most cost-effective way to mail.

Here in North Dakota, I've found that United Parcel Service is often as fast as and less expensive than the post office in shipping large envelopes and packages to editors far away. My husband (a professional photographer) and I often send out bulky packages of photo transparencies that would cost plenty to mail, considering insurance or registration and special handling. UPS packages are automatically insured for one hundred dollars at no additional fee; they're also delivered to the addressee's door and must be signed for, like more expensive postal categories. Charges vary according to parcel size and distance, so it's worthwhile to frequently compare costs and advantages from your own geographic starting point.

Despite the horror stories told about mail service, I've never had a truly bad experience, except just once . . . and I've never been certain that the manuscript was lost in the mail and not in the editor's office. Many accusations of postal ineptitude turn out to be excuses for checks not mailed in the first place, manuscripts lying under pizza boxes on the corner of a desk, or assignments not quite ready by deadline.

You can enlist special services for super-rush delivery, like couriers—Purolator, Air Express, and others. The expense is considerable; it has cost me twenty dollars to ship a manuscript one thousand miles, with delivery guaranteed only in two working days. That compares poorly with the post office's own special express mail service, which guarantees delivery in twenty-four hours or less to selected cities. Its cost depends on package weight and distance.

Just in case you run into delivery problems—the jet carrying your express manuscript falls from the sky, perhaps, or there's a fire in the magazine's mailroom—locate the least expensive copying service in town and establish a routine of duplicating every manuscript you mail. Naturally, my one lost manuscript was the only one I hadn't copied. To save sixty cents and a trip to the local library's Xerox machine, I risked the painstaking reconstruction of a story from long-forgotten notes and enthusiasm just as distant.

You should be able to get commercial copies for ten to fifteen cents. Or find an office with a copier and work out a monthly repayment system at their own cost of a penny or two per page copied. If you can't find either a coin-op machine or a friendly business, you have two final options: Try your local school district (since schools run on copies these days), or purchase a small home copier. These begin at about a hundred dollars, but require costly paper and chemicals that increase your per-page cost, not to mention your supply problems. The quality produced by small copiers isn't what you expect of the big, dry-copy machines, but as a last resort, it's better than smudgy, illegible, over-corrected-and-revised carbons.

The mailman is the number one solution to your problems of geographical distance from publishing markets. Your second answer is the telephone. But like postage, telephone costs can add up quicker than a wink when you're not paying close attention.

Telephoning is better suited than mail for gathering some kinds of information. If you need to closely question a source, if you need to gather quotable statements and opinions, if you want frank answers on controversial questions—the phone is usually more effective than a letter. You're able to direct the kinds of responses you elicit, and you can probe for the real story behind a pat answer. Most people are highly reluctant to commit themselves on touchy subjects in a letter; they're more likely to do so when talking to a friendly voice.

Letters, of course, have their purpose. When you need to obtain data that may have already been assembled or which is factual and straightforward, the mail is clearly a better approach. A letter can also serve as an introduction and prelude for a phone interview.

But when time is at a premium, telephone calls are your best information-gathering tool. They can accomplish much the same as a personal, face-to-face interview, but save you the expense of travel from your out-of-the-way location.

Telephone interviews and inquiries are an enormous money-saver when you work at a distance from your sources. From North Dakota, my calls connect me almost instantly with anyone in the country; trying to make those contacts in person would be prohibitively expensive and require untold hours among the Moonies in the Denver or Chicago airports. Yet long-distance rates being what they are, the bills can still stagger you at month's end, added onto the thirty-five dollars or so your monthly services amount to.

It isn't really cheap to call anywhere from North Dakota except to other places in North Dakota. I've found there are ways, however, to cut twenty-dollar phone interviews down to size, and to avoid paying for your subject's "hmmm"s and "let me see"s. You may find it unavoidable to first contact your sources during normal working hours, the exact period during which the telephone company, in its wisdom, charges its most businesslike rates. It's easiest to contact many people at work—also most courteous, unless your questions are of a specifically personal nature.

But to phone someone unannounced is to reach him far from the peak of his answering powers. I've found it more effective to first make a concise daytime (full rate) call to explain my project and how I hope the subject will fit in. Then I arrange to call him back at a mutually agreeable time, after he's had a chance to gather his thoughts and take care of the impatient salesman waiting in his office. One important element that makes the call-back time agreeable on my end of the line is that it be after 5 p.m., when rates go down, or otherwise avoids peak rate periods.

Now, 5 p.m. in North Dakota isn't necessarily 5 p.m. where my subject answers the phone. If I'm calling west to Rocky Mountain or Pacific standard time zones, I'll reach him at 4 p.m. or 3 p.m.—still in the office, and at a less hectic time of the day. Yet since the call is placed from Bismarck, I get to take advantage of a 20 percent after-5 discount (larger perhaps where you live). On a long call, that quickly amounts to real savings.

Calling people in the eastern standard time zone eliminates my advantage after lunch. But we get up early here in North Dakota. Since the time you *start* your call determines the rate you're charged, I can call eastward any time before 8 a.m. and qualify for a discount. This even applies if I stumble, bleary-eyed, to the phone at 7:59 a.m. The whole call would then be at the lower rate, no matter whether it lasts a minute or all morning.

Writers further west have an even better situation. While 7:59 in Bismarck is 8:59 in New York—just a little early to catch many editors or agents at the job—the mountain and Pacific time zones add additional hours to the differential. That breakfast-time call from Cheyenne, Wyoming, is 9:59 in Manhattan; the same call from Portland, Oregon, would reach the editor at 10:59. All this finagling results in savings worth the computations: Calls placed between 11 p.m. and 8 a.m. your time are discounted a whopping 60 percent.

If you can arrange to call your interviewee back when he really has more time and leisure to talk—say on Saturday, or before 5 p.m. Sunday—you'll get the same discount of more than half the usual rate. And even on Sunday evenings, when all America calls dear Mother back home, you qualify for 35 percent less than the going price.

What are you going to do with all these savings? One

good place to apply them is to your other telephone problem: what to do when you're away from home and the client or editor finally calls you back.

You have two options short of a full-time receptionist's services. One is those telephone answering machines. The other is a live answering service.

The machine has its advantages. I started out with one, a good model which cost several hundred dollars. It was clearly superior to cheaper models simply because it was voice activated. That is, I didn't have to listen to my own voice saying "Nancy is not home," and so on, before every message when I retrieved my calls.

I hated it. I dreaded taking messages off the tape, partly because about two-thirds of them were preceded by a comment about how the caller despised talking into tape recorders over the telephone.

I did not research whether they preferred no answer at all because I can't afford to miss calls, not even once in a while. Instead, I invested in one of Bismarck's big-city luxuries, a hookup with the single local telephone answering service.

The service picks up my calls on the fourth ring. Three rings gives me time to grab for the phone no matter where I am or just long enough to finish typing the sentence I'm composing. If I really can't be interrrupted, I let the service catch the call and phone later for the message. (If you've got suspicious friends or in-laws, they may begin to wonder if you're really gone when the service tells them you're out . . . or if you're just avoiding them.) Though a certain percentage of callers don't like my service any better than my former machine, the majority tell me they much prefer talking to a live human.

There are drawbacks. Once in a great while I return a call to a mystified person who left a message for the plumber—who uses the same service. The other negative is the cost. I pay forty-five dollars a month for the privilege of having my calls covered from 8 a.m. to 6 p.m. six days a week; costs are sometimes higher in larger cities, but this seems to be about average. Just one important call that I would have otherwise missed makes up for that monthly billing, however. I count it as one of my best business investments.

If no commercial answering service serves your area, you might consider setting up your own by enlisting the help of a reliable family member or neighbor who spends the day at home. Unless the person lives with you, you'll have to invest in a second phone line to his home plus a monthly service charge for this extension; it will cost you no more than the installation fee you'd pay for hooking up with a professional service.

My answering service also has secretarial help available for typing, transcribing tapes, and mailings. Their cost for transcription is now about ten dollars an hour—the transcriber's hour, not per hour of recorded tape. The going rate for typing manuscripts is about $1.50 per completed page.

Good secretarial services are worth a healthy price. I've had better help for lower cost, though, by hiring a moonlighting secretary working on a freelance basis herself. All I normally require is retyping of heavily edited or revised manuscripts and occasionally transcribing interviews, though I usually decode tapes myself to refresh my memory of the discussion.

Entertainment and travel are big parts of your business overhead. Fortunately they're the ones you can most easily control. Of all your business expenses, these are definitely the most fun.

By business entertainment, I don't mean taking clients to Las Vegas or buying them fifty-dollar-a-plate dinners . . . although there might be reasons for you to splurge on either one someday. I'm more concerned with fifty-cent cups of coffee, occasional lunches, perhaps a drink together after hours.

The government recognizes these treats as a legitimate expense of doing business. You might as well go along with them. Since I prefer to meet clients on neutral territory—neither their office nor mine—I practically live at a pancake house a few blocks away, where the pots of coffee I've purchased could fill one of the smaller Great Lakes. (This is one way to minimize the liability of working out of a home office, by the way. I could do my writing in the runway of our local airport and they'd never know.)

You need to keep track of these expenses for your own

budgeting and for the Internal Revenue Service at taxtime. Jot down your expenditure in a daybook along with who you coffeed or lunched with, his business, the date, and the matters you talked over.

Impressing people with lavish lunches is not necessary to establish yourself as a professional. Picking up the bill for coffee definitely is. You ought to expect to spend a modest amount each month for entertaining clients, sources, and editors (if you're so lucky as to nab one when he's in your part of the world).

As a rule of thumb, I try to hold expenses down to no more than my usual weekly lunch money—twenty-five dollars or less. I let clients whom I meet with frequently set the pace for expenditures; it's not unreasonable to expect them to reciprocate. Sources and those whom you're courting for business are another story. Still, it's best to hold cost to a modest level. You don't want your entertaining to interfere with the serious purpose of these occasions, which is to exchange business information.

Travel is the flip side of the coin. You can't play the host to all your sources and editors; you have to go to many of them. Telephone calls and letters won't always preclude travel expenses, either. Some things must be done in person. It's almost impossible to obtain photographs in some situations, for example, unless you're on the spot to take them yourself.

But travel can break your budget in no time. Take it from the North Dakotan: Distance makes travel costly in both money and the time it takes to get there and back.

Yet you can tame the monster of travel costs. The secret is good planning.

I never go anywhere on business with only one objective in mind. Flying only from Bismarck to Minneapolis costs over a hundred fifty dollars per round trip, and two nights' lodging and meals can swallow another hundred even on the cheap.

It takes a very good story to justify two hundred fifty dollars in extra expenses, along with several days' nonwriting time during which I can't count on earning a nickel. But if that same trip results in material used for three or four or half a dozen other projects as well, it becomes a bargain in terms of both money and hours.

Time that you'd squander watching situation comedies in your hotel at night can just as well be spent pursuing an interesting new article idea, collecting quotes and case histories for another story, checking the local university for experts who might lead to other sales, or digging through museums and cultural centers for new perspectives or more depth on accepted ones. You can use spare hours to make fresh contacts with editors of publications whom you've already met, or new acquaintances who may one day buy material from you. And if you really do have an extra hour or two before your plane leaves or while you wait to make connections, the most fascinating coffee companion in a strange city is always a reporter for one of its leading newspapers.

Average out the cost of your trip over the number of waking hours it allows you to spend in a new locale. You'll see that you can't afford to sleep late and call it quits at the cocktail hour. If you need a break, take a nap when you get home.

If you really can't get that much material in Oshkosh, you can explore flight layovers in cities along the route. They're usually available at no extra cost or for a very modest boarding fee. And alternate routings by air may hold some benefits, too. You can fly from Bismarck to Chicago, if you so desire, nonstop; by way of Minneapolis; or via several milk runs that put you within shouting distance of nearly everywhere in eastern South Dakota, southern Minnesota, Iowa, and southeastern Wisconsin. If you don't fly, the bus and in rare cases the train may allow you similar flexibility with routes and stopovers. Your plans are even more adaptable if you drive.

Need I mention that *any* travel expenses must be meticulously recorded in your daybook? Keeping receipts for all meals, cabs, and other incidentals is a good idea. You'll definitely need your hotel receipts at tax time. (As a general rule, your conscientious daybook is all the proof needed on expenses of twenty-five dollars or less. Receipts are always required for larger amounts.

Does it seem to you by now that you need a bookkeeper to keep track of all these details? Not a bad idea at all. During your early stages of freelancing, however, I doubt you need more than a good filing system for every receipt and bill and that faithful, ever-present daybook to record little financial bites that add up to respectable deductions at year's end.

Files, daybook, and accountant. Even before you launch yourself full-time, I recommend you find yourself the best accountant in town who deals with self-employed people.

My own is the cream of the crop, a certified public accountant whose firm deals mostly with big (but impossibly dreary) industries and business concerns. For about a hundred fifty dollars a year, he prepares our increasingly complicated tax returns, takes care of filing estimated income declarations and quarterly prepayments of taxes, and stands ready to advise me in times of panic. His advice has saved me ten times his fee. I've even suspected he enjoys working with someone not worth millions, but always full of interesting, complicated freelancer's hang-ups. Find yourself a tax wizard with similar tastes.

Your accountant can fill you in on all the deductions you're entitled to for, mark my words, your days with the short form are over. Among these unsuspected boons are educational expenses related to improving your professional skills (though not going into a new line of work); periodicals and reference works related to your professional pursuits; depreciation on your typewriter, your furniture, your answering machine, and any camera paraphernalia you use for freelancing, plus the portion of your home costs attributable to a home office. The rules of home office deductions have recently been tightened up considerably, so be sure to ask his advice on this entry.

When I began freelancing I was haunted by the oft-repeated statement that you have to show a profit on paper two years out of five to convince the IRS that your business and thus your deductions are legitimate.

During my first two years, I showed a net loss on my tax returns. Of course, this does not mean I failed to earn anything during those years. The total of all the deductions I was allowed—business-related expenses of every kind, depreciation on equipment and tax credit due me as a new business—exceeded my gross income. That's a common situation with businesses small and large, and one you'll almost certainly encounter as you begin freelancing. It's no cause for alarm; its effect on your tax liability, in fact, inspires rejoicing.

I shouldn't have worried about that two-out-of-five rule as it turned out; the tax bite in my third and subsequent years has put me firmly among the ranks of those writing checks on April 15. Nevertheless, my accountant assures me that the profitability rule is meant only to weed out hobbyists' less-than-legitimate deductions. If you pursue your writing career full-time, you too should have no trouble demonstrating you're in it for the money.

4

Make Them an Offer
They Can't Refuse

The care and appreciation of freelance writers is a brand-new art throughout most of the country, including the special corner where you live and intend to earn the income you've chosen as a goal.

Dealing with exciting new possibilities, it's no wonder you think first of the advantages freelancing can provide for you. They're the golden possibilities that attracted you in the first place. The freedom, the flexibility, the fame, the financial rewards. . . .

Does it surprise you that those who'll hire you, editors and clients alike, learn to love freelancers for the same endearing reasons?

The **freedom**—to honestly criticize a piece of work to their hearts' content without having to reconcile their attitude with the office goals for realizing employees' human potential (and face their all-too-human urge for revenge).

The **flexibility**—of calling in someone new to take a crack at a job that's had the regular staff stymied or which, no matter how they try, still sounds a tad stale or bound by the same old company line.

The **fame**—the ability to take advantage of a writer's reputation and experience without having to pay the hefty salary he'd undoubtedly demand (if you could snare him) as a full-timer.

The **fortune**—or the financial advantage, at least, of giving nary a thought to the freelancer's Social Security, unemployment taxes, pension fund, health insurance, profit-sharing plan, or multiple state, federal, and local tax withholding programs.

Freelancers present a whole range of benefits to clients beyond their glorious way with words and their charm, wit, and delivery of finished manuscripts by deadline. Why else would so many successful magazines rely heavily on freelancers' contributions when a quarter of the writers in America would gladly die for a chance at any staff position they cared to create?

Working with freelancers can be neat and clean: They do the assignment, you pay their bill, your bookkeeper enters it under "miscellaneous fees and services," and you're home free, with no ties to bind you.

Working with freelancers holds obvious advantages to those who already know their many good points. But what do you say to the guy in Muncie who's never even seen a freelancer, or who once paid his sister-in-law five bucks an hour to write an awful brochure and thinks of professional writers in terms of gratitude for loose change?

He's used to working with freelancers in other areas of his life. His doctor and dentist in private practice are freelancers of a sort. So's the man who remodeled the kitchen, the photographer who shot his daughter's wedding pictures, and the accountant who comes in to handle his taxes.

But all those people have an advantage. He knows exactly what to expect of them, and has some idea—from years of personal experience—what to be prepared to pay them.

You're almost certainly a new factor for him. He's wondering what he'll pay an hour . . . and for an hour of what?

So it's up to you to initiate those novices, your clients (and a few editors of smaller publications, to boot), into the mysteries of how a freelance writer can brighten their lives.

Consider these points:

Your fresh, unjaded viewpoint. You are, after all, an

outsider to his publication, his agency, or his firm. Matters that are more of the same old grind to him and his employees are almost sure to be new ground for you. As an outsider, you bring your own set of experiences and prejudices and your own perceptions to his subject, whether you're doing a story on the home applications for the minicomputers he manufactures or an annual report explaining higher-than-usual research costs and lower-than-usual profits to consumers as skeptical as you.

Editors value the variety of viewpoints they gain by assigning stories to freelancers. Staff writers sooner or later develop a certain uniformity of attitude and style, whether by official decree or habit. After my own years with a newspaper, I saw the world around me in pretty much the same way as the reporters who sat beside me, behind me, in front of me, and over by the water fountain in our city room. That uniformity, conscious or not, has its drawbacks: For one, staffers are likely to perceive new developments in the ways they've understood the old. They sometimes miss striking new angles and story elements.

The same is true for commercial clients, with added implications. Someone who knows his business inside out but can't write a sentence without sweating is not likely to instinctively know what he wants in the way of written communications . . . or, if he's sure, he just may turn out to be wrong.

Witness all the thousands of brochures handed out across our country that promote businesses and agencies with a picture of the whole staff, a chronological history of the concern (year by year! no omissions!), a line or two about why you should call on them, and their phone number. All that may be of great interest to the guy who makes out salary checks for all those smiling faces and who struggled for twenty-five years to get the company off the ground. It does not make one whit of difference to the average recipient of that dull but costly presentation. Unless one's own face or that of a highly desirable stranger of the opposite sex is in the photo, the whole thing is sure of a short trip to File Thirteen.

Only a freelancer cowed by too many years within the salaried fold would ever allow that internal perspective to be presented with a flourish to a cold, uncaring public. You know, as an outsider, that it bores you to depression and does nothing to communicate a real message to those it's meant to reach.

The same fresh viewpoint goes for writing investigative stories involving publications' sacred cows (admitted or unacknowledged) and handling stories outside an editor's usual frame of reference. Why shouldn't it apply to commercial clients in identical ways? As a freelancer, you're closer to the public than the average editor or client who hires you. You're in a position to know what's going on outside the ivory or pre-stressed-concrete tower in which they're doomed to work.

Here's another way freelancers are worth their fees, no question asked: *As translators.*

Never thought you'd make your living as a professional translator, did you? But don't head for the United Nations yet. Your services are badly needed at home, wherever you find home to be. As a communicator who takes a maze of technical gobbledygook and turns it into clean, clear, meaningful English.

Translators are prominent in every variation of the freelance trade. Science writers take scientific research, as understandable to you and me as lines and dots chipped in rock by prehistoric savages, and turn it into readable, yea, fascinating verbiage. Writers with other "hard" specialties such as economics, medicine, and legal matters perform the same sleight of hand through the medium of their own backgrounds and their typewriters.

Commercial clients need your translation services just as badly (and sometimes much, much worse). The person whose business correspondence begins "We are in receipt of your letter of the thirteenth" (and commits further horrors from there on) may actually be a warm and wonderful human being, eager to say what's on his executive mind—but unaware of what a stuffy and inaccessible front that suit of verbal armor presents. Or perhaps communication is neatly avoided through the traditional jargon of the trade. Letters from lawyers are the classics of the genre, where even the stiff, formal salutation creates despair in its reader.

I've translated sets of form letters into English for state agencies; a ninety-six-page commitment law into brochures with a fifth-grade reading level for the Mental Health Association; and tons of hyperbolic travel literature into simple what-to-see-and-do stories for travel magazines. You might find yourself translating government regulations, new research on weather control, or violent environmental objections to a billion-dollar dam project. In any case, the task is essentially the same—to turn meaningless verbal meanders into a message that can touch the public. No one does it better than a freelance writer.

Besides your ability to refresh old information and to translate technicalese, you have a third advantage that makes sense even to potential clients who have never worked with freelancers before.

You are available for temporary or special assignments. While a publication may hesitate to hire new staff to work on an intense yet temporary project, they should have no such concerns about "renting" a day, week, or a month of your writing time. That is, after all, the essence of the freelance business deal: the knowledge that when you're done, you'll say goodbye, shake hands, and walk off into the sunset.

From the employer's point of view, your short-term availability is an extra plus. It enables him to contract for a share of your working time and take advantage of your strengths without paying the full annual upkeep on your expertise. He doesn't have to commit himself to keeping a specialist busy when the current project is finished.

Neither does he have to love you. He doesn't have to worry about whipping you into the ideal Corporation X automaton. Nor do you, in turn, have to resign yourself to working forever for someone who's not your idea of perfection.

The temporary nature of your freelance assignment is part of the reason for this low-pressure interaction. But there's another factor I think you'll like, especially if the strictures of serving as an employee have gotten on your nerves. As a freelancer, you're the peer of the people for whom you do assignments—not a subordinate. Your special qualities get a little more respect than they did when you worked within the system. And you yourself are free to savor the vagaries of individual clients' personalities and work habits while respecting the value of each other's achievements. The happy ending for your freelance jobs is that there's no forever after to be endured.

The fourth selling point for freelancers is that your clients don't pay for your coffee breaks. Nor do they sponsor hours you spend in interviews for stories that never work out, making out your personal invoices, scanning the morning paper for story ideas, or dreaming of the day you crack the major markets.

When they hire a freelancer, they pay only for what ultimately benefits them—researching, interviewing, writing, presenting the assignment. Since it's pure working time unadulterated in the thousand ways employees are kept (or keep themselves) artificially busy, you can justify charging considerably more per hour for the work you perform than you'd ask or receive on the forty-hour week.

Most clients grasp this advantage immediately. Though your fee can sound high to someone paying staffers five dollars an hour, most editors and clients appreciate the volume of time their workers spend accomplishing nothing during the average day.

They appreciate, too, the other kinds of genuine savings you represent—savings the novice freelancer may not even understand clearly on his own terms:

By contracting for your services, they avoid paying the employer's contribution to your Social Security benefits. (Employers match the big bite taken out of workers' paychecks with an equal contribution of their own. That's currently 6½ percent of gross pay.)

They avoid the expense of health insurance, life insurance, or any similar benefits that go to their employees. The cost varies; on our family policy, my husband's employer kicks in the better part of a hundred dollars a month.

They don't contribute to a pension fund for your golden years. They don't pay unemployment tax to cover your possible claims. (That's where unemployment checks come from for the formerly employed, in case you didn't know, and why freelancers usually can't qualify for unemployment.)

They don't worry about including you in the company profit-sharing plan, guarding your occupational safety a la OSHA, or even finding you a desk and a typewriter in a semiprivate cubicle. You don't load up the secretaries' workday. And they never, never give you a paid vacation.

Finally, as a freelance contractor, you don't show up on their employment rosters. In some businesses and public positions, this is a genuine asset. Some business owners wish to remain in the small business category, since employing more than a certain number of people can bring them under the scrutiny of more government regulators and necessitate compliance with additional reporting requirements.

Government agencies, too, on occasion appreciate a solution to their manpower needs that doesn't require another entry on the payroll to be justified to legislators. In North Dakota, it is sometimes a political liability to have employees on staff whose function is clearly labeled "public relations." Political opponents rhetorically suspect (sometimes with cause) that the offending party is actually doing political work. In such situations and their counterparts in your own area, contract freelance writers can be an ideal and economical solution to the public's genuine need for understandable information from government.

These pluses for your clients add up to the reasons your income goal is within your grasp. Whether it's $20,000 or whatever you set for yourself, it represents good value all around—a respectable level of payment for what you do best, and a bargain for your cost-minded clients.

Which is fine, good, and encouraging. What you want now is a way to translate these neatly dovetailed needs into dollars: specifically, the number of dollars which you must earn to make your freelance writing self-supporting.

You must establish two figures to use as tools for carving out that living. One is the minimum total annual income that will justify leaving your salaried job. The other is the hourly sum you have to recover to reach that goal.

Twenty thousand dollars is not an arbitrary amount for me. It represents approximately what I'd earn in a comparable salaried position—a bit less, perhaps, than in some kinds of work, like corporate relations; a bit more than in government information; quite a bit more than I might expect to earn as a reporter for most of the dailies in my part of the country.

All things considered, it's an amount that someone with my experience and skills can reasonably expect.

Perhaps it's not the most justifiable figure for you. Look honestly at your own professional writing level and investigate the going rate for similar salaried employees in your own area before you select some number out of the blue.

If you have a decade of news media experience or have worked as a writer in public relations or advertising for more than a few years, you clearly are justified in expecting to earn at least the equivalent of your present salary. Your skills are established. Your background has contributed to a certain stature in your community (or can be translated into that kind of reputation in the new community you're planning to move to). You've proven over the years that you can work on schedule, that your writing is purposeful and to the point, and that you're familiar with the kinds of assignments which you'll be proposing to take on as a self-employed writer. If this picture is you, you can confidently count on rapidly reaching the $20,000 level or much higher.

If, on the other hand, you're just beginning to work as a writer, your first year's goal should be more in line with the paychecks you'd earn at the salaried jobs for which you qualify. You can count on steadily increasing your rates to achieve a substantial living as you gain experience and credentials, and as word of your writing spreads. But you clearly cannot hope to equal from day one the income potential of one who has exercised skills for years that you just now are hoping to demonstrate.

Your goal is a private matter, so set it at a level you can live with. Both over- and underestimating carry dangers. If you expect too much, you may not reach it and become discouraged; you may also have to charge rates out of line with what your work is really worth, and thus cripple yourself by limiting the number of clients willing to pay that much to hire you. Underestimating your worth simply results in less income than you should be bringing home. Your clients will never pay more than you ask; you'll be giving them an unexpected bargain.

Arriving at your goal is the most difficult part of setting up your business. Modesty and high hopes clash, and—if you're like me—you vacillate between valuing your worth too highly and much too little. I can only advise you to look at how much you must make to keep your obligations covered, and then at the kind of background you bring to freelancing. Then take a leap of faith to establish a level which sounds reasonable. You can revise the figure as you go along by taking on more jobs, by working more hours, or by adjusting your hourly rate. But do remember that it's much more pleasant and psychologically rewarding to revise your expectations upward than to have to trim them down, so a conservative figure is a wiser choice than the sum of your wildest dreams.

When you've picked out your goal, however tentatively, you're ready to establish your initial hourly income projection—the rate by which you'll bill some clients and judge other flat rate assignments.

Add the overhead expected over your first year—including office expense, telephone, entertainment, and projected travel—to your desired income level.

Combine these two figures to arrive at the gross income you'll plan to make during your first year. Then divide it by the number of weeks you expect to work (usually fifty, with a margin for vacationing). What results is the weekly goal you'll be shooting for.

Take the $20,000 goal and projected overhead of $300 a month for a writer with a home office. Over the course of twelve months, $23,600 would have to be received to cover income and expense. Divided by fifty working weeks, that's $472 per week.

If you presumed you'd work forty hours a week, you'd arrive at an hourly figure of $11.80.

That's an easily achievable return, I've found, but it doesn't take into account the peculiarities of the writing business, which seldom allow you forty hours per week solely devoted to writing.

You'll spend many, many hours (especially at first) in necessary tasks from which you can't directly recover a cent: calling on potential clients, researching article suggestions in the stacks at the library, keeping books on income and expenses, and performing all the other duties required by any new business. So add a margin into your billing fee to cover some of this time. Increasing that $11.80

to a flat $15.00, for example, would cover approximately ten hours of nonpaying labor per week without extending the length of your workweek.

(Of course, these figures are all hypothetical. You may well find yourself working longer weeks—and occasionally shorter ones—after you've begun your freelance business. But averaging is the only way you can set an hourly fee, so pick numbers that sound right to you.)

The hourly rate you come up with will be the yardstick by which you judge all kinds of writing jobs. You'll use it directly only in setting bills for some commercial clients or those who hire you for editorial work. But it will be the implicit standard by which you judge whether any assignment is a worthwhile one to accept, from writing books and magazine articles to ghostwriting, public speaking, teaching, and any other applications of your craft in which you become involved.

Writers can find it hard to separate profitable assignments from those ultimately less rewarding, especially since the check that finally arrives in the mailbox isn't the only measure of how well they've done. Those dollars have to be considered compared to the time it took to earn them . . . and here your computations can be put to immediate and gratifying use.

Your hourly standard shows you whether each project will help you reach your annual income goal, or whether it represents, at the bottom line, a setback to your plans. A magazine assignment paying several hundred dollars, for example, may return considerably more than your goal on a per-hour basis if it depends on research you've already assembled or can be wrapped up in only a few hours. Another article that seems much more lucrative—a major market story with a price tag in four figures—could ultimately be less profitable (at least in dollars and cents) if it requires vast amounts of time and expensive telephone and travel bills not covered by the publisher.

You also use your hourly rate when commercial clients and editors play guessing games with you. At first I was invariably stumped when faced with an assignment for which the fee wasn't preordained. I could no more produce a reasonable estimate than resign myself to just accepting whatever minimum the wily client might offer. To this day

I shudder when an editor asks me what I think an accepted manuscript is worth—an experience that's neither as unusual nor as heady as one might at first expect.

You won't always quote an hourly figure: "Oh, I work for fifteen (or twenty, or thirty, or more) dollars an hour." Some clients do prefer this. But the majority of those I've worked with, and every single editor, want a lump sum. With the aid of your rate, you can figure one out, based on the number of hours you expect the job will take to complete . . . and you can also set a maximum amount of time you'll devote to the work for that price you quote, with a ready figure to mention for extra labor involved beyond your estimated hours.

In my experience, businesspeople and government officials often have preferred the hourly fee approach, while nonprofit associations (charities and professional organizations) and private citizens seem more secure with one figure for the whole job. Perhaps it's because of their experiences. Those who often work with professionals (lawyers, for example) at an hourly rate are less intimidated by a fee that exceeds minimum wage by more than a couple bucks. Those who think of assignments in less ordered terms and who themselves make modest salaries, on the other hand, are easily sent to the brink of cardiac arrest by the amount you require per hour. But they can see the reasonability of a lump sum fee that sets a reassuring upper limit to the bill they'll expect to pay.

What will you do when faced with an appealing assignment that doesn't meet your goal? You have a choice. You can weigh its ultimate worth to your career, as in the case of by-lines in prestigious publications, or decide it will be so much fun you can consider it only partially work.

Or you can negotiate the payment up to a figure closer to what you require. As you gain experience, you'll find this option open to you far more often than you'd expect. When a client or editor offers you an unacceptably low fee for an assignment, he's already hooked—he wants it, or he'd not have made the offer. You can generally counter it with a statement that the work involved is considerable and that, while you're anxious to take it on, you'll need a bit more money. Nine times out of ten, you'll be offered a higher sum; if not, refer to your first option above.

Bargaining is an accepted part of freelancing, though those who bargain with freelancers are loath to let you know it. Most publications' payment schedules are tentative at best; they'll pay more for work they really want, that's in demand, or that's produced by writers they want to work with. But neither editors nor local clients will tell you this, and they seldom make a first offer of more than the minimum they could conscionably pay.

You won't offend editors or clients by asking for more than they offer if you must to bring reimbursement within your income guidelines, and if you're worth what you're asking. You may not always get more, though I've found you usually do. But you'll almost never be thrown out on your ear, branded an ingrate, and told never to darken their hallowed doors again. If you are, forget them; they don't deserve you.

Many writers have found that it's quite possible to be both very busy and very poor. If you're taking on freelancing as a business, it's your job—not your editors' or clients'—to see that you make a living from assignments you complete.

Every rule, though, has its exceptions. Though you need to be ever conscious of your hourly rate, you may develop, as I've done, a second category of assignments: work you do free, for love instead of money.

After you've become established, I'll bet you have the same experience that I've encountered with charity and volunteer organizations. Everybody in town seems to have some modest proposal they're waiting to ask me to write for them . . . as a donation, because their cause is so just and noble.

The nerve of some of these perfectly nice people can be astonishing. Men and women whom you've never met and will never see again call at unpredictable hours to ask you to chair publicity committees and perform all your regular professional routines—for free. Youth groups, churches, candidates for everything from PTA president to political office—all have approached me at one time or another to do for free what I do for a living.

Practice the word: *No.* But don't apply it heedlessly to every plea that comes your way as automatically as the dog next door howls at the sound of a police siren.

I do take on certain of these requests. But I don't do as many as I did before I became wiser and more cynical about their motivations. I apply a true-false test to them.

True or false—I really care about this cause.

True or false—I want to make a contribution toward their goals.

True or false—I owe the person making the request a favor, or I admire what they're doing, or I just feel benevolent today.

True or false—I can handle this request with a minimum investment of time, and it won't interfere with work for my paying clients.

I do not do for free what an agency or group normally pays to have done. . . by others. Ever. I do not take on even simple projects just because it's easier to do than to turn down, or just to get a particularly persistent recruiter off my back. If I'm only mildly interested in the cause, I give what my civic-minded neighbors give: money.

Part of the reason you'd better feel good about causes to which you donate your writing time is that good feelings are just about all you'll get out of your work. In some few cases you'll make contacts or stumble across information that can be translated into articles or commercial work. For the most part, though, the worthiest causes come equipped with no such promising connections.

You can't take a donation of your services off your income tax, either, even though writing free for a worthy cause takes time away from your income-earning pursuits, and time is money. The best you can do is deduct out-of-pocket expenses run up while doing good works, like car mileage, office supplies, and postage. This makes you one of the very few persons to donate to the cause who does it solely and demonstrably for love, not money. Even the guy who digs down to give them a dollar can take it off his taxes.

So choose your causes and favors carefully. Your mission in your community is to help it learn to appreciate, work with, and remunerate freelance writers. You'll do nothing to establish this praiseworthy principle if you undercut the value of your own profession by helping bystanders associate the written word with casual and cost-free efforts by volunteer publicity chairmen.

When you do give, give freely and with enthusiasm. That's the spirit you want people to remember when they think of the only freelancer in their part of the world.

Ultimately you'll work out a balanced diet of writing assignments that meets your income goal and provides you with the kind of variety you need to mature as a writer and maintain your own enthusiasm. Some work naturally excites and challenges you more than other kinds. Magazines and books, for example, may cause your writing juices to start flowing. Yet, because they sometimes pay beginners a limited hourly rate of return compared with other assignments, you'll want to balance them with more lucrative but sometimes less exciting commercial projects, local editing jobs, or forays into the world of audio-visual writing.

Likewise, local commercial work demands balance. While it can, at times, pay higher rates for work of relatively less intensity, it also can be stultifying to limit your efforts solely to brochures or publicity or radio ad copy. You might reach your income goal with somewhat less effort, but you'd lose the invigorating challenge and variety that add up to the joy of freelancing.

The need to earn income to support your household doesn't have to limit your spirit of adventure. Quite the opposite. Use it as an incentive to try new topics and techniques, expand your writing horizons, and keep in touch with the spirit of discovery that accompanies so many newly mastered skills.

Freelancing is one long voyage of discovery . . . not only now as you begin, but as you go along from year to year. Your horizons are limited only by the vigor with which you explore possibilities waiting for a writer in your corner of the world.

5

Magazine Writing
for the Nonmetropolitan

You can learn a lot about the mechanics of magazine freelancing from the dozen books that even the tiniest library stocks. Half a dozen issues of *Writer's Digest* or *The Writer* will fill you in on other niceties—wise querying, current market needs and editorial shifts, the experiences and observations of the lofty ones who have already made their mark as writers. Oddly enough, the launching pads for their literary successes are seldom cities served by the same county fair as yours.

But all that copious information about margins and copyright laws, writing techniques and self-addressed stamped envelopes, doesn't answer the question that burns most brightly before writers who live far from publishing circles:

Can you honestly make a living writing for those glossy magazines that beckon from the racks of the local drugstore? Your informed question is, not whether it can be done (freelancers do it every day in New York City) but, can *you* do it? Saddled as you are with an unlikely address, limited local stores of celebrities and research material, and a dearth of seasoned veterans to emulate, the odds, despite the books' and magazines' optimism, seem more chancy than that bright advice suggests.

Here is what the other books haven't told you:

No, you probably can't.

Not at first, not totally, not from where you call home . . . and most important, not if your idea of magazine markets encompasses *Harper's*, *Saturday Review*, *Playboy*, *Reader's Digest*, *National Geographic* and the *New York Times Magazine*.

In fact, this chapter doesn't really belong at the beginning of this book at all. Selling to national markets, while it's the delightful dream that keeps employed would-be freelancers grinning into the dark of night, is not likely to be the mainstay of your writing career in the boonies. Frankly, it is not the backbone of mine.

Yet it's the first thing you thought of when you picked up this book (and my own thoughts once would have tallied quite nicely with yours). So let's look at those fascinating national magazines first—you'd be thumbing past less glittery subjects to get to them anyway.

The outlook is neither so dazzling as you'd make it with three magic wishes, nor so dark as the scoffers would have you believe. It is, simply, partly cloudy. (Or partly sunny, if you're the kind who sees glasses as half-full and never half-empty.)

You may be able to hit the so-called major markets—the top magazines with general circulation throughout the country or the world—with a well-honed query and a magnificent job. Sometimes. But "sometimes" doesn't pay the rent, doesn't justify leaving a salaried job, doesn't add up to the independence and self-determination of your dreams.

If these are the only markets that can make you happy, keep your job and freelance on the side.

You can, however, make practical preparations for those sometime sales and make a living writing for magazines (as well as for other, local markets) if you broaden your idea of magazine markets worth your while, and narrow your sights to the stories with which geography has blessed you.

There are writers in nearly every state of the Union and province of Canada who support themselves today on just this principle. They—and I, here in North Dakota—have learned something from experience that books haven't told us in explicit terms before:

Certain stories are inherently easier to write and sell from an address that's thousands of miles from the editorial office. Some resources are so valuable they almost insist we specialize in them. And some stories are so hard to sell, or expensive to research and write, that they really are better left to our mega-urban counterparts while we fish in more productive streams.

We've also learned that certain types of magazines are better markets than others for writers who live in nonmetropolitan locations, that certain editors are more likely than most to have an open door for beginning freelancers, and are ready to guide them through the long and mysterious learning process that master writers reminisce about as their apprenticeship.

Remote writers learn to turn up and mine these congenial markets. They rejoice and take note when they find the good ones where competition (for one reason or another) is less fierce than in the top offices that are besieged with submissions every day of the year.

To successfully write and sell magazine nonfiction from your unorthodox location you need, in short, to make the best of the ways in which geography has blessed you, and minimize (or avoid) side issues that might hold you back.

Right now, before you add to their daily workload with stunning queries and flawless manuscripts, let's take a minute to consider the plight of those editors you hope to sell. There are two things that worry them about you: whether someone in the boonies has enough experience and talent to come up with what they want, and whether you're just too far away for them to help you find it.

I have dug through the mail of several magazines published nearby and, though my samples are each specialized, I can vouch for the basis of editors' trepidations when facing the stack of unsolicited manuscripts known as the slush pile. Frankly, editors do get an enormous amount of junk: oddball stuff, poetry (sent to publications that have never used so much as a couplet), amateur nostalgia, sentimental tributes to mothers and parakeets and lost lovers, and astonishing manuscripts that really do arrive written in longhand with No. 2 pencils on tablet paper.

We may assume that you and I are not responsible for

any of these mortal sins. But I've also noticed, in these editors' mail, some heartbreakers that strike a chord. They're stories or queries that almost fit the editors' needs, but belie their initial promise under close scrutiny by a discerning reader. They're too bland, or too stale, or too much like another article either printed by the competition or on the boards for next month. Or they're perfect for an audience—someone else's, one that's wealthier, or older, or more family-oriented, or just more consumed by the detailed fine points of using widgets wisely.

Multiply my local sample by the volume of mail received daily in national magazine offices, and you realize this torrent of near-misses spiced with outright disasters is bound to dull the hopes of the man or woman who must read it. Unfortunately for us, the bulk of these rejects carries addresses of writers who live outside New York . . . for there are simply more of us.

If you have the faintest sympathy (or understanding) for Pavlov's dogs, you can learn to commiserate with editors who come to associate weird (to them) addresses with material that's hopelessly unusable. No matter how badly they want to find the occasional jewel in the slush, they're bound to view your envelope's return address with a bit less than pounding heart and rising expectations.

But if they do get to your query with hope intact, they recognize—as should you—that some stories are more easily written from the boonies than others. The others are the ones that require detailed editorial input or, to the editor, more negotiation and cooperative effort between him and his writer. If your query falls into one of the trickier categories, another handicapping factor enters into your plight: distance, sheer distance.

It's more convenient for the editors I know in Fargo to work with fellow Fargoans than with even the most promising comer in Grassy Butte. It's easier—at least, it seems easier and faster—for a New York editor to knock heads with writers conveniently sharing the same telephone area code. It's cheaper, too, when you consider long-distance telephone rates and breathless waits for reply by express mail. One step further down the path to publication, the editor finds the same advantages in writers of conventional address for communicating second thoughts, further suggestions, and requests for the article's arrival at his door. A rewrite that never leaves the boroughs of New York can often be accomplished in mere days. Contrast that with the iffy delivery of transcontinental mail from New York to Nevada and back.

Face it. We all prefer the simplest route to reaching our objectives. Can you really blame an editor for relying on a stable of nearby proven professionals instead of taking chance after long-shot chance on us deserving outlanders? He has only a few sheets of paper and our word to go on when he judges whether we're up to producing the irrefutable, amazing, world-class copy he feels his publication demands. All the SASEs in the world can't make his life easier at that point. (Okay, go ahead and accuse him of Manhattan myopia if you want to. But you know now there are other, better causes than the big-city provincialism to which we love to ascribe our rejections.)

You need to be aware of these odds against your brainstorm when it lands on an editor's desk. Yet you need not be intimidated by them. You can provide your own editorial insurance of the kind that's worked for other writers equally isolated from editors' acquaintance, who do manage to sell consistently to every magazine you can imagine.

The most obvious insurance is to be meticulous about tailoring your queries or unsolicited manuscripts for the markets you submit them to. The editor's first question is whether your article fits his readers' interests and needs, and whether it fits into the issues he's currently at work on. If he can immediately answer a tentative yes, you've crossed Hurdle One.

Do check back issues as thoroughly as you memorize a magazine's requirements in the current *Writer's Market*. Read the competition as well to get a feel for each magazine's subtle differences and the topics that are currently hot. (If the competition has a story on your idea this month, don't expect your editor to buy it just to keep up appearances.)

Once your idea passes that first test, other questions present themselves because of your unknown address. One is whether you—an unknown writer from somewhere the editor may not have heard of or even be able to pronounce—are capable of carrying out the assignment you propose.

The editor's tool for digging the truth out of you is the "on spec" go-ahead. He's agreed to take a look at it, period. No money is committed; no title is added to that issue's article budget in ink. If your work doesn't meet his standards, or even if unrelated factors, like another story in a competing magazine next month, ruin your chance of a sale, you receive nothing in return for your effort.

Unknown writers or those with only minor publishing credits usually can't avoid being told to pursue an idea on speculation. (Avoid it? As a beginner, you'll nearly raise the roof with excitement when you get your first such conditional "Yes, maybe.") But one way to minimize the problem that the tentative go-ahead is meant to counter is to tell the editor enough about yourself to give him some degree of confidence in your ability to deliver.

You don't need to recount your life story—unless it's a dilly and you want to peddle it to *People*. However, there's no sense in not mentioning your very best credits, whether local or regional publications, salaried writing experience, or published articles in minor and medium markets.

Writing experience isn't all that counts in your favor. If you have special expertise or background that qualifies you for the topic you wish to tackle, by all means detail it. Especially be sure to bring it in if your query covers a complex subject you might otherwise seem unlikely to match up to—technical or medical topics, for example, or subjects requiring a highly informed opinion. Your source material and the authority to handle it well are the heart of your query. In fact, these stories for which you're unusually well qualified may be your strongest bets. Writing style can be patched up if the material is good; but if the subject's clearly over your head, the story can't be saved by any brand of editorial grace.

Editors wonder whether you can dig up needed data from your out-of-the-way location. I've found them easier to convince if I casually suggest my sources up front. A story on overseas travel to the American West became more salable when backed up with discussions with the European-based travel marketing director for the Old West region, who works every day with cowboy-happy Germans and Scandinavians seeking help with travel plans. Another story on "the new museums" was surely received more thoughtfully in light of behind-the-scenes access to half a dozen of the very best new-style centers on the West Coast and across Canada.

You do have to sell a little harder to get queries accepted from afar. Forget the advice to be brief if brevity hurts your case. Often all you're doing is allowing the busy editor to rule you out more quickly. I don't, of course, mean two-thousand-word queries. But tell your own story well enough to sound professional. A breezy fifty-word note from the boonies suggesting an idea to an editor who's never heard of you is as inappropriate as overalls and work boots at the Four Seasons, and will create a like impression.

You do face limited alternatives when selling yourself on paper to an editor you've never met. But that's not all bad. The query system saves time and money by weeding out the stories that will never work, and it does make use of your good points—for isn't writing prose that persuades what you do best?

You needn't remain an invisible person known only by your postmark forever, though. Becoming established as a distinct individual is vitally important for those of us at a distance who can't drop in to remind editors we exist. And it *can* be done.

Your own professionally designed letterhead and envelope help promote this distinction. In lieu of the sight of your face, they're a way to help an editor recognize you. Granted, they're superficial and tell nothing about your many good qualities besides taste in stationery. But they're a visual cue. An editor who debated over my query a few months ago or remembers the cover letter on a purchased manuscript is likely to recognize, however vaguely, my black-and-gold design when it comes back carrying another proposal. The advantage is slight but cracks the ice ever so gently.

You know how hard it is to visualize a person you've never met—and how hard it can be to remember that this invisible person is really out there in a spot that's no more real to you. I try to take steps to become three-dimensional to editors who have (or should have) already bought stories from me.

Once someone has accepted that first fateful manuscript, he's not likely to get rid of me. Badgering him, of course, is probably suicide. But I do try to keep my name and letterhead before him with additional queries, compliments on an issue I particularly admired, and updates on stories he may have considered but rejected "for the time being."

Your objective is to remind the editor you're a real person. Since he may be a little uncomfortable working out of arm's reach of your developing manuscript, ease his worries. Don't be afraid to pick up the telephone and call to clarify suggestions you're unsure of or to warn him of new developments that may change your premise. And if unforeseen circumstances unavoidably delay your story past its deadline, by all means let him know! Don't let him wonder if you're still out there.

You can use the phone to half-sell articles to editors who already know your work. Though they'll probably want a written query on the subject anyway, the call can let you know whether the coast is clear before you research a new topic. One editor whom I've not yet managed to sell has even asked me to call him before submitting new proposals, since both of my previous near-misses were scuttled not for themselves, but because they were too close to other assignments that beat them to his desk.

By calling, of course, you not only find out if your query would be in vain—you add the sound of your voice to the one-dimensional portrait you present by mail. A person you've talked to is that much more real.

When making those calls, though, observe the courtesies of all good business contacts. Have a definite proposal or question, not a fishing expedition ("How about a story on North Dakota? Or something maybe on teenagers?" Guaranteed failure!). Have a solid reason for butting into his working day. Any less genuine a motive is immediately obvious to the busy person on the other end of the line.

Telephone conversations help. Yet you aren't really fleshed out in a stranger's mind until he's met you and traded comments in person. All the writers I've talked to agree that editors who know them are more likely to purchase their work, given a basically sound proposal in the first place. Meeting editors is not as easily accomplished as finding their phone numbers, but it can be done.

You can encounter some editors at writers' conferences. I highly recommend it. A good writers' conference brings you together with your quarry in a relaxed yet business-oriented atmosphere—a much better atmosphere to make your contact than, say, running into him at the dry cleaner's.

Gerry Engh, who lives in western Wisconsin on a farm that could easily illustrate a calendar, advocates a more direct approach to meeting editors. "You just have to invest in a hike to New York City and put yourself in front of their desks," she says. "To hit major markets consistently, that's the only way to go."

It has worked for her. Her credits include articles in *Reader's Digest, Saturday Review, Parents', Redbook,* and other top magazines. "After you've met an editor, you become a person, not a name. You're more likely to get hard assignments instead of lukewarm go-aheads on speculation by mail. Once you've hit with an editor, of course, follow up with periodic re-visits with new ideas."

Gerry's first market trip from Wisconsin to New York was, she says, as cold a call as one could make. She had only a year's worth of local writing credits and had never sold to a major market before. "It was sheer selling for me," she says. "I was quaking inside, but worked hard to appear confident and enormously enthusiastic. I'd done my homework, thoroughly researching two ideas for every editor I met and having a sketchy idea of a third to use at the end of the visit."

Did it work? She came home with enough assignments and on spec go-aheads to keep her busy until her next New York trip a year later. "I've met many talented writers at writers' conferences who've been working longer than I have but who've only sold to minor and medium markets by following the query method by mail," she says. "I think my trips to New York are a major reason my experience has been different."

The New York market trip is not a spur-of-the-moment vacation. Done as Gerry does it, it's a grueling four or five days of meeting two editors each morning and two more each afternoon.

Write several months in advance to tell the editors when you'll be in the city and would like an appointment. If you haven't heard from them a few weeks before your departure, call to confirm a day and time. (In fact, write and confirm anyway.) This early planning pays off in more than good will. It allows you to take advantage of airline advance ticket discounts that mean substantial savings: North Dakota-to-New York fares, for example, are cut by as much as a hundred dollars when booked in advance. (Airline discount rates may require departure on certain days of the week or for a visit of a certain length. Check with your travel agent before you start writing editors.)

Did Gerry find New Yorkers reluctant to talk to her at length? "Oh, no! They seemed to enjoy talking to somebody from Wisconsin," she says. "Actually, it's an advantage not to be from New York. 'Different perspectives,' and all that."

If you, however, can't make a personal trip to New York this season, there are still ways you might encounter editors closer to home.

Top editors of national magazines are not unheard of on the lecture circuit and scattered college campuses. Lenore Hershey of *Ladies Home Journal* was booked into our local community college last year. *Reader's Digest* regularly takes part in student seminars at colleges across the country. Pat Carbine of *Ms.* covers a lot of territory, as do various *Playboy* staffers and editors from *McCall's*, *Redbook* and dozens of other major and medium magazines that circulate across the country.

The sponsors of these lectures can be useful people to keep in touch with. The speakers they book usually have extra time in town, since small city airline schedules effectively rule out in-and-out flights. The sponsors—a college department, a women's club, a writers' conference—may be able to arrange a rendezvous for you during a lull in the visitor's schedule; you may even end up going to lunch or showing your visitor around town. If the sponsors are short on time or staff, they may be grateful for your assistance, which is certainly gilding the lily.

I'm not suggesting you ambush an editor when he least expects it—that's fairly boorish. But, by appointment, you can talk over your common interest in writing and casually suggest several ideas tied into the local landscape and tradition that are bound to be of current interest to your guest: a social problem that's been outstandingly remedied in your community and could inspire similar solutions in other towns, for example, or a historic site with a long, colorful history buried beneath those dry stones and dull inscriptions. If you've chosen your brainstorms with the editor's publication in mind, nine times out of ten he'll suggest that you mail him a query or get in contact with one of the staffers who handles the department into which your subject falls. Either way, you have a valuable foot-in-the-door. When your letter arrives on his desk back in the big city, he'll probably remember the interesting person in the charming town he visited so recently and pay closer attention to your suggestion.

If you're a writer from North Dakota or Mississippi or an equally unlikely spot, you're more memorable than you suspect. Once met, you're not one of any crowd, but a curious and interesting exception.

Make the most of this geographical edge by becoming a three-dimensional human being to those whom you want to sell. The best antidote to distance and geography may just be fighting fire with fire—highlighting your exotic location as a positive and memorable characteristic rather than a fateful misfortune.

The best prospects for not-in-New-York writers

Your address is much more than a source of amusement to metropolitan magazine editors.

It can be a handicapping factor if you misjudge its impact on the kinds of stories you're trying to sell . . . or, if you use it for all it's worth, it can have a neutral or even a pleasantly positive effect.

If you are really serious about making a living as a writer where you've chosen to live, you owe it to yourself to be realistic about what you can and can just barely sell. I am sure that someone, somewhere, is selling exactly the kinds of stories I'm going to tell you to avoid, for sooner or later you can accomplish anything you set your mind on. But as a self-supporting writer, you need to keep an eye on your own cost—in time and money—in selling a longshot as compared to selling a story that's accepted quickly, easily, and with less exorbitant out-of-pocket expense to you.

For our purposes, there are only three categories of stories to be written for nationally circulated magazines:

Those that virtually demand the peculiar New York viewpoint or access to that singular city's resources; those that could be written almost anywhere and your living in San Francisco or Tulsa or Tacoma influences only your final telephone and postage bills or has no effect at all; and those where your own location, for one reason or another, is a tangible advantage.

The first category is, fortunately, the smallest. Some magazines use this type of story almost exclusively—New York magazine, of course, being an excellent example. The stories in this group range from high sophistication to the depths of urban crime. Fashion, home furnishings on the trendiest levels, gourmet dining, the foibles of the jetset—all are out of reach to most of us, unless we invest unusual effort and expense. So are exposés of gang life, subway safety menaces and the urban drug culture. Just as national politics is tough to cover from anywhere but Washington, D.C., so the purely New York piece is not a likely winner from the Texas Panhandle.

But your stories don't touch the very heights or depths of city society? An urban location can still make a difference in the salability of your article if it's of a certain type. Some medical and self-help stories simply sound more believable with big-city experts quoted than they do from the mouths of sources elsewhere in the country; it's conditioning, but a fact nevertheless. A psychiatrist in Bismarck can be every bit as accomplished as one practicing in Manhattan, but his pronouncements won't have the same ring of authority—unless he's talking about the effect of deep winter on sanity, or the psychological problems of farmers, or unless he's fresh from a New York practice.

Stories related to industries headquartered in metropoli are also best written (or, more precisely, best sold) from those locales. That's fashion's advantage in New York, or movie gossip's edge in Los Angeles. Those appropriate addresses for freelancers reassure editors that they have access to the best information of its kind—that they have absorbed their subject, by some process of osmosis if nothing else.

Even if you've absorbed the city's sophistication during long years spent working there, you can't expect to take more than nostalgic memories when you move to Montana.

Your degree of authority depends on current access.

Any of us could hop a plane and be in New York for dinner tonight, so it's unfair to say that we are totally without access. But the cost-benefit ratio is too low, when you count air fare, living expenses, and the time it takes away from your typewriter. City stories are a bad investment for those of us living and writing elsewhere. They cost us far, far more to write than they do our metropolitan counterparts.

Fortunately, the vast majority of magazines don't concentrate exclusively on the highly localized metropolitan viewpoint. Read any major women's magazine this month and you can't miss the wide range of authors' addresses that give hometown credibility to every kind of article, from food to family problems. This nationwide angle is so important that editors actively seek outside viewpoints. An editor on *Redbook* who spoke recently at a writers' conference in Michigan said her nonmetropolitan origins provide her with that edge. "I've always thought I had an advantage in not being from New York myself," she told the gathered writers. "I was one of 'us' rather than one of 'them.'"

Many of these location-neutral stories, once an editor's decided to look at them, can be written as well from one city as another, and require fairly equal amounts of travel and other expense for most writers wherever they live.

For location-neutral stories, you have three excellent sources of information on which stories have the best prospects of piquing an editor's interest—short of managing to meet the editor in person or having any sort of inside help.

First you'll consult the annual edition of *Writer's Market* or one of the other market directories. In regularly updated entries, the staffs of thousands of magazines lay before you exactly what they think they want (and don't want) to see. Many mention free sample copies and writers' guidelines. I request these whenever they're available, especially for publications not stocked in our local library nor listed in any of the periodical indexes. I've found the sample copies most helpful. The guidelines tend to be little more than an extended version of listings in the market directories, but may offer clues about whom queries should be addressed to, annual special editions, and specific needs or not-needs which space prevents from inclusion in the annual directories.

In *Writers' Market*, as well as in monthly market reports in *Writer's Digest* and other writing publications, editors stress time after time that freelancers should study their market listings closely. It's such obvious advice that it's taken for granted; yet overlooking this one unmistakable step can be very costly for the remote freelancer.

Sending gun control stories to hunting magazines and sophisticated sexual humor to the women's supermarket periodicals is clearly a waste of postage. But worse, it's wasting an opportunity to lay groundwork with an editor who could come to respect your judgment. Your very sharpest observations on what fits into a given publication are none too good for any market you approach. Misfit queries only confirm some editors' preconceptions that distant writers aren't likely to understand and satisfy their needs.

The price of a few stamps may seem worth investing in a shaky query on the off chance that it'll strike someone's fancy. But add to it the hour or so it takes to put together even a casual idea and the ill will garnered by wasting an editor's time, and you'll probably conclude that the attempt to sell a magazine its first prosepoem in two decades is too expensive an experiment to indulge in. Selling well-tailored ideas and articles at a distance is risk enough for most of us.

Your second source of pre-query information is the familiar *Reader's Guide to Periodical Literature* and the more specialized indexes at your library. You can learn in a few minutes whether the topic you're working on has been used where you hope to place it or in similar markets in recent years.

The current issue of the magazine is your third available clue to what sells and what doesn't. Study its masthead, which lists editors and senior staff of the magazine. What subjects are handled by staffed departments? (In a women's magazine these may include food, fashion, interiors, and health. A men's magazine has its own established set of staple topics covered in-house, as does almost every category of periodical you study.) While selling stories in these areas is not impossible if your angle and information are just right, suggestions for subjects the magazine desires but which aren't handled by full-time staff are more likely to be chosen.

The table of contents offers other hints. Look not only at the topics but at who has written them. Eliminate those that are regular features with the by-line of a known staff member or contributing editor. Scrutinize the writers' biographies often included at the end of articles or near the bottom of the first page. You can learn quite a bit about the writers' locations, experiences, and the qualifications you hope to match. Travel stories, for example, have always encouraged me with their mention of writers' home bases in Iowa or Wyoming.

References to the writer's years on staff with the magazine you're reading offer less hope. If all those familiar faces are now out in the field competing for the present editor's consideration, an outsider's chances are significantly weakened. Also note whether author credits are listed. The line you're looking for is: "This is his/her first appearance in our pages"!

The articles written by writers most like yourself suggest the most fertile areas for your own efforts. There are sure to be exceptions galore. But as a beginning, try applying this technique to weed out the weak areas from those where your chances are strongest at the moment. Don't try to duplicate published stories—X-ray them to see how they're joined together. How are comparable themes slanted and approached? What form do they take most often—essay, anecdotes, interviews? What kinds of anecdotes, what quotes, what expert opinions have been included to make the author's case? Even the editor may not have considered his needs and preferences in this kind of detail before. Yet he's provided you with a neat and clean model to demonstrate exactly what he's deemed relevant and suitable in months gone by.

You don't have to be in New York to come up with ideas for the kinds of stories that remain. What you will do is listen closely to the people around you—your family, neighbors, and business associates—for indications of the kinds of joys or problems that concern them most. TV and newspaper headlines will provoke other thoughts; so can a trip to a trade show, a random overheard comment, and any number of other everyday stimuli.

No matter where you live, you'll find certain kinds of stories that are not place-specific but which are easier for you to research and write with a voice of authority. That same sensed authority in your writing makes these stories easier to sell to editors than other ones, just as fascinating, that are beyond your (reasonable) reach out there in the boonies. It's up to you to find out what your authoritative subjects are.

That good old *Reader's Guide to Periodical Literature*, dog-eared by now, is the source book for finding how the nation's eyes (and editors) see your part of the world, if they glance your way at all. The topics already associated with your address are the ones you'll sell with the greatest ease—for me, rural life, climate extremes, and the burgeoning western energy industry; for you, whatever editors associate with your part of the world: agribusiness in the Midwest, ecology in the Pacific Northwest, gambling in Las Vegas and Atlantic City, country music in Nashville.

Strangely enough, I've found that editors of even the most innovative, forward-looking, groundbreaking publications are more likely to buy ideas they half-expected when they looked at your address than they are to pick out the really exciting, entirely new topics that catch your own eye. Baldly stated, what you take for granted may be of more interest to them. What's been written about most often is the more, not less, valuable for this past exposure.

A few years ago I was trying very hard to sell the idea of coping with severe winters through home applications of solar energy to the editor of a general-interest market. He was more interested, he said, in traveling south during the crisper months—but how about a story on amazing new strains of wheat and other grains reaping harvests that would thrill farmers of yore?

The energy shortage has since made solar heating—pardon me—a much hotter subject, while inflation has taken its toll on flying south for the duration. But at the time I'd missed an important point: Annually increasing grain yields are so common around here that I hadn't separated them from the rest of the scenery. Yet farmers today are getting routine yields far better than my father's bumper crops of the mid-1960s. While I was more interested in what was unusual from my point of view, the locally commonplace was of greater interest to those who didn't take it for granted day to day.

Leave shockingly atypical newsbreaks to the newspapers, who still subscribe to the "man bites dog" school of journalism. Modern magazines are more interested in an analysis of the more familiar "dog bites man" that adds new insights to man-dog relations.

Another difference between newspapers and magazines is the way articles are built. This was an important realization for me, resulting partly, no doubt, from my own newspaper experience and partly from my reliance on papers for information that leads to article ideas and stories.

A newspaper story stresses the local side of any subject. It often starts with a general observation—that elderly people are having a hard time living on Social Security checks, for example, then immediately narrows it to a specific local case—that half a dozen widows in a run-down part of town admitted to reporters they stretch their meatloaf with Alpo.

Most magazine stories, on the other hand, use specific anecdotes and statistics to build up their general themes. That's where your local sources come in. Your neighbor may tell you about a problem her family has met and conquered, and it may suggest a possible article. But unless you aim for one of the first-person departments, such as "My Problem and How I Solved It" in *Good Housekeeping*, or plan to turn out a confession piece, this one family's story is of limited interest to most magazines' wide readerships.

But it can be the stimulus to start gathering supporting data to identify a widespread problem and indicate how readers everywhere can solve it. Your local material has value, for it's the basic building block. But you'll need anecdotes and quotes from other locations, research among authorities who can back up your observations with facts, and enough material to flesh out your originally local subject into an article that those who never will meet your neighbor can appreciate.

You can accumulate your supporting data without

traveling all over the country cross-examining total strangers. Your starting point is—surprise!—the information resources you have at home.

Remember my suggestion that you get to know your librarian while you're scouting out your community? Buy him or her a cup of coffee and talk about what you're working on these days. (With librarians' interest in writing and writers' in libraries, you have the makings of a natural alliance.) Ask for suggestions on sources. Get a tour of the stacks. Even a small library can usually be counted on to contain some titles relevant to your subject. Better yet, an alerted librarian will keep your interest in mind when reading book trade publications for news of new issues and even when deciding which new books to add to the collection.

Most community libraries are now connected, some by computer and others by Teletype, with larger libraries in their states. You can greatly expand the number of books at your fingertips by using this free service. In North Dakota, I can get almost any title issued by a national publishing house within a day or two through the libraries' computer hookups with each other and the state library itself. It's not only far less expensive than ordering needed reference materials through a bookstore: I've found the libraries to be ten times as fast in securing what I need.

The second stop in gathering data is to talk to local experts in the field. If my story involved the juvenile justice system, I'd talk with police assigned to young offenders, to the state reform school staff, the Law Enforcement Assistance Administration in the state, local mental health workers, schoolteachers, and so on.

Few of these people are likely to have the deep, solid voice of authority that a national magazine article requires. But they do each have something that can lead to that authority—connections and background in their own professional fields.

I have had fine results with this borrowed range of contacts. Since most public workers and executives in private industry now take part in professional associations, national training workshops, and regular conventions, they may be acquainted with the national authorities you want to locate. I have never been refused when I've asked a local expert for an introduction to a prominent national figure whom he or she knows personally. Most are glad to do it, since having such high-powered friends in their own professions enhances their reputations.

These local experts have another resource—their subscriptions to national publications and journals in their fields. Smaller libraries like Bismarck's seldom subscribe to specialized trade publications and you'll never find them on newsstands. Yet people have a habit of saving back issues of periodicals that relate to their work. You'll probably find someone, in the course of your hometown interviews, who has complete collections of several different publications which you can borrow for background information and insight into new developments in your subject area.

Your local experts can also help fill you in on the meaning and implications of technical material you turn up elsewhere. While your time with a prominent national authority, even with the benefit of an introduction, may be short, your friends back home will be glad to discuss the facts you've gathered and explain them in your subject's context.

When we think of interviews, we usually picture a face-to-face question-and-answer session. When the face you want to interview is a thousand miles away, you can use two cost-effective interview methods at your disposal and never enter an airport: your post office and your telephone.

You can get the information you need by courteous use of these two conveniences, often more easily than you could book a personal interview even if you were willing to spend the money to travel.

Despite all the complaints we heap on it, the U.S. Postal Service really is the remote writer's best friend. Use it to send a letter outlining your project and your questions to the experts whose opinions will help you most. You might want to pose your questions in questionnaire form for easy reply. Or you might ask your subject to call you collect at his or her convenience—a quicker and sometimes easier way to get answers to involved questions.

Or you can use your letter as an introduction and follow it up with a phone call. In either case, keep your questions to the point and the time required to answer them brief. Those that can be answered by yes or no won't get you the explanatory, quotable answers you need for your story. But those that can't be answered halfway adequately in two or three sentences won't often be returned at all.

Stamps and phone calls cost money—they're part of your writing overhead. Don't be afraid to use them enough to get the best of what they can offer. Supporting quotes that you didn't get so you could save ten dollars in long-distance charges might cost you the sale of a story worth hundreds, and in which you've invested hours and hours of time.

But sometimes even the smartest use of phone and mailbox can't get you what you need, and you have no alternative but to go to your sources in person. Under such circumstances, travel costs can be a good investment. Like all good investments, business trips should be made to pay.

We've already considered the multipurpose travel expedition that offers you time to explore more than one project while at your destination. To get the very best returns on your primary purpose from your travel investment, however, be intent on gathering all the impressions that you'd never get by letter or telephone: your subject's surroundings (sight, smell, taste—in decorating, perhaps, or via sips or samples), relationships with others you meet, habits, pastimes, emotional pitch. Then use these clues in your article to enhance its color and credibility.

When you have solid, firsthand knowledge that you've paid good money to assemble, use it as fully and vividly as you can. Those details are the evidence that you've really done your away-from-homework.

So far I've mentioned stories in which your location is a drawback and stories in which it's a neutral factor. But there's a whole Santa's bag of surprises left that are your location's gifts to you—the stories in which where you live or want to live is a positive asset.

I've sifted out five kinds of stories that are easiest to sell from the boonies. I've sold articles in each category with what I've come to believe is greater ease and far less risk than is involved in trying to crack the general-interest topics. They include:

■ Travel and history.

- The outdoors.
- Personal experience.
- Religion and inspiration.
- Rural living and suburban living.

Besides these, there's an enormous sixth category that we'll consider in a bit. But first, let's look at the possibilities these present.

Travel and history: What could be more perfect for writers living hither and yon? What counts in travel writing is not where you call home, but where you call home from. Your location puts you near a range of travel destinations, no matter where you live, that makes up an automatic low-cost list of salable topics.

History often fits into this category because so much travel is historically oriented. Together, travel and its historical sidelights can have a market nearly as broad as the whole range of national magazines.

Besides those directly connected with travel—and recreational vehicle (RV) magazines—*Trailer Life, Travel and Leisure, Travel/Holiday,* for example—general consumer magazines like *Better Homes and Gardens, Esquire* and the *Saturday Evening Post* offer regular vacation articles slanted toward their particular readerships. A variety of customer publications also concentrate on travel topics, from the airlines' in-flight magazines (*Northwest Passages, TWA Ambassador*) to motor club magazines (*Discovery,* or any of the state Automobile Association of America magazines and tabloids) and those mailed to owners of makes of vehicles, from Volkswagen's *Small World* to *Accent.*

During my years as assistant travel director for the state of North Dakota, I was engaged in a pursuit that I've since learned was headed in exactly the wrong direction. Our staff attempted to attract travel writers to cover our state by touting little-known historical landmarks and well-hidden meadow bowers. Oddly enough (we thought), they seldom snapped up these fresh, never-before-covered stories that we practically filleted before their eyes.

A principle already mentioned, that what you take for granted in your locale may be just what turns an editor on, goes double for travel and history articles. Those writers knew—and I finally learned myself—that our almost-secret tips wouldn't distract an editor from his three-day-old Danish. What travel editors prefer, instead, is application of the fresh-but-familiar principle to places that people really visit. A new slant on Mount Rushmore still sells, though that hand-carved mountain may be the only travel illustration in the country that has graced a few hundred thousand license plates as well as every self-respecting publication in the field. Overemphasized or not, people still want to go there. If you can hang a new angle on the trip, you'll sell the story.

National park stories usually sell. Stories on absolutely breathtaking parks minimally maintained by county government and located two hundred miles from the nearest transcontinental highway do not, not unless there's something mightly special you've dug up out there.

Teddy Roosevelt, Calamity Jane, various mountain men with peaks named in their honor, and General Custer help sell travel stories to major markets. Brave but obscure cavalry second lieutenants, lyrical but little-known Indian chiefs, anonymous sodbusters and missionaries who founded Protestant splinter sects in the middle of cornfields do not. Those stories can be sold, of course, if you dig up the drama and pathos and humor in them. But you won't sell them to the big travel markets. They've got bigger fish to feature.

Historical monuments marked today by only a pile of stones and a plaque will not sell (unless possibly accompanied by a luxurious resort-style RV park). Virtually anything in Hawaii or Alaska, however, probably will, as will Mexico, Texas, and Florida in winter, lakes where either the fish or the resorts are spectacular, and annually superlative fall color descriptions.

A surefire way to deduce which destinations may capture the editor's interest is to study the tourism ads in the publication for which you hope to write. As with an enormous percentage of cosmetic, automotive, and fashion articles, what you read about travel in a magazine's editorial content has ever so much to do with the advertisements that surround those stories.

Some magazines are entirely obvious about this connection. When the Old West Trail tourism group bought a major block of full-color advertising from the *Saturday*

Evening Post several years ago, a Wyoming writer who knew of the purchase offered—and sold—an equally imposing travel story on the region. The copy ran amongst the paid advertising; though the story wasn't exactly bought and paid for by those lucrative ads, its content was certainly suggested by them. Likewise, some magazines—*Glamour* among the most obvious—carry tourism copy only to please travel advertisers; a certain amount of favorable editorial comment is virtually a part of advertisers' agreement with the magazine. (Like other commercially wise publications' travel departments, the *Glamour* travel column is staff-written.)

Other publications, especially those focusing sharply on travel, have much less of a direct cause-and-effect relationship between advertisers and editorial content. But I can assure you that none of them would be adverse to a good, legitimate story that happens to concern a major advertiser. Look to the ads for clues on immediately salable topics.

I can mark the beginning of my own sales in the travel and history field very precisely. It was when I realized what I should have known back when I marketed tourism—that prominent, accessible regions make the best proposals, especially when captured with a new slant that makes them come alive again. A good share of readers peruse your articles because they've already been there and want to relive those good times in an untrite way, not because they're currently planning to go or just expanding their horizons.

So what has your location equipped you to make fresh, exciting, and intriguing to this mixed bag of past and future travelers? Your best starting places are the ones you deem most obvious. If they're near an interstate highway, you're in luck. Research by my former agency demonstrated that travelers seldom take side trips more than an hour from the four-lane, and the energy crisis makes that even more credible. If you can fly to your destination and use mass transit or rental vehicles to get around, you may have spotted one of the travel hot spots of the 1980s: work it for all it's worth.

Keep seasons in mind as you ferret out travel tips and historical yarns. Several editors I work with assure me that summer-oriented stories are a glut on the market, especially in the RV-camping field. Winter stories, on the other hand, are prized, since many of us in the northern states just don't write them (and southern writers apparently get very tired of them). Unfortunately, the North Dakota travel story set in winter does not exist; no editor in his right mind expects readers to be fascinated by a trip to the land of thirty below zero. Similarly, Phoenix in summer is a bit iffy, as is Seattle in the soggy season.

Travel writing has provided dozens of authors with a living, and hundreds more with a favorite specialty. One of the full-timers in the field is Don Wright of Elkhart, Indiana, who has recently moved from a freelancer to a contributing editor of the *Trailer Life* group of publications. Over fifteen years ago, as an impecunious college student, Don was writing and selling travel and outdoors articles to their publications and others. (He never seriously considered freelancing for a living, though. "Everyone, but everyone, told me that freelance writers starve to death.") When he graduated, he got a job in journalism and forgot about his not-inconsiderable freelance credits.

He was manager of the *Omaha Sun* in 1976 when those dreams were abruptly resurrected. The editor of *Trailer Life* called Don to ask if the magazine could reprint an editorial he'd written about RVs and the energy crisis. Reminded of his submissions of more than ten years before, she asked if he had any article ideas they might consider . . . and he responded with an almost instant list of sixteen likely possibilities.

"One story led to ten others," he recalls. "Soon I was spending every spare minute doing stories for *Trailer Life* and its sister magazines, and making as much from my weekend efforts as from my full-time job."

He reduced his newspaper duties to part-time several years ago, then left the newspaper world altogether in 1978. Today his output averages just under twenty stories a month, including RV test reports, travel stories throughout the Midwest, and a regular column in one of the company's trade publications. Travel has provided a rich vein of articles for him, including many that also fall into the next category of best-sold remote topics:

The outdoors: Don's travel pieces segue neatly into the

outdoor field as well—a distinct category which not only includes some adventure travel but also all the outdoor sports, from hunting and fishing to mushroom hunting, running river rapids and just about anything one can do where Nature's at its best or simply its most obvious.

Outdoor stories find their way into the Big Three—*Outdoor Life, Sports Afield,* and *Field & Stream*—right on down to dozens of state and regional publications including my state's own *North Dakota Outdoors* and *Dakota Country.* As with travel, material in the outdoor field has appeal for editors of general-interest publications, from conservationist periodicals to fraternal publications of the Elks and other orders to the glossy major markets.

Your address confers a special benefit here as it does with travel. The wilder and woollier your surroundings are presumed to be, the better you may be presumed to know your field (and stream). Stories sold specifically from my own area include how to fish the state's great river reservoirs (where one of the best fishing holes is above a flooded former cemetery from which coffins were long ago removed), hunting waterfowl in the prairie pothole country, and canoeing on the seasonally boisterous Little Missouri River through the badlands.

If New Yorkers can be expected to know Greenwich Village, Broadway, and how to hail a cab in a rainstorm, you can associate yourself with prairies or lakes or mountains. There is a thriving handful of outdoor writers in Minnesota who know those lakes and the woods that surround them as well as they know their markets. Another small group of successful writers (and photographers) live around Jackson, Wyoming, in the Tetons close by Yellowstone National Park; they're first with elk herds and geysers. All across the country, as you identify an area rich in outdoor writing possibilities, you spot another collection of writers who've made that ground their own.

Your geography is ready to equip you, as theirs has staked them, with its own varieties of the wilds. Even if you live amid the smokestacks of the Ohio Valley, there's something waiting for you. Hike out and look it over.

Personal experience: If your geographic angle is full of possibilities, consider your own experience. It's portable.

It's inalienably your own, yet can touch the hearts of complete strangers and illuminate universal truths. And nearly every category of magazine in the country uses personal experience stories in one form or another.

Lois Duncan of Albuquerque, New Mexico, has specialized in applying her personal life to her professional endeavors. She considers everything that happens in her life as potential story material—her children's problems and joys, her funny and sad moments, her friends' problems and triumphs, and comments she overhears wherever she sets foot.

As she has done, you can explore a multitude of applications for your experiences—first-person tales of drama and homely tensions, major magazine articles that use your own experience as a springboard for stories of broader scope, inspirational articles, juvenile nonfiction, a variety of fiction markets, and more.

Her own credits demonstrate the success of her years in the personal experience field. She's sold well over three hundred articles to publications ranging from denominational magazines to *Redbook*, *Seventeen*, *McCall's*, *Good Housekeeping* and other top markets.

One of the reasons that personal experience articles are universally popular among editors is that they appeal universally to readers, who see their own lives reflected in another's story. An advantage that your location bestows upon these manuscripts is the not-from-New-York writer's experience may be considerably closer to universal in the United States than that of the urbanite who frequents Bloomingdale's, Regine's, and Lincoln Center. Non-New York experiences, whether they transpire in Kansas City or Nephi, Utah, are perhaps more applicable to the majority of readers accross the country. Why else do all those New Yorkers write about their childhoods in the hinterlands?

Your locale colors your kinds of experiences, too. I've published stories on polka festivals and church lutefisk suppers. My mid-America upbringing, which occurred not so long ago, has provided other material: recollections of hot summer days spent in "prairie air conditioning," the damp coolness of a pre-recreation room stone-walled cellar; and reflections on the best good old days of all, which were of course in 1969.

You have your own savings account of experiences, whether hunting agates in Montana or landscaping with cactus in the Southwest. The place you start from adds flavor to your experiences; your insights provide the nutritional value that makes these stories so meaty to nearly every kind of magazine.

There's almost no way you can avoid having salable experiences happen in your life unless you sit very still and breathe evenly—and even then you can become a spokesman for meditators or catatonics. Survey your own life and that teeming around you. You're carrying some of your best stories around with you and may not even know it!

Religion and inspiration: As travel stories blur into articles on the outdoors, personal experience moves neatly into the religious and inspirational field. These stories in their most internal form can be a subcategory of personal experience—or strong, hard-hitting journalism in other applications.

Spiritual stories await you in almost every community in the land. Nonmetropolitan America, we're told again and again, is closer to its churchgoing roots; that affinity literally extends the Bible belt from coast to coast.

Religious stories can be moving little essays of personal awakenings or hard-edged news of churches facing and solving problems. Turmoil in many denominations, like that in the Missouri Synod of the Lutheran Church, provides stories of controversy, personal antipathies, and rediscoveries. Cults like the Moonies (eminently visible in small towns all over the country, and unavoidable in most cities) provide more possibilities, as do the big-money evangelical crusades that move through communities such as Bismarck; the struggles of small churches facing extinction due to rural population loss; and crusading Christians (and followers of other faiths) applying their religious principles to social ills.

The myriad publications offered by every religious denomination and not a few sects are an accessible market that nearly everyone can sell. But the religious market doesn't stop there. General consumer magazines, recognizing that churches and religion are a vital, familiar part of readers' lives, often publish stories of an inspirational nature. The *Saturday Evening Post* and the new *Argosy*, for example, both carry stories of religious flavor—the *Post* in a generally devout tone of voice, *Argosy* in a vein of interest in churches' tax-free property holdings.

The religious markets have a reputation for poor rates of pay, somewhat offset by their willingness to consider simultaneous publication with their counterparts serving other denominations. (A Catholic who reads your story in one of her publications is unlikely to encounter it later in a magazine that serves only Presbyterians.) Four sales of the same $25 story add up to $100 just as surely as one for a hundred bucks does.

Some of the religious markets, however, do better than this stereotype suggests. *Guideposts*, a nondenominational publication, pays up to $300 for full-length manuscripts and $100 for shorter works. *Christian Life* pays up to $175. General-interest publications that purchase inspirational material pay the same for the privilege of publishing it as they do for secular stories.

Rural and suburban living: As religion is an accepted part of nonmetropolitan life, so are a variety of other topics that range from the homey to hard-nosed economic issues.

The percentage of Americans who make their living from farming has been decreasing for years, from an estimate of over 90 percent in colonial times to less than 5 percent of Americans today. But don't let this fool you. The back-to-the-land movement of a few years ago, supplemented by hundreds of thousands of new food and hobby gardeners, wood-burning-stove stokers, ex-urbanites fleeing city tensions for the supposed rewards of their own pieces of land—all have combined to make farm and country living stories a better bet today than they have been for years.

You needn't be a farmer to write for this market. *Sunset* has demonstrated that even sophisticated Californians have an avid interest (as writers and readers) in gardening, backyard living, appreciating nature, and other bucolic pastimes.

As with each of our five special categories, rural living stories meet their markets in magazines designed specifically for these interests, but also overlap generously into other categories of general- and special-interest publications.

Farm and rural markets run from the agricultural trade magazines—which use general-interest as well as highly technical stories on how to raise more oats—to family life (*Farm Wife*, *Farm and Ranch Living*) and more specific topics, like gardening, crafts, and avocations (how about *Horsewoman?*)

Rural living queries also tend to take root in the new wave of magazines that focus on the allure of living in the country: *Country Gentleman*, of course, but also *Mother Earth News*, *Ideals*, and many more. General-interest magazines, too, use rural stories that fit their own special concepts of who their readers are—female activists in small towns and on farms for the women's magazines, country readers sick of a steady diet of crime-ridden urban bad news (*Grit*), and members of religious denominations who share the small-town or country viewpoint and range of problems and experience.

Rural life reflects the roots of a majority of Americans, whether their bumpers sport "Big Apple" stickers or their barns are ads for chewing tobacco. There's another bounty waiting in your area—from personal reminiscences of pioneers to ethnic traditions still kept alive, from small-town-neighbor ethnics to the fine art of schottische. Blame it on the Bicentennial . . . or *Roots*, or city insolvency, or all the TV commercials that feature a front porch, a rocker, and Granddad savoring a frosty glass of a chemical-based drink mix with his grandchildren at his knee. "Just like your Grandma used to make."

Whatever the reason, you're now in precisely the right place for these kinds of stories. It's about time, isn't it?

These five big, fat categories have something else in common in addition to being the most congenial to us outlanders.

The magazines that specialize in these subject areas are almost without exception published in the kinds of places where we ourselves live. Tennessee. Ohio. California. Wisconsin. The New York-centered offices are a minority in company like this. Is it coincidence? However so, let it be a lesson to you not to overlook pastures close to home, where the grass just might be greener than you think.

Most of the magazines that use stories from the sixth

group of geographically gifted topics aren't published in New York, either. They're trade magazines, which, though never seen by the public at large, outnumber all others by a hefty margin.

They won't win you a lot of fame. But they will serve as steady, dependable markets for many of the close-to-home stories that cost you least in travel and research time. Payment ranges from puny to excellent; an average story, in my experience, earns between $75 and $200.

Trade magazine editors are honestly fun to work with. They talk to you. They take time to explain why one idea works and another doesn't. They are glad to hear from you. They really want you to succeed in selling them something. And those with whom I've worked pay regularly, dependably, and a lot faster than some of the glossier publications.

Finding these markets is half the challenge. *Writer's Market* lists hundreds, but that's just the top of the barrel. A foolproof way of finding out which trade magazines serve members of industry in your part of the country is to ask. Drop in on an acquaintance who works in the field you're interested in covering; ask to see his trade journals.

The average businessperson has them stacked all over his or her office, creating guilt as they accumulate faster than anyone could keep up with them. Every industry is served by more than one trade publication, some by a roster that seems overwhelming, many of which are published weekly instead of monthly.

These magazines exist to bring helpful, specialized information to readers working within their fields, and also to provide an advertising vehicle for all the companies that want their readers to stock, sell, or consume their products. Some are house organs for dealers in a particular network—owners of Standard Oil service stations, Rexall drugstores, Mercruiser boat dealerships. Others address all members of a profession in a geographic area—*Commercial West* for banks in the Ninth Federal Reserve district, *TravelAge MidAmerica* for travel agency ticketers in the 13 Midwestern states and corresponding provinces of Canada.

Your business friend will be happy to lend you as many copies as you can carry away, possibly only if you agree never to return them. If you can't locate a business contact in an area that appeals to you, try the library of your community college or post-secondary vocational school. Since they educate people for the local job market, they usually have relevant trade magazines on the racks.

There are two ways to sell to trade magazines. One is to try to become a regular contributor, or stringer (which we will consider in its newspaper applications in a later chapter). The other is to query and sell articles of interest to them just as you sell articles to the consumer magazines.

You absolutely have to research trade magazines' needs and policies before trying to sell to them. Those borrowed back issues are your best way; or write the editor, explain your interest, and request several recent issues to study.

I've found that most writers I've talked with have a somewhat outdated idea of what these magazines buy. They're still hoping to sell the universal story—on cutting employee theft, perhaps—to noncompeting publications that go to dentists, plumbers, grocers, hardware store owners. Or they have a local success story in the field whom they propose to interview, photograph, and make a star in the magazines his colleagues and competition read.

Most of the trade magazines I've worked for look down their noses at these approaches. They've grown vastly more sophisticated—in layout and story content—in the past ten years than the rough-edged publications uninitiated writers picture them to be. Why not: Some of the trades have profit potential that consumer magazines only dream of achieving.

One reason why you might underestimate the trade markets is the books about writing for them that are stocked by libraries like mine were written fifteen or twenty years ago, before these trends began. So do your homework.

What trade magazines look for are stories that can inform, aid, or occasionally amuse their readers. One shop's experience can be useful if it presents ideas that can help other readers improve their businesses or illuminate new trends within the field. Horatio Alger these stories are not—they're hardheaded, well-informed explorations of current practices.

Don't overlook them. They can keep you afloat and teach you the freelancing ropes in a way that very few other markets ever will. Competition is less fierce, though standards are just as high. They may be just the markets you've been searching for.

How national magazines fit into your income potential

You *can* sell stories to national magazines consistently if you apply these suggestions and your common sense to marketing them—especially if you first escape the long-shot psychology of writers who don't believe they've got much of a chance of hitting their target.

I know writers in diverse diverting locations who make all of their income from magazine sales, who make much of it this way, or who supplement occasional sales with one or more of the many additional writing markets we're going to look at next. Those who are making substantial incomes from their writing share a viewpoint toward magazine work that you'll have to adopt if you're to reach your income goal.

Being published in a magazine isn't an honor for you. It is how you make your living—the sale of a handcrafted product for a predictable sum of money. As such, it deserves your serious attention.

As a full-time freelancer, you'll no longer have the luxury of languid sales efforts, of feeling out doubtful markets through optimistic trial and error. Nor can you continue the part-timer's standard sales tactic—writing articles strictly on spec or sending them in cold, to sit out their indeterminate terms in unknown editors' slush piles.

You can learn how the income-earning imperative changes your viewpoint simply by quitting your job to experience freelance stress firsthand. Or you can save your fingernails from being bitten to the quick by looking at magazine writing from the most rational vantage point: how those editors whom you court so attentively can do their part to satisfy your own needs.

There are two pitfalls I've learned to avoid. One is pay-on-publication markets. The other is markets whose payment sounds good until you figure in how much it really costs you to write for them.

Either situation costs you hard money—the first through iffy, unspecified future dates of payment that might never come or might amount to far less in buoyantly inflated dollars; the second in time and research costs that you'll never recover when the check finally comes through.

I sold six stories during my first month of freelancing, totalling $1,500. It sounded good when I gloated to friends and acquaintances. I'm glad I got at least that much reward out of it, for the reality was somewhat less impressive.

Two paid within weeks of acceptance.

Two paid, as promised, on publication . . . but publication came 13 and 24 months after the stories were sold.

Two met tragic fates. One was published just before the magazine went down the drain, and I was never to hear from it again. Not, you may be sure, because I didn't try.

The sixth story has been in limbo for years. The magazine has gone through three editorial staff purges to date, after each of which I've been assured my story will be scheduled soon. The story is so outdated by now it's as good as dead. In the meantime, it's provided me an education in how some editors work. The head of one of the new regimes actually called me to ask why they had the manuscript, whether they'd accepted it, and what they were going to pay me for it.

The moral of this sob story is this: Don't be so eager to sell that you overlook your own best interests. If you're living on what you make as a writer, you probably cannot afford to balance someone else's budget by taking payment in inflated dollars two years down the road. This habit is entirely reprehensible; try it on your own creditors someday, offering to pay for what they've sold you after you've finally used it up. Regrettably, the practice of paying only after a story appears in print is commonplace, especially among smaller markets.

I don't mean to paint all P-O-P markets with the same broad brush. Some are truly conscientious about it, scheduling stories within reasonable times and paying promptly after those issues appear.

But why let an editor fatten his files with your copy for an unspecified portion of infinity? If you're just getting started and need the credits, perhaps these markets are worth selling. I speak from sad experience when I suggest that, under almost any other circumstances, you avoid them like the plague.

Not to put more time and money into a story than you'll be paid for it can be more difficult than spotting P-O-P's. It can be just as damaging to your cash flow, however, since it leaves you with a negative balance.

Keep track of the actual hours you put in on every story. That means not only at the typewriter, but research and reading time, hours spent getting to and from interviews as well as conducting them, out-of-pocket expenses for office supplies, travel, telephone and postage; and any other costs that you can trace directly to the assignment.

Oddly, an assignment that carries a payment that sounds unusually good sometimes proves to be the costliest; major market assignments sometimes set this trap. They may pay two or three times what you're accustomed to earning from smaller markets. If they require four or five times the effort and expense that the smaller market demands, the bargain becomes less impressive.

The potential value of a by-line does sometimes outweigh the immediate bucks. A major magazine credit really can improve your sales record to some degree. In that sense, an assignment that costs rather than pays can be viewed as an investment in your career.

Once, it's an investment. More than once, it becomes a case of pricing yourself too cheaply. You are not a beginner petitioning the big time from an unlikely locale forever. At some point you bring experience and well-developed talent into play on every assignment you accept, and your time is worth more than it was before. When you sense that this is true, let the world know. You're not a beginner forever; nor should you receive beginner's rates.

Some magazines automatically increase the rates they pay after you've sold several stories to them. Some—beware—do not. They count on writers' natural resistance to talking about dollars to keep their work priced low. If you gulp down your embarrassment and say, "I think this is worth more money," you may be as surprised as I have been. Every single time that I've stammered that I would not accept what was offered, I have gotten an increase with hardly a murmur of protest. (That worries me too. If they accepted my demand so easily, I should have made it sooner or asked for even more.)

You can write for magazines for the thrill of it while

someone else is underwriting the cost of your bread and butter. When you're really on your own and depend on your writing for a living, you'll realize that thrills don't keep the lights burning.

Writing for magazines as a full-timer is a business. A freelancer is a businessperson. Treat your work with all the respect of a mason pricing a fireplace or a utility company making its case for a rate increase, and market it as well as any salesman who sizes up his customer before he begins his pitch.

The difference is that you pursue your special business for both love and money. Unless you can live on love, keep an unblinking eye on the money.

6

Easy Access Markets:
No Matter Where You Live

Be they ever so humble at casual glance, the publication markets closest to your home are bound to be a mainstay of your geographically exotic writing career.

Take them for granted, do you? Don't. They offer you solid assistance in reaching your annual income goal—assistance that goes far beyond the checks they send in payment for your work.

Regional markets are accessible. They smile upon a writer with an out-of-the-way address, since it's one they share. You face much lighter competition in winning their support. And they brighten at the fun, but minor, story proposals that are of such a limited nature national magazines barely deign to reject them. Regional magazines consider, even desire, the minutiae of local appreciation and discovery.

To the writer intent on making a good living by his craft, regional publications—both magazines and newspapers—can provide a rock-hard foundation for every kind of income-producing undertaking.

Take national magazines and book publishers. Regional publishing credits, while not as good as by-lines in last month's *Playboy*, provide incontrovertible evidence that you can write and that at least a nearby editor or two has successfully worked with you in the past. Clips from these publications fatten your portfolio and lengthen your list of professional credits. The stories you develop first for them may also turn into nationally marketable material; if so, your regional editors will have underwritten a good bit of your research.

Even better, the work you do for regional markets gives you visibility as a writer in your own territory. Unlike many other kinds of endorsements—which, along with fifty cents, will buy you a cup of coffee—this one is readily converted into cash. Articles regularly carrying your by-line in a regional publication give credibility to your claims of verbal fluency. In fact, they may even preclude your having to make those immodest claims as your reputation precedes you.

Your regional by-lines are a credential that you can use to secure every kind of nearby writing assignment—editing your own publications, writing as a ghost or a public information consultant, working with audio-visual programs or radio and TV, lecturing or teaching. Those credits can be used to lead directly to the level of writing income you desire.

Business isn't the only relationship you may develop with your regional markets. I, for one, love them, too. They are the ones that welcome me with arms open widest, with proud blurbs about my achievements in their editors' columns on contributors, and with long, pleasant lunches at downtown dining rooms that serve the best burgers in the state along with a glass of beer to fortify the literary banter.

I am not alone in loving my regional markets for themselves as well as for what they can do for me. Writers who work for them generally harbor a growing fondness. Some make their entire incomes from assignments for the gamut of local magazines. Others, like those of us in the Dakotas, find them only the relish for our meat-and-potatoes writing; the gamut here is pretty quickly worked. In either case, these are among the most enjoyable markets for which you can write.

Their readers love them, too. National publishing credits may get you little perks like an author's entry in the *Reader's Guide to Periodical Literature*, circulation in the hundreds of thousands (or more), and bags of enraged letters from everywhere if you touch a sensitive spot a little too roughly.

But do they prompt lovely older ladies to introduce you at church potlucks as "our own local celebrity"?

Do they get you invitations to speak to homemakers' conventions?

Do they put you on a first-name basis with the clerks down at your local magazine and book shop? I thought not.

What Gael Greene is to New York and Bob Greene to Chicago, I'm a bit of to North Dakota. You can be one of the name writers in Idaho or West Virginia. Regional markets do that for you.

Money is the big stumbling block for many writers who have considered—and decided to pass up—the magazines and newspapers in their neighborhood. Newspapers, for example, are generally conceded to be low-pay, troublesome markets for freelancers. Regional magazines vary. They range from a top rate of multihundreds up to a thousand dollars for *New Jersey Monthly*, *Yankee*, *Alaska*, and other commercially successful titles, to three to five cents a word for *Florida Keys*, *Inland Shores* and more; and right on down to a word of thanks from *Beautiful Idaho* and not a few additional markets.

When it comes to writing for nothing, you'll have to examine your need for visibility very carefully indeed. In my opinion, no professional writer ever needs to be that visible. But the other markets, even those with relatively puny payment of a nickel a word, may not be the bad bargain they first seem.

For one thing, most of these markets expect pretty much what they're willing to pay for. That means you'll seldom be asked to perform extensive research and run up big travel and telephone bills for stories they're buying for fifty dollars. Because these stories draw on your existing background knowledge of an area, they are fast to research and write, so they may still return you the hourly rate you've set as a minimum for your work.

(As a basic principle, I do not write for less than my minimum just for the sake of added reputation. If you feel you badly need the experience of working with an editor at the beginning of your career, you may choose to violate this rule. But I'd caution that if you need experience this much, get it before you begin to freelance full-time on a self-supporting basis.)

The vast majority of regional magazines fall somewhere into the one- to three-hundred-dollar range of payment for full-length stories. At that rate, I know you can make these markets pay their own way for your efforts on their behalf, and still enjoy all the side effects of writing for them as a bonus.

Before you begin to bask in their benefits, however, it will serve you well to figure out just what is meant by a regional market so that you can take roll in your own area.

Regional markets are characterized by one fact, and one alone: they serve a readership united solely by its interest in a particular city, state, or region. That's the one thing they have in common. Their readers live on that hallowed ground, or lived there once, or know it only in their hearts. So every scrap of content in the publications, from book reviews to recipes, has some bearing on their locale.

Beyond that, regional markets exhibit as much variety as the magazine field in general. *Vermont Life* editor Brian Vachon, who has written a book on regional publications, divides the field into quarters: city magazines, positive regionals, environmental magazines, and guidebooks. (Guidebooks are treated in Chapter 8.)

I add newspapers to that list, with a few cautions. They aren't the wide-open markets that the magazines certainly are. Yet they have the same potential for carrying your regional articles, which, if pursued to the limit, can provide its own rewards. Since they're a different type of market from magazines, we'll look at them separately.

The regional magazines share some good points. Their editors are eminently and emphatically approachable. They want to talk to you—not just open a letter that has to be answered, but sit down, talk over ideas, and share some thoughts on your common love of your location.

They don't really expect you to be a polished professional convincingly scarred from the major market battles. A goodly share of their contributors often are nonwriters or part-part-timers fascinated with one perfect story idea or a tremendous love (sometimes even beyond words) for a single facet of the spot you all call home.

Because of their size and the good local supply of professional writers, some of the city magazines work with a more sophisticated crew. Even there you can be assured of standing in good company. Full-time serious freelance writers are rare, friend, very rare in most regional editors' offices. Says Vachon in *Writing for Regional Publications*, "There aren't many full-time writers in these parts. For my money, there aren't enough part-time writers either. I'm always on the lookout for new talent."

The city magazines look to me like a dedicated newspaper reporter's dream in content and bright presentation. Unlike the regionals I know best, they're usually commercial ventures dedicated to picking up where their local news media leave off—the real story, untold or unfinished in the daily news columns, or examined at length for new interpretations and new insights.

If your area is served by one, I highly recommend an expert on the subject, Art Spikol. A columnist on nonfiction for *Writer's Digest*, he's former executive editor of *Philadelphia* and author of the book *Magazine Writing: The Inside Angle*. His book includes a lengthy chapter on city magazines that discusses in detail their needs, their attitudes, and the basic propositions that account for their being one of the fastest-growing markets in the country.

City magazines investigate all kinds of lively aspects of urban life, from where to buy the most generous ice cream cones to who controls the local porno scene. If they live to investigate, the regionals serving my part of the country (and most of the rest as well) belong in a quite separate category, for they exist to extol.

North Dakota Horizons and its genial, generally gorgeous brethren across this great land ring out with the sound of self-discovery and not a little pleasure at what they find. People read *Horizons* (as they do its counterparts across the country) for a fix of self-satisfaction with their place called home.

With the best available photography and exacting graphic production, *Horizons* (and *Arizona Highways*, *Inland Shores*, *Manitoba Moods* and dozens of others) strives to serve up the best parts of life in its territory. The closest it will ever come to an exposé is an expansion on the journal notes of Lewis and Clark on their trips through the state while exploring the Louisiana Purchase. Its approach to consumer affairs is assignments on local arts and crafts. The nearest thing to dining reviews is its one-page recipe section noted strictly for its glorious full-color food illustration of wholesome North Dakota products.

North Dakota Horizons exists to make us proud of North Dakota. And more: to provide a glimpse of home (from its most photogenic angle) for the thousands of Americans who have their roots here but who've been transplanted around the planet.

Writing for *Horizons*, and for your local magazines which parallel its sunny, optimistic approach, is almost pure fun. Stories on the characters, districts, and pastimes you hold dearest can be natural material for their pages. While they do receive a striking volume of strange ideas ("My Amazing Pet Rabbit Fluffy") from those who don't understand what they're about, they are entirely open to legitimate suggestions and submissions. The editors welcome small voyages of subtle exploration.

Those small voyages are the ones you're most eager to take—but don't leave without a chart for navigation. Submitting prewritten material over the transom is a poor policy when dealing with regional magazines, unless you're absolutely sure ahead of time what the editor wants.

Fortunately, regional editors are perhaps the most approachable and helpful of their profession. Those I know are friendly, interesting people, overworked but always eager to help you find your way if your sense of direction is even a bit awry.

Their accessibility may come as something of a surprise; after all, their staffs are minuscule, their duties maximal, and their time fractured daily into a dozen phases of magazine production. But letting you go off to write an assignment half-informed only adds to their workload, for it almost always means they'll have to revise your finished product. The editors I know despise revisions.

So make an appointment and get to know a regional editor today. Discuss several story ideas you propose to cover. Ask about needs for coming issues; not seldom will you find the editor engaged in filling up more than one at a time. Ask about the slant he prefers on regional stories or profiles—or read the magazine faithfully, for the slant becomes almost instinctive after you've been exposed to it often enough.

You can find out about a magazine's prejudices if you push the right buttons during these visits. *Horizons*, for example, has an unwritten ban on photos and eulogies to abandoned barns and farmhouses. Though some of the most striking vistas in the state are brought to life by the bittersweet silhouette of a tumbledown family home stark against a plowed field, the magazine officially finds no beauty in it. Memories of the Great Depression are still too vivid to its sponsoring organization, the Greater North Dakota Association. To them, the empty houses cut adrift suggest family tragedies during the dust bowl era rather than an artistically pleasing weathered landmark.

Oddly, editors' prejudices run the entire gamut of possibilities and are as unpredictable as they are arbitrary. Vachon, at *Vermont Life*, definitely prefers stories of those living now in his state to the escapades of expatriate Vermonters. *North Dakota Horizons* editor Dale Western, on the other hand, has never been averse to a story of a North Dakotan who's made it big (and "showed 'em") anywhere in the world. He argues they contribute to North Dakotans' pride in the quality of people the state has reluctantly exported since the end of the homestead boom.

The best stories I've found for our own regional magazines all distill the essence of what North Dakotans find most distinctive—ethnic groups and their special holidays, history pieces (rooted firmly in current events whenever possible), and interviews with prominent or remarkable North Dakotans, from the governor's warm, farm-bred wife to a colorful horticulturist with tips on picking the right tomatoes to an elderly artist who escaped from under Hitler's thumb. (She now creates icons and coddles homeless cats in a striking old house on a hill north of town.)

There's another tie that binds the best regional stories. They're ready to be illustrated, either with a camera held in your own capable hands or by one of the proven photographers all regionals save up for golden opportunities.

The illustrations are the reason for many, many

acceptances. I would go so far as to say that, given a good cerebral story with only head shots to brighten its gray columns of type, or a weaker story with striking photographs just begging to be taken, you're usually much better off pursuing the photogenic topic. Leave the other for the newspapers.

Controversy, similarly, is a factor in choosing your topics. There are two kinds of controversial topics for the regional magazine: those arguments that raise the stock of its chosen territory, and those that probably don't belong between its lovely covers.

The controversies in which *Horizons* specializes are on the order of whether ancient migrating peoples really carved the outlines in the chiseled rocks lying in farmers' pastures (for romantic and conversational purposes we have held that they did) and whether researchers who several years ago declared Fargo the windiest place in the nation knew enough not to spit into that stiff breeze.

The kinds of controversy it isn't interested in include political, social, economic, artistic, and technological dogfights. The reason is partly practical; lead time can be a full year, clearly ruling out any stories of a timely nature. The rest is purely pragmatic. Regional magazines' readers are united in only one principle, their love for a particular piece of geography. People who dote on prairies may share friendly "how do you do's," but are likely to make the oddest of bedfellows when it comes to matters of more subjective opinion like politics, religion, strip mining, and the boom in shopping malls. The rule on controversy is generally this: If it isn't upbeat, it's probably a bad bet.

The sponsorship of regional magazines can tell you more than just who will sign your paychecks. The positive regionals are often published by governmental bodies—state or local—or by quasi-public organizations, like the chamber of commerce, who have a stake in elevating the image of their promised land. When in doubt, look for advertising: While these magazines seldom take ads, privately owned publications always have it. If there's nothing but unbroken stretches of intriguing photos and prose inside, the magazine is almost surely deriving much of its budget from its publishers' direct support and the balance from subscriptions.

Magazines published by private companies are a bit more likely to take on highly charged controversies. While constrained by the same common interests among their readers, they're still in a position to experiment with their contents. How do you find out their inclinations? Just ask. That's always the best way to get an answer.

The sunny, positive regionals serve a general audience. Another type of regional publication is aimed at specialized groups: environmental magazines for readers concerned with the natural state of their region; regional farming publications, regional business magazines, regional entertainment tabloids. They're similar to the magazines that serve a national audience interested in the same specific concerns, but they're sharply limited to matters defined by a geographic area.

Many otherwise undefinable markets fit into this category of regionals. *Southern Outdoors* is one of them. *Corporate Report*, covering business in the upper Midwest, is another. So are the *North Dakota REC [Rural Electric Cooperatives]* Magazine, with its firm sense of place and its focus on farm families, and a little thirty-two-page monthly distributed free to travelers in the Bismarck area, called *The Greeter*.

Circulations can vary from a hundred thousand to a single thousand readers. Some are sold by subscription and on newsstands, while others lie in wait in motel rooms or go to association members as a benefit of paying their dues.

The most minor of these pay contributors nothing. They depend on their audience's amateur field reports or an executive director's efforts. Most, however, do rely on professional help. And there's where you can come in.

These special regionals may not shy away from controversy, provided it's of vital interest to their readerships. And the topics that interest them can be much broader than you'd predict, since even the most avid businessman likes humor and travel and entertainment, and the most go-get-'em hunter can care about conservation, hunting ethics, history and tradition, cooking and interesting personalities.

Controversial topics are of a more carefully prescribed nature. Government exposés won't find a market at a regional business magazine—unless they're of immediate interest to its businessmen subscribers. Scandal and investigative pieces can be welcomed if they have direct bearing on the publication's readers, but will be ignored if you miss the vital basic tie-in.

Granted, these publications aren't likely to assign the most sensitive pieces to those outside their organizations, at least not until their work has been proven through less touchy submissions. While well-documented articles supporting the group's positions may be considered, they have to stand up to the most rigorous standards of accuracy and interpretation, or the publication's sponsors open themselves to charges of bias and misrepresentation. Embarrassing them with inaccurate or incomplete research—particularly on topics with direct bearing on their own fields—is guaranteed death for the well-meaning freelancer who slips up (even just once).

Clearly, regional magazines can't be lumped into one or two well-defined stereotypes. They vary as much as do the areas they serve, not only in subject matter, but in attitude, approach, and the appeal they offer their readers. They're a challenging group of markets which you can develop without great expense right where you live today.

Regional readers are hungry for articles about the territories they're loyal to. If you can write to satisfy that hunger, your locale has opened up a whole new range of markets for your services.

Newspapers

Newspapers as freelance markets? They provoke two kinds of reactions from freelancers, both somewhat unjustified.

Beginning writers overestimate them as a market. They don't understand that papers rely almost solely on their staffs and wire services for the copy that crams their daily editions.

More experienced freelancers tend to ignore them altogether for exactly that reason. To them, "newspaper markets" suggests the Sunday magazine supplements, or the occasional big-city paper that does buy a certain number of freelance manuscripts for its weekend editions. Any less a newspaper than this looks like a hopeless situation.

Surprises happen to both groups.

Beginners waste untold hours querying newspaper editors or trying to peddle pedestrian stories they've already written. Usually their letters go straight to File Thirteen (the editor's wastebasket, alternately known as the round file). Newspapers, unlike magazines, are not set up to deal with would-be freelancers. Their editors work in a demanding atmosphere of imminent deadlines, and only the kindliest are likely to respond to the sight of a self-addressed stamped envelope with an explanation.

Occasionally the freelancers win, against the odds, and see their unsolicited articles make it into print. They're surprised—at both the minuscule size of their checks and the casualness with which their opus is met.

Both the beginners and the seasoned writers are half-right about selling to newspapers. The beginners have a point: Newspapers do demonstrably obtain articles, columns, and news stories from writers not formally a part of their staffs. Almost every newspaper in the nation, weekly or daily or any other, can be relied on to buy some material from freelancers if their work sounds too good to miss and they're capable of writing what they propose. It may not happen often, but it's never never out of the question.

The veterans are right, too: newspapers are not the plushest of markets. If you manage to sell to them, you may be rewarded with a check that couldn't buy hamburgers for even the smallest crowd. Ten to fifteen dollars is not a bad payment at all for a story, according to the supplement editor of a local daily. At rates like that, full-timers can't afford to dig too deeply into the newspaper field.

But there is a way to make newspapers pay. Three, actually.

You can sell occasional stories to more than one noncompeting newpaper. This is most often done in the travel and lifestyle fields, where freelance purchase budgets are most likely to be found.

You can follow the example of other freelancers who have made newspapers their prime markets: Ann Landers. Erma Bombeck. Art Buchwald. You too can develop a column or regular feature package and syndicate it yourself to as many noncompeting papers as you can reach. The minimal payment from any one of your clients is then multiplied by the number who send you those little checks each month. Self-syndication need not be national, either; it's worked for freelancers on a regional or even a state basis.

You can, of course, develop a column and find a syndicate to market it for you. But the money will probably take longer to mount up, and the feat of impressing a syndicate is a bigger, longer job than most beginners can afford to invest their time in.

Or you can develop an ongoing relationship with one (or a couple) newspapers that take an interest in your region.

All three methods are variants of the same principle. To make freelance newspaper writing pay, you have to increase your published volume and get it in as frequently as you can.

Half a dozen writers in my own state supplement their writing or salaried income with self-syndicated newspaper columns. Another, who recently left the area when her husband was transferred, made a name for herself as a stringer for the local daily and eventually earned herself an invitation from a national newspaper feature syndicate. Other writers—regularly plying markets outside this state—have become familiar names to readers of the several dozen far-flung Sunday newspapers which feature their work from time to time.

To sell to newspaper markets, you must find a gap in their staffed coverage and devise a way to fill it.

That's why travel writing, to name just one area, is a relatively fertile field among the nation's larger newspapers. Readers are interested in travel to every corner of the globe, and travel industry advertisers are interested in reaching those readers at a time when their receptivity is at a peak. Voila—the travel section.

But even major papers are reluctant to treat staff writers to what they presume is a life of one paid vacation after another to gather original travel stories. (Travel writing really *is* work, no matter what editors may suspect, but the point is still valid.)

It's more economical for them to search out freelance travel articles from professionals who have already been there, or who amortize the cost of their own research travel over a series of articles and topics. Besides saving money by buying freelance stories, editors can get a wider selection of writing styles and vacation destinations than a limited travel staff could provide.

Smaller newspapers are less interested in travel freelancing because their markets don't include enough potential travel advertisers to carry an entire section. They may still group ads together with some editorial travel copy, but their wire and news services provide enough articles to make a credible, if less than dazzling, showing.

So what gaps do these newspapers suffer from? It's important to know, for gaps in their coverage are the portholes through which you can peep into these markets' workings.

Don't look for big areas of white space next Sunday. Gaps are more subtle than that. Instead, consider material that would interest the paper's readers, that's not currently being offered, and that has a logical tie-in with local advertisers which will excite the ad department. Editors and reporters are loath to admit it, but the advertising angle has more than a small impact on publishers, who in turn influence the editorial staffs they employ.

When citizens band radios were just becoming a craze, dozens of local newspapers—our own included—suddenly discovered CB columnists. The local CBers gravitated toward these columns. Advertisers with CBs to sell were bound to notice and gravitate a bit themselves.

The same reasoning lies behind the photo, gardening, home improvement, and beauty columns and stories you find scattered throughout city newspapers. Which came first, the readers or the ads? Either way, an alert writer turned up to take advantage of the situation.

An obvious gap—say, in material of interest to retired people or those on the verge of retirement—provides you with your opening. If you can spot it and prove that a local audience is waiting for it, chances are the editor will agree.

Does that mean one story on senior citizens? You might be able to sell it, though your odds depend entirely on how open the editor is to "monkeying around" with writers outside his staff. But even if you sell it, you'll be only a bit ahead; the payment is generally paltry and the impact on your career minimal.

You can overcome both problems by offering not one story, but continuing coverage of the area. That usually emerges in the form of a column, a regular piece of more or less uniform length that can be depended on to serve the same audience week after week. It simplifies the page editor's task, and also greatly improves your proposition. Building a regular readership is, after all, both the editor's goal and your own; he can hope to attract only a handful of readers with sporadic material.

You can use the postal service to introduce yourself to the editor of your newspaper, but don't count on getting an acceptance by return mail. Or ever. A much more effective approach is to make your proposal in person, backed up with material that demonstrates your skills as a writer and the depth of material available to you.

Most columns are proposed in the same way, whether by an outside freelancer or a member of the staff: The writer develops the idea and checks to see whether it duplicates copy already in use or too easily accessible at no charge to the editor. Public relations representatives, for example, could be all too willing to fill for free the gap you've found.

The next step is to write not just one column, but enough for at least a month. While an editor may seriously consider your idea on the basis of three articles, he's more likely to have faith in your productive capacity as well as the strength of your theme if he can see six to a dozen samples.

The samples should be as close as possible to what you envision for the finished work. They should be presented in standard manuscript style—typed double- or triple-space with the first sentence beginning about halfway down the first page. Don't bother to have it typeset or resort to other gimmickry; the newspapers will take care of that side of production and are used to working with nonfancy typed manuscripts.

Develop a list of enough ideas to carry you through a few months as another demonstration of your idea's potential. One of the editor's first questions will be whether your premise is broad enough to sustain itself over a period of years. Yes, that is *years*. Every newspaper, from the smallest to the mammoth, will want to be reassured that you can sustain the column over a substantial span of time.

Writing a regular column is a grueling assignment, whether you're doing it as a freelancer or as a staffer. I wrote two columns for most of the eight years I spent at a newspaper, and can attest to the desperation and impending dullness you face after you've written on the same kinds of topics for years and face another ironclad deadline—and have run as dry as a glass of burgundy.

The relative shortness of newspaper columns—many run no more than 600 to 800 words—is deceptive. Behind those well-chosen words is a need for thorough background research and a deep well of variations on one basic theme. Don't take on a column project if you doubt you can sustain it. Six good months followed by one or two that falter won't help your reputation a bit, though no one will realistically expect every single column to be a classic.

Selling one editor is the first step in any kind of self-syndication. If you secure a column or an assignment to a permanent area, like reviewing films or books, you'll quickly find you put more time into that one regular project than you can hope will be rewarded by a single newspaper's payment.

With your first editor's knowledge and permission, you can approach other newspapers with the same material. Obviously your stories must have more than local appeal to be marketable outside your community. Many columns built around hobbies or activities or advice rely mostly on general information and can be broadened enough to serve readerships in several areas.

The most important caveat of multiselling is this: Never, never offer your material to another editor whose paper competes with your first. Competition doesn't stop at cutthroat intercity rivalry. Even small circulation overlaps must be considered, for what you're selling must be offered exclusively in each subscriber's territory. Weekly papers in separate counties seldom compete with one another. On the other hand, even small city dailies often do, with a larger newspaper nipping at the heels of a daily in a smaller town within its area. If you must make the choice, you're better approaching the smaller paper than the larger; it imposes fewer limits on the other contacts you can make.

What kinds of columns and regular material might succeed in your area? Some of the more salable topics include the outdoors, hunting and fishing, personal sports and recreation, homemaking skills and human-interest profiles and anecdotes. In each case except the last, the audience is well defined both to the editor and to the advertising manager. As for human-interest stories, newspapers have an almost insatiable hunger for them. But touching people's emotions is a tricky technique that not everyone can manage.

Humor is another deceptively appealing area. A strong localized humor column would appeal to almost every editor. Oddly enough, there seem to be more would-be Erma Bombecks around than anyone would have suspected from the glum tone of much kaffeeklatsch conversation. That every newspaper doesn't already have one of its own demonstrates how many aspiring humorists fail to amuse anyone but themselves.

Wayne Lubenow defines the field of humor writing in my part of the country just as Erma Bombeck sets the tone for housewife chuckles and Mike Royko for sardonic wit applied to Chicago politics. Wayne's weekly columns, accompanied by a second feature, appear in thirty-two North Dakota weeklies. Another column and other special material show up twice a week in the tabloid *Midweek* in his hometown, Fargo, North Dakota.

Wayne has been a popular columnist in the state for over thirty years, first with a succession of daily newspapers and then as a full-time freelancer. He began applying his witty observations to the weekly, rather than daily, markets in early 1971.

"I started with just nine papers. It was a question of survival," he says. "A buddy in an ad agency suggested a self-syndicated column to me just before the annual North Dakota Newspaper Association convention. I went on up there two weeks later and talked to a few guys, and I was suddenly in business." He added more of the state's hundred weeklies as they watched his column's popularity soar, until reaching the present comfortable 33 percent two years after sending out his first column.

Each of the members of the Lubenow Co-Op—"a pretty loose name for us, since all we have to go on is a handshake"—receives a column of about 600 words each Friday along with a short North Dakota feature story suggested by one of his editors. The price for the package is twelve dollars per paper per week. "My big competition, believe it or not, is Erma Bombeck," he says. "They can get her for three dollars. But she isn't going to drive out their way during a January blizzard to write a story they want to see in print."

Lubenow's work appears in another overlooked newspaper market, too—*Midweek*, the highly successful shopper distributed to all the homes in the Fargo vicinity. That continuing relationship matches the revenue from fifteen or so of his country weeklies to bring his annual income, he says, considerably above what he could expect from any salaried job. And that's not counting assignments for *Horizons* and nearly every other regional publication with money in the budget for a contribution from a top regional name writer.

"My writing is a means of survival. My clients have a wonderful incentive system," he says. "If I don't write, I don't get paid. I've never missed a deadline for a column since I began. You have to understand that I'm completely undisciplined. Sheer economic pressure keeps me going. I just sit down at the typewriter every day, stare at it, and maybe open up a vein. . . ."

Wayne's forte is family humor; his kids have grown up and mirrored all the stages of his readers' homelife over the years. But your backyard resources don't have to be limited to your own spouse and children to prosper in the newspaper markets.

How about your whole community—its news, its controversies, its characters? You can become neighboring newspapers' eyes and ears at home as a correspondent or stringer.

Many publications have correspondents stationed throughout their service areas who feed them updates on local developments in the hinterlands. Newspapers need their stringers more desperately than most. No matter how large their staffs or how eagle-eyed the assignment editor, no paper covers every story its editors would really like within its circulation area. If you're on the spot—the right spot to fill a gap in their coverage—you can find yourself another kind of beneficial relationship between the news and you.

Where stringers are needed is outside the city where the newspaper office is located. That may mean in a city's suburbs or outlying towns served by the county seat.

Papers want news of these areas, for their advertisers desire those customers' attention, and the circulation influences the rates they charge for ads.

But these peripheral subscribers commonly share one predictable gripe about that major newspaper: It never carries news of their own towns unless something really extraordinary happens, and that something is usually a natural catastrophe or horrible crime. They envy the kind of ongoing attention the paper gives its primary area, from its coverage of civic meetings and issues to personality pieces and features on local leaders and groups.

If you're living in one of these dissatisfied, overlooked communities, here's one chance that your address will elicit genuine interest and even relief (unlike the guffaws you get on a bad day in the Big Apple). Provided you can demonstrate that you're a capable reporter with time to maintain a reasonable level of coverage, you may find you've got yourself a job.

The job of a stringer isn't usually salaried. Most newspapers pay according to the total inches of copy you produce or the number of stories called or mailed in.

Your most important quality is not that you write like Hemingway, but that you're on the spot. Some newspapers regularly work with stringers and actively replace those who move or retire in a certain locale. Others are open to the idea but seldom go out of their way to seek correspondents.

In either case, your best route is the most direct one. Drop in to talk with the editor, calling first to make sure you choose a time when he's not swamped with work (and crabby). On a larger daily, talk with the state editor. Find out what kinds of news interest them and offer to submit your first samples on an entirely nonbinding basis.

Good freelance stringers find that they can generate a surprising number of local stories for their editors. Sometimes ideas are offered by the editor who's their contact at the newspaper; they may have been kept on the back burner for lack of someone with time to take them on.

With a topical column, the key to decent earnings is the number of newspapers that purchase it. Stringers stretch out their earnings rather differently. The more stories they produce, the more they earn. But they also can borrow a single page from the columnist's book and investigate the possibilities of serving more than one paper at a time.

This works best for the lucky few whose communities are within the prime interest areas of more than one daily newspaper who do not consider each other competitors. More common are situations where you can write about your community for both a neighboring weekly and a larger daily. These two kinds of papers usually don't see themselves in a neck-to-neck race for subscribers, so strong material may be marketable to both with fresh treatments and different angles.

Before you approach any additonal editors, however, be sure to get the approval of your first contact. Going behind his back may cost you both markets.

You should be aware of two more peculiarities of dealing with regional newspapers. One is that few are really set up to handle the standard freelance tools of query letter and SASE. On most of the country's papers you're going to be a curiosity in the city room. Take nothing for granted; ask whether they keep score on your earnings (and check them yourself), and offer to bill them if they prefer. And present your inquiries and ideas in person or by phone. If you write and mail them, rejection is as likely to be the harried editor's wastebasket as it is the U.S. Mail.

Another problem is the fervor with which editors defend their staffers' territory against encroachments from the eager would-be freelancer. The way to get work is not to tell an editor his staff writer is rotten and you can cover his beat better. Nor is it usually worthwhile to try to sell material in an area that's close to any staffers' turf.

Try instead to find true gaps in coverage and take steps to make that ground your own. Once you've sold your services to an editor, you'll be in the enviable position of the writer who got there first. All that you've got left to worry about is turning out great copy as regularly as you've promised—and believe me, that is quite enough.

Other stringing assignments

Though newspapers are the most numerous markets that might seek stringers in your part of the country, they're by no means the only ones.

Stringers can act as on-the-spot reporters for a number of

organizations. Some are strictly news oriented. Others depend upon your growing network of contacts and background knowledge of your area. All view your location as an asset, for you can help them stretch their coverage into cities they'd never reach in any other way.

I have been a North Dakota stringer at different times for a national consumer magazine, United Press International, several trade publications, a national association with an interest in legislation, and a Washington, D.C., consulting company whose clients are vitally interested in the economy and regulatory climate in North Dakota.

My friends have managed other correspondent jobs: for *Time* and *Newsweek*, for an activist women's newsletter, for nature and ecology groups, and for consultants preparing feasibility reports on North Dakota construction projects and business development.

Some of these assignments are a real snap to identify: they are occasionally advertised in larger state newspapers. During the past six months our local paper has carried want ads seeking part-time stringers for a coal publication, a banking industry newsletter, and several anonymous advertisers who used a blind box number for replies. (I was tantalized but too busy to answer their ads.)

Other openings are passed on by word of mouth. For 18 months I provided abbreviated daily coverage of North Dakota government and politics for United Press International, which has staff offices nearly everywhere around the world except in the state of North Dakota. The Minneapolis bureau chief responsible for the state inquired at the capitol about reliable correspondents. An acquaintance who had seen my work in regional magazines recommended me.

But many good opportunities require you to seek them out. They have this in common with most newspaper stringer slots—the opportunities don't quite exist until you create them by offering your services.

I have an informal relationship with several trade publications in industries I follow closely. I set them up in just this way, starting cold and simply asking whether they needed local information support. I knew they had a clear interest in Dakota news from watching their circulation and keeping an eye out for important developments within my territory. I studied most over a period of several months, subscribing to some (many are free on request) and reading others in the library or by borrowing copies from friends who received them. The critical point was whether they seemed to have contacts already within the territory I could cover for them.

In most cases the answer was clearly no. In more heavily populated states, you may end up with a few yeses and maybes . . . but even then publications with real interest in developments in your area may not be at all averse to having more than one stringer stationed in your state to field local news.

Writing to offer to serve as a correspondent can be an invigorating exercise for freelancers. The reception can be a great deal warmer than the one that greets the average unsolicited magazine query. The editor of one publication for travel agents wrote me by return mail to say she was "honestly delighted to learn of a potential stringer" in my area.

Include samples of your published work and any personal background that qualifies you to report on the industry. Most editors don't expect you to be a ready-made expert, though background does help. If you have any experience at all in the industrial or business world, it will help you sound thoroughly promising. You'll find that most editors are more than willing to help you nail down the basics of their business if they're confident you'll turn out to be a productive stringer who'll be around long enough to justify their time and effort in your early months.

Consulting companies, another field for freelance stringers, are a mysterious outside force over much of the country. When a group of Bismarck business people was considering whether the community could support another new luxury motel, they contracted with one such company to explore the market. When North Dakota wanted a feasibility study on a new governmental social program, they brought in a consulting firm with a national reputation. When a problem seems to beg for further study—for instance, the need for better transportation in a rural area whose citizens are too few to guarantee it will return a profit—a consultant is often the answer.

There are dozens of national consulting firms, working in

various parts of the country. Most have one factor in common when they're faced with a study in your community: As the proverbial outside experts, they lack familiarity with local ground rules and givens. By hiring your native expertise, they can save a tremendous amount of work in accumulating the background knowledge they need to give their reports credibility.

Watch your local newspapers for word of impending consulting contracts. These items turn up most often in government news reports, but also appear in the business and finance pages and around the local chamber of commerce. You need to reach these companies very early in their planning stage if you're to be considered as a local stringer, so your own early warning system can make a great deal of difference in your prospects. (A friend at your chamber of commerce office is always a good source, as is any friendly face among the city fathers.)

To consider your help, the consulting firms need information on your reporting skills, your reliability, and your local credibility. (A local contact who's earned a reputation for exaggeration could completely undermine their own work, so they're justifiably suspicious.) Local references are a must. A recommendation from the governmental body or company that has hired them is the most persuasive reference you can have. You may find that local executives familiar with your work are most amenable to recommending you.

Fees vary, but are generally on the healthy side. Work may be assigned on either an hourly or piecework basis. Be sure that your expenses are covered, either directly or through a substantial fee. Telephone calls to distant head offices and volumes of data shipped cross-country can quickly run into a substantial expense.

If you live in or near your state capital, as I do, you have an excellent source of stringer assignments that are almost yours for the asking. During legislative sessions a broad range of clients are anxious to receive fast reports of bills introduced and enacted that affect their interests, either for news value or as their own early warning system.

Energy, for example, has been a hot political issue in North Dakota since the late 1960s. A wide variety of special-interest groups and industry newsletters and magazines, all highly interested in regional developments, are located at such distance that they're forced to depend on local help. (Little North Dakota legislative news ever hits the national news wires.)

Some who watch your legislature with interest would like more active local help—part-time lobbying, perhaps, along with this news of relevant actions. It's up to you whether you want to take advantage of these possibilities. Lobbying pays very well, even in its more casual part-time forms. But I suspect that any business affiliation with a special-interest group damages a writer's credibility as a gatherer of news, since politicians are highly sensitive to these connections. Lobby only for groups you can truly support and defend. Otherwise, you're safer turning away tempting plums that can put you in a compromised position.

The best advice for unearthing all kinds of stringer opportunities is not to be afraid to ask whether a potential client is interested. If he's not, you'll never hear from him. But if he really is open to establishing a local contact, he'll greet your offer warmly.

Regional markets can be a solid backbone of your freelance income and a source of pleasure and reputation—a nearly perfect mixture of payoffs. Once you've explored their possibilities and considered their contributions to your overall income-producing strategy, I think you'll savor them as well, one of geography's commitments to your career prospects.

Your location is an asset in all these regional markets. If you've got the address they want, you ought to flaunt it.

7

Photography
(Picture the Possibilities)

Photography is a mystic art. It demands an artist's eye, and a vast investment in equipment and professional training. Only a gifted few can rise above the Thanksgiving dinner snapshot and the Polaroid head-and-shoulders portrait to create true photographs—creative, useful, salable images.

Out here on the prairie we call that sort of statement buffalo manure. You may not be the next Ansel Adams or David Muench, but I know you can learn to take serviceable, reproducible photos that will enhance your writing, both in communication value and in sales.

Nothing can add more to a story than appropriate photographs.

Situated as you and I are, getting those good photos when and where we need them is largely up to us. You have to come up with the visuals for which your writing projects cry out. Either you line up someone to serve as the second member of your writer/photographer team, or you learn to cover yourself with a camera.

Photography can add directly to your annual income through the sale of photographs themselves to a wide variety of markets. But its biggest contribution to your freelancing career is in the increased salability it lends to your writing: to magazine articles, books that hinge on visual explanations, and commercial projects of every kind, from putting out a newsletter or brochure to publicity shots and audio-visual projects.

In big-time publishing, arranging for illustrations is supposed to be your editors' responsibility. They are in charge of selecting photographers and assigning them to complement your words. They want the best of both worlds, after all—verbal and visual—and they strive to get it by this two-step, two-assignment process.

This picture dims watt by watt when you reflect upon the realities of the geographically unconventional writing life. Number one: You are far, far away from those editors' offices, and from the photographers they're used to working with. Ergo, the expense of travel to the sites of your likeliest subjects (not only fares and food, but idle professional time spent in airports and aboard jets) is a small lump hard for the finance director to swallow.

Number two: Your subjects are sometimes as foreign to editors as the sight of the Ganges at sunrise. More foreign; you can see the Ganges in the encyclopedia of your choice. What I can see from my window and peer at on writing forays is as difficult for the average editor to picture as it is for me to conjure a vision of little old men selling roasted chestnuts, or people actually wearing high-fashion clothes. (We do not roast chestnuts in North Dakota.)

Number three: Many of your best markets aren't the kinds that buy photos and manuscripts separately unless absolutely forced to. The medium and minor markets, including most of those six best-sold categories we talked about in Chapter 5, are accustomed to buying manuscripts and photos in the same package. When half the package is missing they're reduced to searching stock photo agencies for relevant illustrations. That's not too much to ask if your story is about the Eiffel Tower or Fisherman's Wharf or the rim of the Grand Canyon. It's a little tougher if you're mining that vein of writer's gold, the natural ideas provided by your location. Try finding a shot of Battleship Butte, a rosy waitress serving *Fleischkuchele*, or a sunset over Lake Tschida. In most cases, our far-out illustrations are tough to obtain . . . or simply not worth the effort.

Trade stories, travel stories, stories of local characters and pastimes, tales of recreational adventure and the outdoors—automatically become, more salable when attached to a set of sharp, natural-looking black-and-white photographs or a pocketed vinyl sheet of color transparencies. And that's just in magazine work.

Book proposals that require illustration become enticing in direct proportion to the number and quality of photos you can provide yourself. If you can't supply those that play an integral part in your proposal, you're doubling the up-front expense and making the book's preparation far more complex for the editor who'll handle it. The cost of securing outside photos lessens your proposal's attractiveness to the publisher who's considering it. In some cases, it might even make it less rewarding for you: A full-scale photo collaborator would be assigned a share of your advance and royalties.

How-to volumes, the best bet for a first book that's frankly planned to make money, are heavy consumers of photos. Yet they're the kind of straightforward, businesslike shots you can easily take yourself.

These photos conserve your editor's time. They enable him to visualize (even visually double-check) the subject on which you've lavished your well-chosen words. Though they cost him money that's paid to you, who provided them, they reduce time spent searching for art or debating an unillustrated proposal's merits. And they save him a few bucks in the bargain, too. Fees paid for photos as part of a photo-manuscript package are considerably less than he would expect to pay for desperately needed shots bought one by one from stock photo agencies or market-minded photographers.

Since his cost is less, the editor is usually amenable to buying only one-time publishing rights for your photos. Sell all rights only if the purchaser refuses to consider any other terms—and then be sure you get considerably more for their use than you'd otherwise be offered.

Photos whose rights you retain are potentially bankable time and again. Here's where you can cross the line toward stock agencies or wise photo marketing yourself. By placing your topical photos (black-and-white or color transparencies) with stock photo agencies, you can make them available to thousands of editors nationally who may be looking for a shot of the inside of a power plant, or a mother bathing a baby, or a grasshopper nibbling a stalk of wheat. Agencies usually split proceeds from photo sales fifty-fifty with you; they're busy marketing your backlog of photos while you're engaged elsewhere. For information on stock agencies—how to approach them and where to find those suited to your files—consult the current *Photographer's Market*.

As your files build, you may also want to experiment with marketing your stock photos directly to editors, art directors and others who may be interested in using them. Again, *Photographer's Market* provides hundreds of pages of tips on which editors need the kind of shots you've already added to your stock. Several newsletters offer timely information on publications' current needs. The best is *The PhotoLetter*, a biweekly published in Osceola, Wisconsin, whose specific leads are tailor-made for the sometime photographer with limited time to spend on speculative photo marketing. The newsletter also includes regular explorations of the art of selling photo illustrations, from how to mail them most safely to how to take the kinds of photos that sell over and over and how much you can expect to earn from them.

A word lover at heart, I've never willingly conceded that a photo can be worth a thousand words. Ten bucks, for sure—or fifty, or two hundred fifty for the cover of a small-circulation magazine. Words aside, that payment does add up. While you may not make your living with a camera squashing your nose every day, you can count on doing a comfortable bit better if you match photos with every manuscript you send away.

You needn't have the photo staff of the old *Life* at your beck and call to take advantage of what illustrations can add to your work. What you do need is your choice of one of two options: a photographer who'll work with you on speculation to illustrate manuscripts at your own or an editor's behest; or the ability to wield a camera without tremors and doubts.

In an ideal world, you'd only be half of a writer-photographer team. That's how top newspapers always assign illustrated stories (always, that is, when everything is running smoothly, about fifteen minutes a day). That, in fact, is how my photographer husband and I complement each other's efforts. Before you can arrange this ideal team play (with or without wedding vows), however, you need to know what to look for in a photographer.

Your photo collaborator should, above all, be willing to work on the same basis as you do for editors far away. That often means on speculation; he or she should be willing to tackle stories with you without guarantee of payment when that's the assignment you have to go on. In many cases speculative shooting may not be necessary, of course; your editor may ask you to secure illustrations through a local photographer and arrange payment.

You should not, in my opinion, select a photographer who'll only work with you if you agree to pay his rates yourself. You may recoup some or all of that cost in the long run; nevertheless, it makes sense in only dire emergencies. You're adding sizable expense to your overhead if you do this more than once in a while. If your stories don't sell—because of weaknesses of their own, because of the photos, or just because of the phase of the moon or a peculiarity of an editor's taste—you're out the cost of his services.

(That cost can be considerable if you're working with a professional. The day rate in my area is two hundred to two hundred fifty dollars, plus travel expense and supplies, prorated hourly for shorter assignments. You can, of course, find amateurs who'll do it for less. But if you're paying the bill, why not spend enough to get the best?)

Your ideal photo comrade is a freelancer like you. Not full-time, perhaps. He or she may be a commercial photographer happy for a chance at a different kind of assignment, or a newspaper photographer moonlighting, or even one of the multitude of superb amateurs who prefer to reserve their love of photography for spare-time endeavors.

One local freelance photographer, for example, teaches college by day. He'd worked as a full-time photographer for years before deciding to become an educator; during that time, he says, his work had grown routine for him and had exerted less and less creative appeal. Now, with daylight hours spent at other tasks, he's brought a missionary's fervor back to his own photographic assignments.

A second choice is someone who works with a local

photo studio. Those cameramen and -women may be looking for the challenge of a different kind of subject, a nice change from stiffly posed high school seniors, wiggling families complete with itchy pets, and radiantly nervous bridal parties.

If this photographer is your best available choice, be sure that he's familiar with the demands of editorial photography before any film or time is spent in vain. That means experience with black-and-white films and color transparency work. Most studio photographers work with color print film, the kind that yields negatives to be printed on paper. Editors do not want to see color prints, period. They are not used in the color separation process upon which almost all publications depend. (On rare occasions an editor will reproduce a color print in black and white. But sharpness and tonal quality are lost in the process, and it's only for situations where no other choice is possible.)

One advantage possessed by many studio photographers is that they often work with large-format cameras—which give larger images than the inch-wide 35mm preferred by photojournalists. Given the choice of two equally appropriate and attractive transparencies, most editors will pick the larger every time. But they can make do with 35mm very well when presented with no such dilemma.

When you're choosing your photo teammate, use your own facsimile of editorial judgment to assay his work's quality. That judgment should include these minimum standards: sharp focus, good contrast (with a range of tones from blackest black through graded shades of gray to whites that are as clear as they should be), and an ability to "see" a story in photographic terms. In other words, photos must be at least technically acceptable and interesting enough to add a striking dimension to the written word.

There's no sense in leading on a perfectly nice and eager friend whose work is clearly not up to reproducible standards. His photos won't get used if they're out of focus or mushy gray all over or simply so dull that no editor would waste space on them. If you work with someone whose skills aren't at least the equivalent of your own, you can be sure your joint efforts will be reduced to the lowest common denominator. That's usually not good enough in a market where even terrific submissions get crowded out.

Not only are you hurting your own sales, perhaps more than by providing no photos at all, you're raising false hopes and running up someone else's film and processing bills without any reasonable prospect of reward. Do that nice guy next door or your cousin's husband a favor, and don't lead him along on the callous off chance that he'll turn out something—anything—you can use.

Find someone who knows the ropes.

Or learn the ropes yourself.

I am convinced that there's hardly a writer practicing his craft who cannot master the basics of providing his own photo illustrations. I believe this partly because I've witnessed photo teachers each September initiate several dozen students in their very first serious relationship with a camera. By Christmas or Easter those same women and men, many of whom had no experience whatsoever in photography, are making slide shows and producing occasionally distinctive photo essays on their own.

Partly their example, that is, and partly my own experience. As a college freshman dazzled by good-looking photographers all around me at the newspaper, I sank a good part of my savings toward my sophomore year into a Nikkormat and the minimum number of lenses that would win me their respect (three).

The same camera has stood by me for over a dozen years. It has taken thousands of feet of black-and-white photos for publication, for reference, and for fun, along with a fair sampling of color slides.

None of those photos is going to be exhibited in the Museum of Modern Art; nor am I in line to become the next Margaret Bourke-White (or even Candice Bergen). But I've happily applied this wonderful combination of useful pursuit and avocation to dozens of other rewarding ends. Among them:

■ "Environmental" photographs of dozens of people whom I interviewed in their homes, on the open prairie, in meetings, or wherever I could catch them. Every one of them would have been happy to supply me with a black-and-white studio portrait left over from his last job application. But those shots I took capturing them active in the world around them are infinitely more interesting than the spotless self-images offered.

■ Photos to buttress investigative pieces. While these stories are not my forte, I've had occasion to use photographs to back up my own observations. However gut-wrenchingly honest the words, photos add extra credibility to your claims.

■ Copying of historical photos and illustrations of artifacts. In writing stories involving historical events and people, it's easier to get permission to reproduce those fragile, yellowing photos in all their evocative sensitivity if you can copy them on the spot where they're being protected. In some instances you can also get permission to borrow them and have them studio copied. But if you have a dear old woman's only photo of her long-dead parents, and she lives two hundred miles away in Grassy Butte, you're risking a lot in terms of good will and irreparable loss by entrusting that photo's return to the U.S. Mail. If you can snap your own copy on the spot, she'll be happier and you'll be in the clear.

Likewise, historical artifacts aren't always easily toted into the studio for perfect portraiture. Sometimes you can't even talk a leery curator into opening the locked, climate-controlled glass case keeping you from your subject. If you have a camera, you can get what you need. If not, you're in for a lengthy series of negotiations and arrangements from back home. And if the curator's only offer is to photograph the work for you, you'll have to worry about mediocre photos, hefty "service charges," or both.

If you're snapping a picture of the feisty curator himself, you can clear up another hazy area that sometimes handicaps photos' usefulness: the matter of a model release, which assigns to you the right of using your subject's likeness in print.

Many photographers go through life blissfully unaware of the model release, relying on the subject's implied agreement to appear in their work. (He didn't hit you over the head with his cane, did he?) In many cases an official release won't be necessary. But it is vital if the photo is to be used for commercial purposes (as in advertising), or if the picture is to be used to illustrate a controversial topic (sex and the senior citizen), or presents the subject in an unfavorable light.

When in the slightest doubt, get a release while you're making your photograph. At that time it's a mere formality. If you have to go back and get it later, it becomes an issue, or at least a question worthy of serious thought. When the answer turns out to be no, you're honor-bound to refrain from using what may be an excellent shot.

■ Photographic note taking. Lengthy inscriptions, immaculate records of where sites are located along a thoroughfare, and memory-jogging inventories of scenes and sources all save reams of handwritten notes on location. You can't place the museum on the wrong side of town if you've got a picture of its surroundings.

■ How-to articles. Here again, I've only dabbled in the genre. But photos have come in more than handy on stories I've written about crafts like dyeing Ukrainian Easter eggs and quilting, as well as step-by-step illustrations of pit-roasted barbecue beef and other stories-in-the-making.

Not all my photos have been published. Not by a factor of one frame in one hundred, if you must know. But they're still not a waste of my time or money.

When you work in a region that most metropolites find literally unimaginable, photos can be a valuable sales tool. Queries backed up by a few shots of the terrain, the profile, or the finished product you propose to write about are far more persuasive to editors of any stripe than the comment, "I can take great photos to go with my story." Don't tell them; show them. Photos catch everyone's attention, and I'd wager that few editors can resist paging through a packet of prints or slides filed in a plastic sheet for easy viewing.

Some of those editors may decide, after looking at your samples, that the prospects are good enough to call in one of their stable of professional photographers. You've still helped your story sell. Ditto for the times when an editor prefers an artist's rendering to photography. Photos can be the source for art that captures the spirit of a place or personality.

One of my favorite story layouts was illustrated with pencil sketches made from proof sheets of film I'd shot on location. The photos were middle-of-the-road: not bad, not good enough for the magazine's top-notch tastes. But handed to an illustrator who'd never seen the people or places I photographed, they led to portraits so uncannily accurate that one subject's daughter framed her mother's sketch. She told me it captured her like no photo ever had.

I'd warn you, however, to keep a careful eye open if your photos are to be used as the inspiration for art. Since they aren't reproduced firsthand, a wily editor may decide he doesn't need to buy any rights to use them from you. Unfair!

I don't think I need to outline how your camera can help in local commercial assignments. Newsletters or house organs, brochures, publicity campaigns—all are immeasurably improved by well-targeted photo images. You can broaden the range of services you provide your clients and increase the income that results, as well as make your assignments more effective before the public that judges them. While you do charge for your services, your client saves money, too: You can research and photograph at the same time in many cases; he need not pay an hourly rate for a photographer who needs lengthy indoctrination before he can do the job.

If you're going to become a double-duty writer-photographer, your first concern is bound to be equipment. Some photo amateurs never do get beyond this stage, spending their photographic hours endlessly discussing various camera systems' presumed advantages and the hotly debated difference between Ektachrome and Kodachrome films. They're the ones, incidentally, who may have originally turned you off on the supposedly complex and doggedly serious world of photography. Pay them no mind. Their interminable argument disguises the fact that they're too impressed with their gear to sully it by taking pictures.

No, find yourself a working photographer whose advice can guide you through the expensive maze of camera systems and accessories. A newspaper photographer may be happy to help. A working magazine photographer would be even better. But your best guide of all might be a sympathetic low-pressure salesman at a local camera store that caters to professionals.

Don't distrust that dealer too much just because he makes his money selling cameras to folks like you. If he runs the kind of store that serious photographers frequent, he values you as a long-term customer, not just a quick commission.

Once hooked, a dedicated photographer almost always becomes a customer again and again, trading up to more elaborate camera systems or buying and switching accessories or dabbling with the newest developments in darkrooms and flash attachments. That dealer has a stake in providing what you'll reasonably need to take professional-quality pictures. If he's a mutant of the breed and tries to steer you toward Hasselblads or such (the financial equivalent of a moderate Rolls-Royce in these inflationary times), keep looking for the stalwart authority you can depend on.

The most expensive camera isn't what you need. Neither, though, is the rickety bargain you pick up at a discount store or through a mail-order camera advertisement. You *can* save money by buying name brand equipment from lower-priced outlets, I'll admit. But as a beginner, you need the face-to-face service that a knowledgeable dealer can provide you. Leave the cheapies to the men (they're always men) who cheerfully polish their cameras instead of depressing their shutters, and find someone you can count on for education, for repairs, and for future advice.

Likewise, I'd suggest you avoid rock-bottom bargains and make your first camera a member of one of the major reputable photo families. Nikon, Leica, Pentax, Olympus, Mamiya—photo buffs compare them constantly. But the fact is the name won't make much difference in your photos: Its effect is on your first system's resale value. If you decide to trade up to a better system someday or—heaven forbid—throw in the towel on photography completely, you'll find the name-brand equipment holds its value remarkably over the years. Brand X fares less well. The money you save by buying your discount store's weekend special will come back to haunt you at the other end of its useful life to you.

Single-lens reflex cameras are the industry standard. They're those black-and-chrome jobs slung around the neck of every modern newpaper photographer, and they enable him to impress bystanders by switching lenses, screwing on filters in odd colors and sizes, and fiddling around in an overweight gadget bag.

You needn't tote twenty pounds of goodies unless you're bent on developing your biceps, but you ought to have a few basics. Lenses in several sizes provide a selection of ways to capture your subject. As I've mentioned, I bought three when I purchased my camera, and have never seen a convincing need for more.

The 50mm lens that undoubtedly came with your camera body sees much as the eye does, and is known in fact as a "normal" lens. A moderate wide-angle lens—I have a 28mm, though a 35mm is also useful—takes in a much broader view, allowing you to photograph the width of a room or all fifteen people seated around a conference table without backing up unreasonable lengths. (This lens gets a little fish-eyed around the edges, convenient for special effects but a pain when you have no such arty aspirations and want vertical lines to look vertical.) The third lens is a moderate telephoto like my 105mm; with its help, you can get close-in portrait shots without smelling the garlic on your quarry's breath.

These lenses provide one of the qualities an editor hopes to see in a batch of submitted photos: variety. They're perfect for the standard illustration technique of a long shot of the subject, a medium shot, and a close-up or two. (There. You have the secret of newspaper photojournalists' photo essays.)

But editors look for more than giddy variety in your photos. Focus and exposure are the two most important qualities that make or break your photos' chances.

All that's fuzzy in beginning photographers' work is not bad focus. My own problem has always been camera movement—tiny tremors at the time the shutter is released that blur the subject just enough to cause a poor old editor to feel he must clean his glasses. Practice and conscientious effort are the only ways to correct the problem; try taking a deep breath and holding it as you snap the picture. You may also hug the arm supporting the camera close to your body, using your skeleton as a reasonably sturdy bipod.

Are all writers nearsighted? Do they all find it awkward to focus a camera wearing glasses? Just in case you're one of us, here's a tip for easier focusing. Most cameras sold today are equipped with a ground-glass viewfinder; you just twist the lens until the scene you're viewing looks sharp.

If you're nearsighted, of course, sharp to you isn't always

sharp to the world. One solution is exchanging the standard equipment for a split-image screen viewfinder. Then, to focus, you merely peer at an image that's cut in half at the waist; bring top and bottom together again, and sharpness is guaranteed. Alternate models give you double vision and require you to bring the images together.

Exposure depends on the amount of light that hits your film. That's what all the monkey business with an adjustable camera is meant to control. There are two ways to cheat, assuming that exposure isn't instinctive with you. (It is only instinctive with a few highly experienced braggarts, who still sneak light checks from time to time.)

Little things mean a lot when using a built-in light meter, like fresh batteries, so easily forgotten, and accurate calibration of your meter. Changing the battery more often than your thrifty nature suggests is really necessary. You can check up on your meter's accuracy by testing its readings against those of another camera known to be accurate. Take it down to your camera shop when in any doubt.

The second option is a hand-held light meter, more accurate but infinitely more trouble than the built-in kind. Carrying one and being reasonably well versed in its use is a good backup precaution to the built-in metering system. But remember that it's prey to all the adversities that beset the camera's own readings—poor batteries, calibration that's out of whack—plus it adds to the number of gadgets you'll have to juggle out in the field. Unless you're really serious about photography, get a built-in meter system and check it regularly.

When all else fails, give thanks that Kodak and its comrades pack a lifesaver in every box of film you buy. It's that little instruction sheet which you thoughtlessly crumple with the wrapper and toss into the bottom of your camera bag. It carries sound advice on exposures in typically encountered conditions, from bright sun to lamplight. You can rely on it to carry you through when, on location, your built-in's battery starts oozing and you've just dropped your meter into the lake.

Correct processing can have a lot to do with your exposure, too. If you plan to use your photos commercially—and you do, for why else go through all this?—give them the professional finishing they deserve. While you may be able to recoup costs and labor of a black-and-white darkroom if you do lots of photo work, you can also for a nominal amount pay a pro to do all the mixing and fixing for you.

If a pro's nice for black-and-white, he's the only candidate for color. Color processing is a long, touchy procedure requiring precise temperatures, ultra-fresh chemicals, and a totally dust-free environment. Few of us can produce a dust-free environment, try as we might. Unless you do yards and yards of color work every week, it's unlikely that you can save money by processing it personally. Why bother?

Choose your photo lab with the care you applied to finding a dealer to trust. There is a difference between professional photo labs and the discounters whose work is sold through your local dime store: about a dollar a roll, true. But it's also the difference between pockmarked, off-color results and a service that won't cause editors to shudder. Ask a local professional photographer to recommend a lab, or borrow one of his trade magazines and answer a few ads yourself. Don't be concerned, incidentally, if the lab you choose lies at a distance. That's the norm for those of us in the hinterlands, since there isn't enough local volume to justify local processing houses. I regularly deal with processors in Dallas and Seattle, and my only complaint is the occasional delay in mail delivery. But if I lived my life in the organized fashion to which we all aspire, I'd avoid those tense mail watches anyway.

You may be paying slightly more for out-of-town service, but you should make it up in professional discounts on equipment and film at home. As a writer who's using a camera in your work, you are entitled to the professional discount offered by almost every camera store in America. To be offered twenty percent off list price is not unusual; cost-plus-ten-percent is often available for good professional customers. The discount will not be volunteered by the guy behind the counter. Ask!

You can't ask him *all* the questions that arise in learning to use your new toy, however. For your serious photo education, investigate the literature and the classes available in your locale.

The Time/Life Library of Photography offers two dozen volumes of useful information, from the most basic understanding of the field to specialized suggestions. The *Photojournalism* volume is especially good. Kodak offers a number of practical publications, from their *Here's How* pocket guides to more thorough examinations of any facet of photography you might imagine. Myriad books cover other photo fields. One of my own favorites is Lisl Dennis's *How to Take Better Travel Photos*. She avoids the equipment mystique and gets down to the real challenge of using a camera: creating memorable pictures.

Your camera store may sponsor seminars on using various lines they stock. The Nikon School, a traveling one-day course that covers the photographic waterfront, hits almost every state in the country annually; it's worth a trip to take part in it. Other camera systems also offer owners' seminars. Your camera dealer has the details.

Photo courses come in two flavors, good and bad. The good ones are taught by working photographers; for your purposes, the very best are offered by photographers actively marketing their work to publications. The bad ones are taught by everyone else—equipment fetishists, artistes who savor every grain of sand in a photo of a beach but are oblivious to the basic art of documenting action, and well-meaning amateurs who can't teach you any better than they were taught themselves. If in doubt, ask your camera dealer about the teacher's reputation. A good one will assuredly have a measure of respect among his fellow professionals.

One special educational marketing tool may come in handy after you've mastered the basics of how to use a camera. It's seminars offered by professionals on how to take salable photos and then match them to their markets. Like writers' conferences, these workshops at their best present you with an inspiring collection of hints and hard information. Those offered around the country by Rohn Engh, publisher of the previously mentioned *PhotoLetter*, are among the best.

The best way to take better pictures, after you've learned to get film in and out of the camera and take off the lens cap, is to go out and shoot photos firsthand. Lots and lots of them. Then go over your results, resolve to improve your composition or focus or whatever's lacking, and shoot a whole bunch more.

The editor who gave me my first photo lessons always reminded me that the amount of film used is the very least of your worries when you're shooting. Consider your expenditure on equipment and accessories. Consider the time you've spent learning how to operate that camera. Consider the hours and fuel you've used getting to the location where your picture is about to happen . . . and then consider the million variables that make every shot just a little different, and just a little better or worse, than the one you've just clicked off.

Then reflect upon the fact that in being stingy with Kodak's finest, you minimize your chances of capturing that one perfect image. Do yourself (and Kodak) a favor. Shoot photos, and shoot more, and more, until you get what you want. It's the only way your labors will ever come close to the work of the pro photographers editors admire.

Don't think you'll make it? Or you don't want to distract yourself from taking notes and soaking up atmosphere to get involved with this fascinating but potentially consuming sideline?

Perhaps you should reconsider Option Number One. That is, marrying a photographer (or making over the spouse you've already come up with).

There is a thought-provoking number of husband and wife writer-photographer teams out here in the hinterlands. The teamwork's convenient. You know where your spouse is when the sun is setting or the birds ready to fly. It can be terrific fun, and it's one way to share the joys and letdowns of the freelance life with your partner.

Just picture the possibilities. There's bound to be a camera in your future if you're writing from a far-out address. Who minds if it's attached to something with even more potential?

8

Book Writing in the Boonies

After you've watched your best published efforts meet their maker along with potato peels, coffee grounds and last night's well-chewed T-bones, you're ripe to consider writing a book.

A book lasts. It has a life of its own, sometimes longer than its author's and certainly longer than it takes to wrap up what's left from cleaning a fish.

To all writers, a book's a milestone along their path of progress. For the self-supporting writer in the realms outside New York, that book means much more than a publisher's stamp of approval.

The time spent writing and marketing your book may be the best investment you can make in establishing a secure, comfortable freelance income. I'm assuming now that you are not the one-in-a-million author who can crank out a novel that becomes an instant mega-seller. Without producing bestsellers, without, indeed, writing the kinds of books that even seem candidates for that status, you can still enhance every aspect of your writing potential.

When you write a book you gain a credential that can be carried over into every other kind of writing endeavor you're likely to undertake. It's a source of local status that can lead to all sorts of commercial work, with grateful clients happy to hire someone of your reputation. It helps in marketing magazine and newspaper articles nationally and regionally. It's a boost in finding an agent if you decide you want or need one. And having written your first book brightens the outlook immeasurably for a second, third, or tenth.

None of this is immediately bankable. But turning your attention to books early in your career can take care of that imperative, too.

Books offer a financial advantage that's unique among the kinds of writing you may take on as a freelancer: they continue to pay you dividends after you've completed and sold them. Only rarely do magazine articles or audio-visual scripts or newsletters or lectures continue to bring in income after you've received your one agreed-upon fee. But books can return royalties for years after you've moved on to other projects. With a little bit of negotiation and luck, they may also pay for the time they consume in writing with a publisher's advance.

Taking on the writing of books early in your freelance adventure makes good business sense. Royalties, even from modest sales, can underwrite other market explorations or additional long-term projects. They're the one way to break out of the rut of using income earned last month to pay this month's bills. They build up financial security when you need it most.

Since having written a book is also good for lining up other writing assignments, it's hard to understand why so many writers put off this kind of project for years. Hard—but not impossible. Those writers, and possibly you, subscribe to the popular myth that writing a book is a sort of ultimate goal for the would-be author, one not to be taken lightly. So they wait, and someday will increase the horde of elderly authors racing against time.

Few of us who live far from Publishers' Row have been personally connected with the birth or life-span of any book, so we're easy prey for the old wives' (and husbands') tales of the rarity of achieving publication. We shy away from the tremendous challenges we assume to stand between us and a publisher's contract, choosing instead to admire book authors as a special, inspired breed with a direct line to the Muse or connections in the industry.

Yet the evidence points to a different conclusion. More books are selling more copies than ever before. Million sellers are no longer as rare as whooping cranes. Money is being spent on advertising, promotion, and book distribution in quantities more massive than at any earlier time. Bookstore franchises have become a hot item and a fixture in nearly every new shopping mall across the nation.

All the signs point to a reasonably bright outlook for your first book, and an improved picture for others you might offer. All those forty thousand authors, those hundreds and hundreds of publishers and booksellers, have seen something in the field of books, and that something would seem to be money.

So how do you cash in?

Four modes of publishing await your investigation. None is superior to the others in every case. Each is legitimate in its turn, and offers its own sets of advantages and drawbacks to freelancers concentrating on making a good living with their work.

Included are national publishers, the traditional route to publication; regional publishers; self-publication; and sponsored or premium book authorship. If you have a solid idea and are willing to develop it for the audience that awaits it, one of these routes almost certainly is going to result in your Book Number One.

National publishers

Rumors abound that getting a first book accepted by a national publisher is a minor miracle, and that making money from the effort is well-nigh impossible.

These rumors are wrong, and I think I know why.

First, they're based on the market for fiction, not nonfiction, and in that field may have some validity. While popular fiction is selling extremely well, its prospects get fainter in direct proportion to its literary aspirations; unfortunately, first novelists in the boonies seem all too likely to set out to write the Great American Novel and stumble far short of their hopes.

Second, they're often passed on by academics whose prospects of publishing a trade book are just as bad as they fear. Strictly highbrow nonfiction is probably as hard to place with a publisher as self-consciously literary fiction. While their book-in-the-making may win scholarly grants-in-aid and tenure for professors, it will reach only readers who take their material just as specialized and rarefied as the intellectuals can make it.

If you're serious about earning a good living from your writing, you'll abandon literary distance from the crowd and be willing to work on the level of the vast majority of readers: not a gutter-bottom; rather, in the realm of straightforward information.

And if you're serious about earning $20,000 or more per year from your writing, you'll forsake fiction (at least for now) for more salable nonfiction topics.

The book world, more than magazine publishing, is accustomed to working with authors spread out all over the map. You can make the best of your return address, and use it as an advantage in proposing and selling your first book.

Your geography suggests certain book topics that are among those most likely to sell your first time out. Remember the five-plus-one best magazine stories to write from wherever you live? Those same subjects adapt well to salable books that can succeed through any of the four kinds of publishing alternatives you have at your disposal.

The big six, translated into book terms, include these broad categories:

1. Travel guidebooks and histories.

2. The outdoors—how-to books, adventures, reminiscence, conservation, and many more.

3. General how-to guides based on your background and experience—cookbooks, hobby books, home repair, gardening, self-help, and virtually any topic that captures your own interest.

4. Religious and inspirational volumes.

5. Lifestyle books, whether humor (Erma Bombeck's *The Grass Is Always Greener over the Septic Tank*) or semi-instructive (*First Person Rural* by Noel Perrin); in either case, drawing directly from the perspective your location gives you.

6. Books (like this one) aimed at particular professions, from farmers to salesmen to freelance writers.

The prospects have never been better for writing and selling books from wherever you happen to live. The book industry is neither so remote nor so unapproachable as it may seem to be. Whatever topic you have in mind, there is almost sure to be a publisher looking for manuscripts that fall into exactly that category. Think of all those new books coming out this year. Either celestial inspiration is a lot more common than it seems, or writing and publishing a book is a more achievable and practical goal than is generally conceded west of the Hudson.

Gone are the days when writers in North Dakota automatically turned toward New York when praying for their book at night. The metropolis is still headquarters for the largest, best-known national publishing houses. But the industry is growing and spreading out all over the place these days, and New York is definitely not the only place for either writers or publishers to be.

National publishers today can be found in Des Moines, Seattle, San Francisco, Dallas, Cincinnati, Minneapolis, Chicago, and more. Not all are behemoths staring coldly down at writers who solicit their consideration. Many are small, specialized companies with a penchant for books on cooking or history or travel or self-help or how-to guides. Though small, their distribution and promotion may be just as spirited as that of the Great Gray Ladies on Publishers' Row. (In the case of a minor title in a massive company's sales list, they may even be much spunkier in your book's behalf.)

The behemoths don't stare all that coldly, for that matter. Despite its inbred tendencies, the publishing world has to look beyond its ranks for new talent to churn out those tens of thousands of books to be issued next year, and the next, and the next. If publishing were entirely an old boys' network, it couldn't show the growth that's sent sales curves swelling upward in the past decade. There are still plenty of old boys around, but competition for productive new authors of salable books is fierce enough that you need never be threatened by haughty demeanors.

With *Writer's Market's* one hundred eighteen pages of leads and all this interest in books abroad in the land, you have your work cut out for you.

You can narrow the field effectively, however, by considering the book you want to write. If it's nonfiction, you're in luck. Most publishers, even those strong in fiction, depend on solid nonfiction books for their meat and potatoes.

Look for the group of publishers that specialize in the subjects you're best equipped to write. You can page through all hundred-plus pages of the market book as bedtime reading, or you can take a shortcut that is almost infallible. Stop at your library or bookstore and find a variety of recent releases on topics in the same broad category as yours—other travel books, perhaps, or cookbooks, or fishing guides, or whatever you have in mind. Open the covers and look at the publishers' names and addresses. Couldn't be simpler.

While you're there, check the reference volume *Books in Print* to be sure that someone hasn't beaten you to the punch on your pet proposal. You can get some feeling here, too, for publishers currently interested in your subject by watching for a cluster of recent releases which your subject complements.

Finding their names and addresses is a mere beginning for your research. Each publisher may be offering different terms to writers, different advantages and disadvantages for the volume you have in mind. Back again to *Writer's Market*, where you can begin to sort out those that suit your purposes best.

The largest national publishers have clout. Their distribution channels are nationwide. Their staffs are large and often superb. Their names open certain doors for promotion, in some cases, that can result in good market positioning for the book you're planning to give birth to.

But the smaller national publishers have their advantages, too—perhaps greater, depending on what you have in mind. Their scope is far less general than that of the industry giants. They may publish only cookbooks or travel guides, but they know their fields in more depth than the generalized giants could take time to develop. Their staffs, though smaller, are also often dedicated and talented. As a new author, you may receive more, and more personalized, assistance from these individualized firms.

The giants and the feisty smaller contenders part company in the terms and conditions they offer authors. Big national concerns—Prentice-Hall, Harper & Row, Doubleday, and their peers—offer advances against royalties that are, in general, higher than those the smaller houses can afford. A 1975-76 Authors Guild survey indicated their median advance was $5,000. Royalties differ, but a usual rate is 10 percent of retail price on the first 5,000 copies sold, 12½ percent on the next 5,000, and 15 percent on additional sales. A solid but unspectacular nonfiction book by a beginning author might sell 5,000 to 10,000 copies, bringing in royalties in semiannual payments beyond the advanced earnings received up front.

Smaller publishers are often hard pressed to equal these advances and terms. Again, they vary; advances are generally somewhat less, and royalties might be based on net (rather than retail) price of the volume. But they have an advantage that can add up to earnings just as great as those of larger companies. Books issued by smaller, specialized companies may be kept in print much longer than those of the publishing giants.

That longer life in print can increase total sales dramatically. Major firms, faced by the crush of new titles coming up, may remainder their stock of slower-selling titles after a year or less, while smaller companies can keep them alive based on more modest but consistent sales figures. The author benefits through royalties over a longer period and has a better chance to surpass the royalty break and earn a higher percentage on additional sales.

Subsidiary rights—book club sales, prepublication excerpts in magazines, anthologies, paperback reprints and foreign language editions, among others—is the area in which national publishers shine when compared to your other three publishing options.

The standard writer's contract assigns fifty percent or less of the income from exercising these rights to the publisher. (Veterans with some success on their records often get more favorable terms.) It's up to your publisher to take advantage of the potential for these additional sales of your material; national firms often do.

Some publishing personnel have suggested that subsidiary rights are, in fact, a major source of income to many national publishers, producing more income than books themselves. Whether or not this is true, it definitely bodes well for the author hoping to get additional income from his book.

To reap these extra rewards—and to find a publisher in the first place—you need to go back to your income-producing strategy. If you weren't concentrating on earning income as you write, you might sit down to produce your book now, then send it to market to try to find its niche. Or you can commence searching out a publisher before you've invested your time in typing out a manuscript and proceed to write it after you've found a company willing to give you a contract. That's clearly the only way for the self-supporting writer to go . . . risking time and talent only with a reasonable hope of returns.

The rest of your quest for a publisher is familiar ground. The query system you employ for selling your work to magazines is nearly identical to how you interest a publisher in your proposal. Write to an editor at the firm of your choice; you can get his or her name from *Writer's Market* or *Literary Market Place*. Describe your proposal and your own writing credentials. Sketch out your book's prospective direction and the resources it will build on, whether they're your own or dug out of some other mine of expertise.

Back it up with an outline of the book, chapter by chapter—brief but detailed enough to introduce what it's about. Slip it into the envelope you've addressed along with the ubiquitous self-addressed stamped envelope.

And wait.

Surely, there's a better way, you say? Something quicker?

Nope. There isn't. Unless you have contacts (or uncles) in the literary business, or are a celebrity, or the rare prodigy who's utterly irresistible on first sight, you aren't likely to have many other options from your vantage point in Arkansas or New Hampshire until you've proven yourself. It's the old writer's Catch-22: You can't be trusted to write a book until you've proven you can do it, but you don't get a chance to prove it until you've already written one. The query and sample chapters are the way most new writers finally break in.

But don't be crushed by the odds you think you face by querying cold and waiting. It can be done; that's how many, perhaps a majority, of books are really sold from the hinterlands. You're holding proof in your hands that cold queries without benefit of those much-desired connections can turn into warm welcomes. The author wrote a query, based on nothing but a listing in *Writer's Market*, from an address just as out of the way as yours. In a couple of months she was invited to send in a sample chapter to augment her proposed outline. Only a few days later, her mailman presented her with a contract.

The method works. You know it. That's how this book came into being and that's probably how your book will come about whenever you get ready to do it.

Unless you get an agent.

Nonmetropolitan writers I've questioned about agents disagree radically on whether they're the indispensable helpmeets they're often touted as. Some of the authors, who, collectively, have sold dozens of titles, can see no earthly way an agent could have improved their own track records. Others swear by their professional aid and encouragement. The choice is ultimately up to you. It may or may not have a major effect on your book prospects, but one thing is clear: your chances of finding an agent who will handle you are slim until you've put together a track record in major magazines or have sold your first book.

Having an agent is undoubtedly a status symbol for authors in the boonies. Their practical benefits include saving you the wear and tear of marketing your own proposals and having a third party to talk to your publisher about financial arrangements. Your cost is usually ten percent of whatever income their efforts produce.

If you're not adverse to talking about money yourself, and feel you know enough about the going rates to get what you've got coming, you may be better off spending your time approaching editors rather then courting agents. At any rate, put finding an agent on your list of things to do after, not before, selling your first book. By then your prospects will be considerably better.

How do you get one? By much the same method as you sell a publisher directly—a query letter, an outline, perhaps a handful of samples of your best published work. Consult *Literary Market Place* for names of agents or, better, find yourself an agented author and ask him or her to recommend someone. (You don't know any authors? Come now. Write to one whose work you've enjoyed in care of his publisher. Fan letters are always appreciated, especially if accompanied by an SASE for the reply.)

Avoid the agents who offer to read your manuscript for a fee when considering whether to represent you. That may sound appealing to someone from an obscure address, since it does make sense that agents would charge for their time. But you want to find someone who's in business to sell manuscripts to publishers, not to sell quickie critiques to gullible would-be authors. If you want a critique and are willing to pay, approach several agents by mail, describing your work and your credentials; if they show an interest in you, make the trek to New York to negotiate in person.

The important thing is to get your proposals before publishers who might buy them. Whether agented or not, your manuscript can't be sold until it makes that connection with an interested buyer. You can hit it on your first query, as I did, or use up half a roll of stamps reaching the publishing houses most likely to cheer when they open your letter.

But one thing remains. If your book is good, and your estimate of its audience is anywhere near the mark, it *will* find a publisher. It's only a matter of when.

Regional publishers

You may find a publisher, in fact, where you least expect it.

Included in those one hundred eighteen pages of possibilities in *Writer's Market* are more than a few that can be described as regional publishing houses. Think of them as the tip of the iceberg. For every regional publisher listed in the book, you can find a healthy handful tucked away in the oddest of cities, publishing books with sales figures that aren't bad at all and reaching a reading audience on which massive national houses—from their lofty perches in Manhattan—only focus by accident.

Don't make the mistake of considering regional publishers just little bitty versions of the national publishing houses—a sort of junior high school of book production. They're much more than that.

Regional publishing, one of the fastest-growing segments of the book industry, is a specific response to an area in which the national publishers are notoriously weak. They market books of interest to well-defined parts of the country, such as New England or the Southwest . . . and do it with a singleness of purpose that makes major publishers' sales representatives weep.

Regional books are sold through bookstores, of course. But the companies usually saturate their own geographic area, reaching readers wherever they browse—groceries and drugstores, tourist attractions and souvenir shops, libraries, schools, and wherever else they can find room for a stack of copies. They market their offerings through regional-oriented publications, where they're most likely to reach an audience with a soft spot in their hearts for their own shared piece of the continent.

The firms choose their titles with that purpose in mind. Regional publishers specialize in topics that national firms can rarely do justice to. They're subjects with an appeal that may be intense but is limited by geography—natural history, cooking and crafts, nostalgia, historical research, travel guides, hunting and fishing and other outdoor sports, and often regional humor.

Fiction appears occasionally on some of their lists, but its apparent regional flavor can be deceiving. The novel offered to a general audience has always drawn its settings from well-drawn portraits of places like where you live; only rarely is it limited by this background. Not much fiction is really well suited to regional publishers, and few bother with novels.

You don't approach regional publishers because you feel you're not ready to play with the big guys. They can be your best avenue to publication, but only if the kinds of books that interest you interest them, too. Their requirements in terms of writing quality are just as stringent as national firms and even more exacting in terms of theme and accuracy of research. Each regional publisher is individual; seeking, in its own way, to fill some part of reader's unsatisfied appetites for information.

Regional publishers, to be sure, aren't without disadvantages. One is the reverse side of their big strength, the limited area of distribution. For books that transcend the regional market, this can be a handicap. Another is the fact that they rarely, if ever, issue advances to their authors, at least until they've proven themselves through successful dealings in the past. They do finally pay their way, though, through long-term royalty payments.

Like regional publication markets, they are likely to care about the people and places dearest to your own geographically oriented heart. And they can be loyal to their authors almost to a fault. For the author in search of a publisher, with homegrown idea in hand, they may be fertile ground indeed.

Consider a publisher in my backyard, North Plains Press. Its catalog (four-color cover, glossy stiff paper, pull-out gummed order blanks for bookstores) contains a rather typical mix of regional books—a cookbook of "good down-home cookin' from the farm kitchens of North and South Dakota," biographies of regional artists and sculptors, tour guides, historical books, local humor, and nostalgia.

What the catalog doesn't mention is that books published by North Plains routinely go into three or four printings of five or ten thousand copies each, and sales requiring two reprintings per year for a decade or longer are not unheard of.

North Plains Press is located in Aberdeen, South Dakota, a flat, prosperous farming center that makes Bismarck look bustling. Scott Kernan, manager of the book division, says their books' secret of long sales life is simple: "By concentrating on art, history, heritage, and humor books, we seldom publish a title that loses its appeal over the years. And we keep a book in print just as long as it sells."

The regional publishers concentrate their interests and sales efforts within their own part of the country. Seattle's ten regional publishers prefer titles on the Pacific Northwest and sell their books on their home ground. North Plains's best circulation is within a five hundred-mile radius of quiet Aberdeen. While regionals may get their books stocked much farther from home, their promotional efforts as well as their wholesale distribution network to stores tend to rapidly weaken beyond the boundaries of their self-defined territory.

Bob Karolevitz of Mission Hill, South Dakota, is one of North Plains's most successful authors. A transplanted West Coast advertising man, he's written half a dozen volumes for the Aberdeen publisher, ranging from biographical books on South Dakota artist Harvey Dunn to humorous accounts of his own attempts at becoming a farmer. One of his books, *Old Time Agriculture in the Ads*, has sold into six figures since it first appeared in 1971.

Two more North Plains writers live in Big Timber, Montana, and Mission, South Dakota. Another began a book in Deadwood, South Dakota, when she learned that a notorious gambler had been shot in her living room a century earlier and was buried a few blocks away on Mount Moriah; her project became the colorful history of Deadwood's "Boot Hill." A fourth author wrote his book of cowboy humor while residing at the South Dakota State Penitentiary; since paroled, he hasn't contacted his publisher even to pick up his royalty checks.

North Plains, of course, is only one of the dozens of regional publishers that encompass every area of the country. Seattle outdoors author Archie Satterfield has had extensive experience with several, with twelve titles to date published by regional firms, and says he swears by them: "I've developed a hard rule about writing books. If it's about a regional subject and will appeal to people within that region, both residents and visitors, always have it published by a regional publisher."

In an article about his experiences published in the Outdoor Writers Association of America newsletter (April 1978), Archie detailed the four advantages regionals offer his outdoors and travel books. They keep them in print longer; they distribute them to everything from mom-and-pop grocery stores to large bookstores. He's encouraged to work more closely with his publisher, and it's easier to get the publisher to update and revise his books. "He's usually delighted at an excuse to promote his backlist and won't be so busy with dozens of new titles."

If your book has the kind of theme that attracts regional publishers, many of your fellow writers will advise you to take that route rather than trying for a national publishing firm. Ask several regionally published authors in your vicinity for their advice. They'll be happy to steer you away from the occasional disreputable firm and toward those that offer the best advantages to their authors.

Since regional publishing is often done on a first-name

basis, the authors you question may even be willing to introduce you to their publishers in person or by telephone. That personal reference, plus a good solid regional proposal, count for much more in regional publishing than the efforts of some agent way off in New York.

Self-publication

Your third route to publication is closely related to regional publishing. It's also based on writing and distributing a book where its audience is strongest, whether that's within a geographic area or inside professional circles where its information is bound to interest readers.

The difference is that you do it all yourself—not only writing, but planning the appearance of the book, working with a printer, securing a distributor or acting as a wholesaler yourself, and working on publicity. If you have a title suited to its risks, you may be ready to become one of the growing number of self-publishers living nearly everywhere you can name.

Self-publication is said to be the fastest-growing trend in publishing today. But it demands a certain kind of author.

Is your energy boundless? Are you so sure your book has an audience that you'd risk your own money bringing it before the public? A highly marketable idea and professionally produced books could double or triple your financial return if you publish the book yourself, as compared to royalties you'd receive from a trade publisher. The only hang-up is that it also doubles or triples your work (or even more). You have to really believe in your project to become a self-publisher.

There's a difference between vanity press publication and self-publishing, though the line admittedly is just a bit vague. Vanity publishers claim to handle all the costs of getting your book before the public for a fee. You go into self-publishing all too aware that you alone are responsible for distribution and promotion to the public. You deal with a printer directly, and probably pay a bill that's considerably less than what a vanity press would charge you. Then you're on your own—an exhilarating feeling if you're looking for a challenge, or a moment of truth if you haven't yet shed your dependence on contractual security.

Self-publishing is flourishing via mail order these days.

Following the steps prescribed by Jerry Buchanan of Vancouver, Washington, founder of the TOWERS Book Club and Newsletter, hundreds of writers are producing and marketing their own books directly to customers. Their main marketing tools are ads in national magazines (often economical classifieds) and fliers sent directly to names obtained by purchasing mailing lists.

Some of these authors—Buchanan is one of the most visible of their number—have done very well through this method. Others, whose ideas or marketing strategies weren't so sharp, have done less than terrifically. To learn more about the direct-mail publishing scene, subscribe to one of the several newsletters now covering the topic, or kick in the price of one of the books advertised in so many publications. (Don't look for it at the library. These books almost never make it into general circulaton.)

The kind of self-publisher those of us in the boonies are more familiar with is the individual who sells books through traditional retail and wholesale distribution networks, but who finances and plans the publication himself.

Several authors have written books that serve as good introductions to self-publishing. The revised edition of *The Self-Publishing Handbook*, edited by Bill Henderson, offers the valuable insights of a variety of self-publishers. Charles Chickadel's *Publish It Yourself Handbook*, an attractive, well-designed volume, is also a good source book when you're considering moving in this direction.

In the case of some books, this is virtually the only way to go. Wilford Miller of Bismarck, for example, noted fifteen years ago that there was not one book available for students on the native wildlife of the prairie. His conversations with teachers and others interested in the state's outdoors convinced him that such a book would find a ready audience.

But national and even regional publishers showed little interest in a book with such geographically limited appeal, so Bill proceeded to do it himself. A superb and well-known wildlife photographer as well as a writer, he put together the ultimate reference work on North Dakota fauna, found himself a printer by comparing price quotes from several of the state's largest, and went into the book publishing business.

Animals of North Dakota, a trade paperback with lavish illustrations and the last word on wildlife, from bison and elk to prairie dogs and field mice, has sold well over the years. It was followed by *Wildlife of the Prairie* in 1976, which has gone through several printings and still draws mail orders and wholesale purchases throughout the Dakotas.

"A regular publisher isn't interested in books that will sell mostly in a remote, limited area like North Dakota," he says. "That doesn't mean there isn't a market here, though. You can really do quite well if you put the right book out yourself." He cites another self-published book about the state, more general in nature, which has sold tens of thousands of copies in three years on the market. "That book didn't have any competition. It filled a real need that wouldn't have been met any other way."

The most serious hurdle in self-publishing is that the writer needs to have enough money to invest in printing the book before any sales can be made. But there are ways around that, too. Some writers have found printers willing to absorb some of the risk themselves and take payment for their services over the book's sales period. Others have turned up "angels" to finance their projects—a church diocese for a book written by a priest, an ecology-minded farming group for a book examining the strip mining industry.

Finding a backer is not so difficult a proposition if you've chosen a subject that is almost sure to pay its way once it has reached the salable stage. The more successful self-published books in my part of the country have fallen into a couple of categories.

One is material of proven interest to a limited but avid group of readers. Self-published city or regional guidebooks come under this category. They may not move well in Bismarck, but the several titles on shopping, dining, and sight-seeing in Minneapolis do well indeed within the city limits. The same is true of books on what to see and do in the Florida Keys, or guides to wildflowers on the slopes of Mount Rainier, or the natural history of the badlands within Theodore Roosevelt National Park.

Others in this group are hobby books, instructional guides for locally popular crafts or pastimes, and histories of nearly any city or region west of the thirteen colonies. For example, books on rosemaling, a traditional Norwegian decorative painting done on wooden utensils, have been best sellers for authors in Minnesota, Iowa, and Wisconsin. A biography of North Dakota's maverick politician Bill Langer was extremely popular within the state; you may assume that not one copy was sold to a nonresident who had no North Dakota roots. Fishing guides to North Dakota's lakes also sell dependably and are hailed with joy by fishermen headed in the right direction.

The other sort of successful book is the one you know you can promote or sell on the basis of your reputation. Local celebrities, recognized authorities within their own fields, and those with a built-in sales advantage (like a daddy in the book distribution business), all have automatically brightened their books' prospects.

But you're not a celebrity? Find yourself one and become an as-told-to.

Don't be deceived by the "self" in self-publishing, however. To produce a book you'll be proud of, you need to enlist others to perform the services publishers invest in the volumes they issue. You need a graphic designer to do illustrations, layout, and cover art. Though all printers have art departments these days, their staff artists will seldom do more than the most basic job of pasting up your copy.

You need an editor. Yes, you do. You can hire freelance copy editors and later, proofreaders; try placing a classified ad or asking someone at a nearby publishing house to make a recommendation. A meticulous English teacher can be a great deal of help if all else fails. Or talk a fellow writer into taking on editing chores for your project (for a fair price, of course) . . . if you're lucky enough to have a fellow writer where you happen to live.

The rest of the help you need is in sales and marketing. A long talk over coffee with the manager of the bookstore you frequent can give you invaluable advice on how to price your book, how to sell it to other stores, area book distribution channels, and kinds of advertising that may help sales.

When pricing your book, remember that retail stores will expect you to give them a 40 percent discount over its cover price if you sell it to them yourself. You can conserve your own time by placing it with the news and book agencies that service all the magazine racks in your area, but they'll want a cut themselves, at least 20 percent or more of the cover price, and you'll have to be willing to take back unsold books, however battered, dog eared, and damaged they may be.

Sales points outside of bookstores also may be a boon to your sales. Drugstores, gift shops, supermarkets, restaurants—all may be interested in stocking and selling a title of interest to their customers. Motels and resorts are natural candidates for selling a book of regional interest. Advertisements in magazines serving the area of the special-interest group you've written for provide other sales possibilities with a bonus: you can keep the forty percent retail markup yourself.

Finally, keep your eyes open for opportunities to promote your books. One regional author of books on farming reaps profits through his extensive schedule of public speaking engagements. He's never without a satchel full of his latest volume for the interested well-wishers who come up after his talk. Bill Miller has sold his wildlife books through booths at teachers' conferences, ads and reviews in state wildlife publications, and workshops with students and sportsmen all over the state.

Let local newspapers know about your book; the contact will usually result in an interview. Most local television talk shows welcome visits by area authors. Newsletters of organizations to which you (or your family) belong may carry reviews, news stories, and advertisements for your book. State conferences for school and public librarians are a must; so is the annual convention of booksellers in your state. Can you get a wholesaler with annual gift or trade shows to put your book on his order form? How about setting up a booth at the state food retailers' convention to catch grocers, who are selling more and more books and periodicals these days along with the pantyhose and Frisbees? Try the local chamber of commerce's annual meeting or regular sessions; your book may be of interest to their members, and a high proportion of their members will be retailers who might stock it.

You have to believe in your book to be willing to pursue its sale with all the zeal it deserves. If you do believe—and if you relish the thought of converting nonbelievers—then self-publishing can really work for you.

Sponsored books

The fourth category of book publishing is a loose one. It includes the hundredth-anniversary history of a prominent local firm; the memoirs of a state organization entering a new period in its collective life; a cookbook promoting one of your state's major agricultural products, and a specialized history text with such a small potential readership among laymen that no commercial publisher would touch it.

This is the broad field of sponsored books. You see its signs in photo how-to guides subtly promoting the advantages of one camera system or in some of the most fascinating profiles of industry leaders or pioneers. In some instances they masquerade as normally published volumes; in others they look like exactly what they are, books that in some way promote the goals of the company, organization, or interest group that paid to have them published.

No commercial publisher would be interested in a book on the history of telephone cooperatives in North Dakota. But the telephone cooperatives' association was. Likewise, the centennial of the Episcopal Church in the state aroused no anticipation on Publishers' Row, but was an occasion celebrated with an excellent and readable volume by Episcopal churchmen in North Dakota.

Sponsored books are the mirror opposites of those published through the other three routes. Instead of a book seeking an audience, you find an audience seeking a book. To get their book, they need to find their author. The author could well be you, a professional writer in their neck of the woods who can produce a readable, accurate, and creditable manuscript to satisfy their pre-established hunger.

These books pop up at the oddest times. The hundredth (or the fiftieth, or the twenty-fifth) anniversary of nearly anything can be the impetus for an official history. The need for a book may result from a promotional push for a product or a group's big membership drive. Or it may appear on the eve of the founder's retirement to chronicle his accomplishments, or memorialize them after his death.

The opportunity for the book may be part of a larger project. Our state Committee on the Humanities and Public Issues, for example, decided several years ago to publish five volumes over ten years dealing with their perspective on the state's history, lifestyle, and people; the project was born because the funds became available for grants to authors and to cover the cost of printing.

Sponsored books—some are called premium books because they're distributed as a free or discount offer—can be an inducement to buy a new product or to try a new hobby or to bank with a particular banker. Or they can be sold at full price as the foundation of someone's hopeful fund-raising scheme. (Make sure you get your payment up front if this is the case. Why depend on a volunteer and unpredictable amateur sales force?)

Do they sound dreary? Don't bet on it. There may be a certain number of tedious histories of interest only to insiders, but they needn't be the rule. One of the funniest bits of regional humor I've seen is a pocket-size "North Dakota Dictionary" sponsored and distributed by an implement manufacturer in the state. It was written by the author who coined the rallying cry "Forty below keeps the riffraff out" and included offbeat definitions of landmarks, personalities, and customs.

Sponsors of all sorts of these books have a stake in making them the best they can afford. The books are meant to reflect brilliantly on their sponsors. A poorly conceived book reflects just about as well as a puddle of spilt milk.

How do you find these opportunities to write a book with full economic security? Like most local writing jobs, it's a matter of listening for clues and keeping up contacts.

An imminent anniversary, mentioned in a newsletter or newspaper article, should be a green light for a proposal to the group (whether industry or association). Contact its president and suggest a publishing project. There are three possible outcomes: You can sell him on your new and attractive idea. You can stumble into a group already considering such a project. Or you can find you've identified one organization where no book will ever be born, for lack of money or interest or visionary zeal.

Your connections within organizations and businesses in your chosen community can lead to tips about upcoming projects. If you're interested in taking on a sponsored book, let your contacts know about your interest. You may be planting the germ of an idea that will eventually grow into a commission.

Watch the newspaper, especially its classified ads, for announced projects in search of authors. Since the job of writing a book often mystifies those who conceived it, their first instinct is sometimes to advertise for more knowledgeable help.

The income from a sponsored book varies with the sponsor's finances and your own bargaining ability. Often groups undertaking their first (and probably only) publishing project have no idea of what to pay. Base your estimates on the amount of time you will have to spend, especially in research and in clearing the finished manuscript with whatever committees are to oversee its publication.

At other times you'll be offered a flat grant or fee. Judge carefully whether it will meet your hourly rates from start to finish. A multi-thousand-dollar sum can sound wonderful until you figure out that it will take the best part of a year to earn.

There are no sure ways to guard against snags, but you can take certain steps to minimize them. Make sure you have a contract with the sponsor, and have your own lawyer look it over to protect your interests regarding acceptance and rewrites. Try to include a passage defining what is required for acceptance—one person's approval, a committee's approval, whatever—and mutually agreed-upon grounds for refusal. To protect yourself, never defer your entire payment until the manuscript has been accepted. Set it up to be paid in halves (half at the start, half at acceptance) or in thirds (one-third now, one-third on delivery, one-third on final approval).

If you can, work out an agreement with the sponsors on how much rewriting you will do for the set fee. Rewrites may become necessary, and not only because of your own work (as a beginning author, you may be readier to take the blame than you should be). The sponsor's goals might change, its administration might be replaced, or committee members might begin to squabble over details.

This sounds like a thorny piece of business; these

problems don't come up often, so don't be put off by considering them. But do think your commission through and try to protect yourself with legal advice and open-eyed negotiations up front. The better you know the book's sponsor and the brighter its reputation, the more secure you can feel. Remember that commercial publishing houses have years of tradition and legal experts to untangle author-publisher snarls, and still some knots can be hard to work out. A non-publishing sponsor of a premium book may be taking on a author and a book for the first time ever. Do as much as you can to make sure everyone involved subscribes to the same ground rules before you commit your valuable time.

If you receive a commission to write a sponsored book, you'll very seldom get a contract offering royalties as you do with commercial issues. If you are offered one, consider the realistic sales potential carefully and the way in which sales would be reported to you. Very few one-time publishers will have the resources to distribute, promote, and sell a book to manage respectable sales; they're even less likely to have the kind of bookkeeping system that insures accurate royalty payments. Unless they guarantee that every member will buy a copy or contract to purchase unsold copies themselves to reach an agreed-upon minimum number of books, your royalties will be shrimp-sized.

These four publishing options offer you different means of producing your book and reaching your annual income goal. Which you choose depends somewhat on the amount of time you can invest in your first full-length project and the amount of return you must reasonably expect from it.

If you have the personality, stamina, and time to be all things to your project, self-publishing a book for an identified audience may be the most financially rewarding route. You may want to choose it if:

■ Your audience can be reached in an area limited by geography or profession or organized interests (like hobbies that are supplied by stores, lessons, and conventions).
■ You have the outside specialists to advise you in editing, production, and distribution, and possibly have a spouse or colleague who can help you with the legwork.

■ You have extra money to invest in printing and can afford to defer your returns until after the book has begun to sell—or you have lined up an "angel" to help with printing and possibly writing costs for a share of the profits.

Regional publishing may be the route that's most effective if your project and your own schedule meet these conditions:

■ It's the kind of book regionals prefer—travel, outdoors and so on.

■ You can write it while continuing to handle a full load of other writing assignments for self-support, without the assistance of a publisher's advance to help underwrite the time you spend in production.

■ You desire a closer relationship with your publisher, both in creating the book and in taking an active part in planning its distribution and promotion.

■ Your book has a long projected sales life and deserves to be kept in print over a number of years.

National publishers, either specialized or general trade houses, might be your best choice if these factors are present:

■ Your audience isn't limited by geography and includes a substantial number of potential buyers.

■ You need to secure at least a moderate advance on royalties to keep you afloat during your writing stages.

■ Your topic is best suited to one of the companies that specialize in books of that kind; or it's one of the few first books of sufficient commercial power to attract strong marketing from a major publisher.

Finally, a sponsored book may be the route to take for your first volume if:

■ Grants are available to you to write it.

■ You want the security of insured hourly payment through flat fees or guaranteed sales among a sponsor's membership or clientele.

■ You come across such a project in your own locale and can handle it in your regular schedule as you would any other local commercial assignment.

■ You feel you need a boost like this to first break into the book world.

Money is only part of the reward of writing your first book as an author of unlikely address. That's rather fortunate, for money is the most variable part of the bargain. It can realistically range anywhere from barely decent at first on up to providing a substantial portion of your yearly income.

When you work on your first book proposal, you'll sample new experiences that may alter your work habits for the better and make a more effective communicator out of you.

The sheer magnitude of writing a book—when compared with anything else you'll take on—demands an adjustment. Eighty or ninety thousand words is awesome. Three hundred manuscript pages is a staggering thought, especially when you've always found that most stories naturally fit into six or eight.

And yet you rise to the challenge and surprise yourself. At least, I did.

While writing my first book, I was alternately faced with elation and despair. I found that I lost all objectivity about the relative merits or faults of what I'd written while I was in the middle of it. On the days when it looked good, I was tempted to do something else to celebrate. On the bad days, I was sorely pressed not to give up.

And yet the pages kept rolling out. One hundred. Two hundred. Three hundred and forty! I'd produced more manuscript, by the time I'd completed it, than I'd put out in any other concentrated period of my writing life. And I'd done it while handling three-quarters of my normal workload at the same time.

My potential productivity wasn't the only surprising insight I gained during that project. I learned more about working with an editor than I'd ever known before.

Working with magazine editors puts you at a distance from their improvements/damage to your work. I've dealt with them mostly in the early stages of proposing and selling a story. The finished, edited copy looked different, when it finally appeared, but I'd never paid close attention to what had happened to my golden prose in the meantime.

Editing and revising a book manuscript is quite a different tug-of-war. For the first time I was working with practiced editors who questioned adjectives and prepositions, and were not amused by asides that had cracked me up at the typewriter. They made small suggestions that pared and clarified my words and large observations that helped mold form and content. I could see my work improve before my eyes, courtesy of their cool (one might say heartless!) appraisal. I'll never bridle at the thought of being edited again.

I learned to give myself a bit more distance with deadlines. Flash finishes are great when you're talking about a thousand words, but a trifle anxious if you're flapping around with six pounds of paper that needs to be turned over to a courier by four o'clock.

And I experienced both pre- and post-partum depression in delivering that book: pre- , because I had last-minute trepidations over just what sort of monster it might turn out to be; post- , because writing books is the most enjoyable assignment I've taken on as a freelancer, and I was genuinely sorry to see the little devil leave.

Don't put off writing your own book until you've achieved financial independence or a lofty, mature, supremely sophisticated view of life. Neither is likely to happen soon if you're sitting on the curb waiting for them to be delivered.

Take a crack at it right now while the idea excites and frightens you, while it can help form the foundations of your balanced diet of income-producing writing. The experience will help you grow as a writer, will enhance the writing prospects that you're growing into, and will teach you just how exhausting, fascinating, exhilarating, and downright fun the writing business can be.

9

Editing, Copy Editing, and the Ghost

Not all who earn a living as editors are in New York. You can be one of the others. Freelance editing takes several forms, each of which can have a salutary impact on your annual income as a writer.

Wherever words are readied to meet the printer, there's an editor sharpening them, nudging them into position, clarifying their expression.

Wherever regular publications are produced, an editor is in charge of selecting material, writing and rewriting copy, deciding on story placement, and overseeing production.

Wherever publishers are issuing books and magazines, copy editors are at work honing nouns and verbs, bringing writers' work into more logical patterns, and making sure the slant stays consistent throughout the manuscript.

Wherever laymen are writing for publication, someone—often uncredited—is helping shape their manuscripts, and polish them into what their nominal authors want them to be.

Many of these duties are assumed by staffers. Publications are edited by full-time straw bosses; book and magazine copy is fine-tooth-combed by wordsmiths on salary, and assistants shine up their bosses' articles and speeches.

But more and more of these jobs are going to outsiders—freelancers like yourself. The boom in new periodicals and increased numbers of books demand editorial attention at exactly the time when publishers are looking for ways to cut inflated costs, not run them up with additional full-time personnel. The answer is freelance help.

Then there are the jobs that are too small to justify a salaried staff professional: newsletters, monthly publications of associations and businesses, quarterly journals whose four-times-a-year schedule and limited revenues preclude a staff of their own.

All of these jobs hold promise for the freelance writer looking for regular assignments to underwrite his one-time and speculative work. The secret lies in finding those for which you're emotionally and creatively suited.

The freelance editor

Editing (part-time) local publications is an ideal position for the freelancer with some background in journalism, public relations, or anything relating to the graphic arts. It is a refreshing change of pace from toiling over your own words and creative worries; instead, you wield a blue pencil over other work, often by amateurs, systematically making a poor piece better.

Just as important, editing these publications can ease the daily urge to work toward your annual income goal. Once arranged, an editing job pays as often as the publication is issued, and just as regularly. The time you spend in locating and interviewing for these jobs is written off across months or years of work. Once you're installed as part-time editor of a publication, you're likely to continue shepherding it as long as you care to. The income it produces becomes a financial cushion you can count on, month after month—the kind of steady support that helps take your mind off money and frees it for more adventurous pursuits, like writing articles or working on a book.

Identifying publications that need your editorial help requires some of the background you've dug up in scouting out your community. You need that inventory of smaller publications potentially looking for outside assistance. You might be surprised at the variety you turn up.

I've mentioned earlier there are only a few periodicals in North Dakota. That's only half-true. Though a limited number circulate to the public at large, there is a herd of others that reach controlled audiences: members of a dozen professions, a wide selection of fraternal and social groups, and special-interest constituencies galore.

A few of the biggest appear before the general public. There's *Bar North*, published monthly by the Stockmen's Association, and the Motor Carriers' *Rolling Along*. There's the Farmers Union newspaper and two publications sponsored by the Education Association. Members of the Elks and other orders get both state and local newsletters. The Highway Department puts out a monthly magazine that's part public relations and part house organ; so does the Social Services Board.

The State Historical Society has its quarterly journal and monthly newsletter. The *Dakota Bell* tolls quarterly for the Mental Health Association. Alumni of every college and university get regular news along with pitches for contributions.

And then there's *Outlook*, among half a hundred others. *Outlook*, sponsored by the Department of Public Instruction, is one of the larger ones. Like most publications that carry on unheralded by the public, it depends on members of the profession it serves for its contents. Over 11,000 copies go out each month to every teacher, school official, and interested third party in the state.

Outlook gets its contributions from department staff members, teachers in the field, and the occasional publish-or-perish education professor. It is not rollicking investigative journalism, though some of its stories are solid as the rock. It never fails to interest and inform me.

It's convenient that I enjoy it, because I'm its editor. Putting together each issue of *Outlook* is a contractual job for me. It takes about one week per month during the school year. That week was bitten out of a reluctant department staffer's time during the tabloid's first year. When he put his foot down (he was so swamped, I hear, he could barely find a spot to set it), the department began looking for someone outside to take it on.

Editing *Outlook* is not like creating Art. It's more like building terrific kitchen cabinets. I enjoy the work and the people, and it guarantees our mortgage payment nine months out of the year no matter what else I do.

Since I began freelancing, I've been approached to edit half a dozen publications and one book. None of them is as glossy as a commercial magazine; many are hanging on by the tips of their fingers, since they're adjuncts of other programs that have their sponsors' priority and attention. Some have folded in the past couple of years, but for every one that's lost, another has popped up to add its own voice.

I've accepted some of these jobs and turned down others—for lack of time (mine) or money (theirs). The surprising number of publications looking for an editor for only a few hours a month, and the apparent trouble they have finding and keeping good candidates, make this one of the most convenient and likely ways for freelancers to underwrite the risks of their forays into magazine or book writing.

Pay for a freelance editor ranges from rotten to excellent. It's always negotiable, based on your qualifications, the zeal with which you can bargain, and the degree of desperation to date of the sponsor who's been looking for someone to take his publication in hand.

The practice of contracting for editorial services for a flat fee is perhaps the most common. It isn't without its own variegacies, however. One is that the fee often bears no visible relationship to the amount of work expected; I know of two comparable monthly publications, one of which pays $750 per month, the other $150. If offered a flat fee, use your hourly rate to compute whether it covers the time it consumes. When the answer is no, consider whether the regularity of payment is worth depressed remuneration and decide accordingly. Again, you can always negotiate.

I've noticed another strong benefit from freelance editing. It opens doors to meeting all kinds of interesting, involved people: your contributors and readers. You get a painless education in the field your client's publication serves, whether it's a labor union or a historical society. Those new personalities and projects supply you with an endless source of ideas for your own writing and an almost guaranteed admission to the national trade publications that correspond to your local one.

For example, my freelance editing introduced me to the

world of mentally retarded adults through a newsletter aimed at those who had contributed to a sheltered workshop and training center. Breakthroughs are being made every year, and are brought to my attention by their immediate applications to the local center. The elements are there for enough stories to keep me busy for months. (Unfortunately, while the stories are there, the newsletter isn't. It's one of those casualties I mentioned.)

Other newsletters and magazines have let me see into the worlds of geriatric medicine and counseling, the arts and the tourism industry.

Locating your own editorial jobs can be a toss-up between staying alert to opportunities and the good old element of chance. I was called to interview for *Outlook* because its former editor, the overburdened staffer, had met me at a meeting to discuss developing North Dakota studies curricula for the schools. I never did follow up that most inviting hint, but that single contact paid off when he remembered my freelancing and suggested his boss call me fully a year and a half later.

Some positions—not always just the best ones—are advertised in newspaper classifieds. These ads are placed by publishers on the brink of panic, who have already beaten the nearby bushes and come up with no likely prospects. I've noticed half a dozen of these in our small local daily over six months' time.

Other ads appear where they can get a good rate: in the publications that need the editors. Make a habit of reading those that interest you. Most are filed by the local library. You can usually get on the mailing lists by calling the association or sponsor, explaining your interest as a writer, and requesting a complimentary subscription. It's a good idea to do this even if you're not currently interested, of course, for the article ideas you might encounter.

Your own writing contacts are the best source of all for these contract editorships. I've had several groups I'd written about call me back months later to ask if I were interested in helping out with their newsletters. I know of other freelancers who've secured editing jobs strictly through social contacts—neighbors, friends, friends of parents, teachers whose offices were across the hall from their husband's.

If all else turns up nothing, remember your friend the local printer. Printers are unsurpassed as a source of scuttlebutt on anything regarding the ultimate application of ink to paper, particularly on their own presses. The same printer who's helped you out with background on graphics and tips on freelance commercial opportunities can often give you leads on who or what needs editing.

He knows which publication, lacking an editor at the moment, has fallen into the lap of an unhappy association president. He knows which clients constantly complain of not having enough editorial experience to do the job they'd like. And chances are he knows when a capable editor leaves one of his choicer publication clients. He has a stake in seeing the position refilled by an ally instead of someone who might take the job to his competition.

And if he's as astute as most members of his trade, he knows down to the sixpence who has the money to afford outside help and who does not.

One other route might appeal to you. Get to know the editors of some of the more attractive local publications, perhaps through your chapter of the National Federation of Press Women (if you're lucky enough to be a woman). Since they're usually in touch with their counterparts at other publications, or at least aware of rumblings along the fabled grapevine, they can give you leads you might acquire in no other way.

Learning to edit . . . fast

You might be stymied because, though you've written reams, you've edited little or nothing in the past. Let that stop you only if you still subscribe to the discredited theory that all editors are impeccable, cold-blooded grammarians with hearts of stone, and stiff upper lips.

The ability to write, to recognize good writing, and to improve the rest is what you need to qualify for these editorial posts. The rest you can pick up on your own through sleepless nights of trying to count out headlines and restless days of wondering how much space the average typewritten page takes up in 10-point Bodoni. (Surprise: Your real problem is that there *is* no average typewritten page, at least among amateur contributors. You're lucky when their copy isn't in longhand.)

The printer who publishes the magazine or newspaper you've taken on is your best source of help and inspiration. His art department will often be responsible for setting type and laying out pages. Your main duties consist of getting the copy in shape and determining what goes where . . . at least roughly. The art department takes over from there, incorporating your instructions with their own familiarity with layout, and paste-up.

Alternately, typesetting, layout, and paste-up of your pages can be handled by a graphics production company, a freelance graphic designer, or even the art department within your sponsoring organization. The last is the least likely, since a group that goes outside for a part-time editor usually lacks personnel trained for specialized type and art tasks. But there are exceptions to every rule.

Publications that do add these services have higher budgets and hopes than those that rely on printers. Undeniably, the presence of someone well versed in graphics and layout simplifies your own job enormously. If you work with a designer, you'll help suggest page design but not finalize it, set placement priorities for stories but not worry about the minor details, and probably end up with a more artistically pleasing magazine or newsletter than you could create by yourself with the help of the printer's art crew.

The drawback, of course, is cost. By using art professionals, you're adding a layer of expense that could otherwise be eliminated by using the printer's modestly priced services. You can often manage to compromise and get the best of both worlds by going to a freelance graphic designer (instead of a larger company that offers this service) and hiring typesetting services from those who specialize in it. Watch for outfits who, like yourself, carry little in overhead and will charge your publication's sponsor only for their time and not for your share of their rent, staff, and office expense.

After you've worked with printers and artists through one or two issues, you'll have learned enough production jargon to hold your own. If you want a more thorough understanding of the mechanical aspects of putting out a publication, try your library or technical-vocational school for reference books on printing and graphics. You might also be interested in *Folio*, the magazine about magazines, though its orientation is far beyond the average sponsored publication that has crossed my desk.

Production aside, the editorial basics for the freelance editor are similar to the rules laid down for editors of any other community publications, whether circulating among a general audience (like a newspaper) or only to your select group of readers.

When you begin working with a publication as its editor, get to know why it exists as well as how it gets into print with your assistance.

What are its objectives? Is it supposed to reflect its readers? Convince them? Inform them of technical material they need to know? Answers to these questions make a difference in the placement of stories and the slant you impart to your writers.

Who are those readers? Just "members" isn't enough of an answer. Are they members by virtue of having donated to a charity? Members in fact? Members of a profession? Who *is* the average member? There's obviously a lot of difference between the readers of the Community Action newsletter and the state Lions Club bulletin, and quite a different approach is required to serve each of them honestly and well.

How does its sponsor feel about its past direction? Should you continue in the same vein, or was the need for big changes at the bottom of your appointment as the new editor? If you don't ask, chances are you'll never find out in any but the most explosive circumstances.

Use your news judgment when laying out the first pages, choosing what will be of greatest interest to the largest number of people.

Concentrate on involving people, not dry rhetoric, in as much of your copy as you can. When you're working with amateur writers, this can be difficult. I've seen some sponsored publications that seem to be filled with the adult equivalents of the boy scout's letter to parents from camp or the cheery instructions on your income tax form. But with encouragement, your contributors will mostly see the light; people stories are really easier to write, anyway.

Use as many pictures as you can get your hands on. Here's where the sponsored publication draws away from the "regular" kind. In all too many cases, it seems that they're a captive medium for fuzzy snapshots and check-presentation pictures of all-consuming triteness. Good photography, however, can raise even the lodge newsletter from the realm of gray (or, heaven help you, purple) prose to an interesting-looking bit of mail that gets read more often than not before it's tossed.

Try to do as little of the writing yourself as you can manage. If that sounds odd advice to give a writer, consider the benefits of involving members of the group themselves as reporters for your publication. They know their audience, and that audience will pay attention to their work. They have the background it would take you months to acquire. Most important, members' or reader's views are the reason the publication came into being—it speaks for its constituency, not (in the best of times) to them.

No matter how nifty your style and how writerly your stories, chances are the readers will prefer to read what the lodge president has to say. If you do end up doing a good share of the writing, try to put it in others' words . . . even under their by-lines, as an editorial ghostwriter.

There's an ulterior motive in this advice, of course. Most freelance editorial jobs seem to be paid at a fixed rate per issue. If you end up doing more and more of the writing—if you let the pressure on the members themselves ease up and slide onto your own shoulders—you can easily find yourself devoting an enormous amount of time to a modest job, with an equally modest return on your efforts. This is fine if you're doing it because you love your fellow Moose, but it's like sinking into quicksand for anyone seriously intent on making a good living as a freelance writer.

When you take on a freelance editorial job, try not to take too much for granted. I speak from experience. When I began doing my first newsletter I neglected to get several points of order straight.

Such as who makes the final decision on controversial or questionable stories.

Such as who has the final word on what reaches the front page.

Such as who's responsible if errors creep into the finished product—errors of policy as well as typographical slip-ups.

Do you think you need to be dealing with cabinet-level bureaucracy before "official policy" becomes an important concern? I ran into these particular hidden tree stumps while doing a newsletter for a nursing home. Every association, every client has its own set of givens. As an outsider, you're liable to discover every one of them by trial and error if you don't have dependable advice.

Editing a house organ for a client is not the time to become dogmatic about freedom of the press. It is, after all, *their* press—not your own. As a matter of policy, I always try to find one person among the sponsors who will be responsible for steering me through the thicket of musts and taboos if the need arises . . . and you may be sure I get to know that person before the need ever turns up.

As an editor, you should have certain prerogatives related to technical points. I try to make sure that I'm the one to decide which stories go on the front page, how unacceptable copy should be rewritten for simple readability, and which members, no matter what, will submit to my blue pencil before their work is reproduced in cold type.

I prefer having a member of the association or sponsor responsible for final proofreading as well. Of course I check the printer's proof myself. But I try to find a backstop—someone whose viewpoint enables him to see errors of theory as well as misspelled names or mislabeled photographs.

Even then error can sneak in. I sent an urgent story for one of my newsletters directly to the printer at the very last moment before the presses rolled. No one but I had time to read it in proof. When the finished job arrived, I found I'd called an influential elderly donor by the wrong first name, an error that would be laughed off by most people but infuriated this very generous—and very touchy—philanthropist. I came quite close indeed to eating the whole job, including the cost of a corrected reprint of all 8,000 copies. Reason prevailed, but I wouldn't want to count on it the second time around.

Finally, when any submission seems to run against my client's current thought on the subject. I like to have my contact look it over before it's used.

Some writers might object to this, on grounds that could

range from freedom of the press to impingement on their professional dignity. That's something you work out for yourself. I don't object to it. I am doing a job that ultimately reflects on my client, not on myself, and I want them to be satisfied (actually, I want them to be elated) with the results. It's all too easy to be sucked into an internal squabble by defending your contributors to the hilt; personally, I don't see anything praiseworthy about finding myself unwittingly in the middle of a dogfight.

As a freelance editor, you can earn the income that keeps your rock-bottom expenses covered while learning lessons that can improve your own magazine submissions as well.

You'll develop a much stronger grasp on the necessity of understanding a magazine's editorial policy when submitting queries.

You'll work more closely than ever before with real live readers, and learn what moves them and what they prefer to ignore.

You'll recognize the variety of reasons that make a good piece of writing unusable under your particular set of circumstances, and experience the desperation an editor feels at press time, when all that's on hand is a feeble humorous essay and three government news releases. You'll understand the art of compromise.

And, if you're fortunate, you'll meet all kinds of sincere people dedicated to what they're doing, whether it's good works or the furthering of their profession. Those new friends and fresh ideas are the fringe benefits of freelancing.

Copy editing—a special knack

Editing takes two forms, each of which suits freelancers of a different personality.

One is these outer-directed editorships, where you're involved in lining up a publication's contents and seeing it through its production period. Required is someone who enjoys contact with contributors and readers, since every editor has to do a certain amount of mediation between sponsor and audience.

The other kind of editing—copy editing—requires different sorts of tendencies. Copy editors are responsible for the fine points of the printed product. Often unseen and even unsuspected, they bring a writer's work into smooth, literate form. Spellings are checked and standardized. Incorrect usages and misshapen metaphors are subtly corrected. Major and minor points in articles or books are checked for logic and accuracy.

The copy editor's duties can be cosmetic or surgical. At their most basic, they require an awareness for detail, an ironbound, inbuilt sense of consistency, good spelling, and a talent for diplomacy. Some writers have these skills or have learned them through past experience as copy editors on staff with publishing houses. Others of a more freewheeling turn of mind may not.

Copy editing can lead into more advanced editing jobs that call for more writerly inclinations (though the finest copy editors share this talent), the assignments that require serious work—rewrites, transplants, reshuffles, and other major creative surgery. The average writer's skills may qualify him more directly for this side of the work, though even here additional insight is needed: a strong sense of market and audience as applied to the copy under the knife. This sense is vital in slanting the manuscript toward its intended audience and insuring the manuscript carries the same slant from beginning to end. Also needed is a sense of logical analysis, not necessarily standard equipment for writers.

A good introduction to this possibly unfamiliar field is provided by Carol O'Neill and Avima Ruder, two experienced freelance copy editors, in *The Complete Guide to Editorial Freelancing*, revised 1979 edition. Included is a list of courses, many by correspondence, that teach editing or copy editing skills, along with a detailed explanation of how copy editors approach a manuscript to play their part in the publishing process.

Can everyone who makes a living as a writer become a copy editor? Not necessarily. O'Neill and Ruder say, "A freelancer should love books; should chortle with glee if she finds and corrects a misplaced comma; should yearn to make every manuscript a great book."

The prospects for freelance copy editing are, frankly, mixed. They depend to some extent on where you live, though freelancers are performing these tasks all over the country. Most publishers, given a choice, prefer to work with editors reasonably near at hand.

The need for freelance copy editors is indisputable. Of the forty thousand books published last year, every one of them required a copy editor's assistance. Many were ultimately handled by freelancers because publishers' staffs were swamped and the budgets included no glimmer of more full-timers.

But competition for the best of these jobs—those farmed out by the largest publishers who, not incidentally, pay highest rates—can be fierce. The field is dominated by ex-editors, who've gotten their lessons from work within the industry and who maintain connections formed during their residencies. They tend to be thought of first when outside help is required.

If you have employment experience in publishing yourself, however, you should explore the possibilities for freelancing, first in your own part of the country, where the competition is certain to be lighter. Regional publishers and periodicals are less likely to have staffs of salaried copy editors and may welcome well-trained freelance talent. University presses are also a possibility; a teaching background in English on the college level would obviously help you secure their assignments.

Ruder and O'Neill found in surveying freelance copy editors that about two-thirds got their first assignments either through formerly working in the field or friendly contacts in publishing. The rest used the same method open to you: writing to publishers to offer their services. Your letter should cover any past experience related to any aspect of editing, since this is the big question in potential clients' minds. You may be asked to take a copy editing test, so be prepared to back up your claims with competence.

Publishers in need of copy editors sometimes advertise in *Publishers Weekly* or the *Freelancer's Newsletter*, published twice a month from Skaneateles, New York. You can buy space at modest cost in these publications to announce your own availability as well. Editors sometimes advertise their services in writers' magazines or professional academic journals, but are far more likely to get ghostwriting jobs from their ads than to reach publishers looking for freelance copy editing help.

Your first assignment is hardest to get. After you've assembled a list of editing credits the going becomes easier.

Your regional clients will almost always remain the best prospects for your work.

Copy editing pays by the hour, as a rule, and it's not on par with what plumbers or even freelance writers usually charge. You can count on an offer well under ten dollars—five to seven is closer to average.

Clearly, you won't get rich copy editing. The difficulty of getting assignments seems to suggest that this is among your less profitable prospects to explore unless you already possess the meticulous eye and professional experience. If you're not already equipped to copy edit, frankly you'd be better off selecting another area of freelance writing and spending the same amount of time mastering it. The time required to break in is unlikely to pay large enough dividends to justify the effort.

But if your background is right and your list of contacts fresh, copy editing may be a way to fill in blocks of time otherwise unspoken for in your freelance schedule. The assignments aren't lucrative in themselves, but add up to another form of insurance.

Life as a ghost

The most far-reaching editing jobs have everything in common with ghostwriting except the name on the bottom of your check. Rewrites are commissioned by publishers; ghostwriters are hired (usually but not always) by the person who'll ultimately get credit for the finished piece.

Why do you really write? For the by-line? The reputation? Or for the income that your writing brings you, along with the satisfaction of a job well done?

Ghostwriting satisfies two out of those three urges, and two out of three's not bad. If you can live without the reinforcement of by-lines on everything you write, ghostwriting presents interesting and abundant opportunities to profit from your skill with words.

You may know ghostwriters best for the "autobiographies" of stars and national heroes. That association, however hallowed by tradition and Hollywood, is apt to have given you a shrunken idea of ghosting's scope. Those few glamour jobs obscure the great majority of opportunities for ghosts that are more mundane but far, far more likely to exist right in your own geographic corner.

Movie stars may not entrust their autobiographies to you any time soon, and you may not know a single celebrity looking for assistance in self-expression. Yet you're living within comfortable reach of a multitude of candidates for your ghosting skills: local businessmen booked to address conventions; elected officials who want their by-line (and the publicity it brings) in prestigious magazines; prominent personalities expected to glitter with witty repartee in person or on paper, but who are blocked or too busy or just too tired to produce all their own material.

You needn't be a writing legend to become a ghost. What you do need is an aptitude for working with people very, very close to the sensitive cores of their egos. Your work has to show them at their best. You have to be cooperative and flexible enough to produce a product that satisfies your own standards as well as those of the person who'll get the credit and wants to be known for only the best of efforts.

If you can uncover the essence of what clients really mean to say, and can work well with demanding but uncertain sources, you're ready to investigate the ghostwriting available in your area. I suspect you'll be surprised at the variety of people who jump at the chance to hire a professional writer to make them look good in print or at the lecturer's podium.

About one-eighth of my written output in the past few years has come from projects I classify as ghosting—that is, any written work which is publicly acknowledged as originating with someone else, and which by agreement I do not claim as my own.

Ghosting can be destined for either written or verbal presentation. I've written speeches for public officials, explaining their complicated government programs (gobbledygook!) in lay terms. I've helped a minister, gifted in the pulpit, add an informal touch to down-to-earth speaking encounters.

I've written statements and helped sketch out positions for not a few candidates for office, enlarging on their own attitudes toward the issues and helping to bring out their real personalities in tense public situations.

I've written articles for politicians and business leaders which appeared under their own by-lines in trade or general-interest magazines. I've helped write a newspaper column under a representative's by-line. I've even come up with the idea and market myself and taken them to the logical person to "front" them—then helped craft a manuscript that did us both proud.

I've written grant applications for deserving educators who, though eminently qualified in their fields, have a hard time producing a professional account of themselves on paper. I've helped smooth out résumés, job application letters, nominations for professional awards, and other odds and ends that together amount to the most fascinating bunch of unexpected undertakings I could imagine. In no case have I falsified information or obscured the client's own style. I've just ironed its wrinkles or tucked back its ears or given it a bit of spit and polish. All some assignments require is to see and follow the thread in the mass of detail.

Why do clients hire writers to do what they're thought to have done themselves? People are routinely judged by their communication skills, I think. A brilliant scientist can come across dowdy and unexciting if his uneasiness with words gives him a stuffy, remote tone. A great speaker and conversationalist can fail to translate his personality to paper. A poor education or uncertain grasp of English can handicap the brightest person. The most astute of these recognize their awkwardness and want to do something about their lack of facility with the language.

Enter the ghost.

You may or may not be able to spot likely ghosting opportunities from afar. Not everyone who gives speeches that would make an English teacher shudder is open to hiring someone to improve his style. Somebody else you consider excellent may, on his own, recognize minor shortcomings or simply expect more of himself and want to add final polish to what's already a fair shine.

Unless you make yourself available, you will be overlooked. The idea of hiring a ghostwriter might not occur to many who'd consider it—not, that is, until an observant freelancer suggests the haunting thought of outside assistance.

The sales techniques that help you reach magazine editors serve you well as a foundation for ghostwriting, too. Back to the good old query. Drop a line to several likely men or women sketching out your credentials and saying you're available if a ghost may be of service.

Think over the professions that might demand well-written work of people to whom a typewriter is a foreign object. How about the local college, where research professors must heed the publish-or-perish imperative? Business people who've been asked to address training seminars or conventions? Scientists and engineers with new techniques for solving common problems? Medical professionals who have something to say about developments in their fields?

Letters aren't the only way to approach these people. In smaller communities, you have two other means of getting your message across that take even less effort—word of mouth and short personal visits.

Those who use the services of a ghostwriter aren't always too ready to proclaim it. But word of good professional help does get around. When you have handled a couple of ghostly assignments, you may find that news of your service has leaked out—perhaps by way of someone "who has a friend" you've helped.

If you want to make a concrete proposal—a journal article, for example—it's easiest to drop in and talk it over in person. Don't use hours of a near-stranger's (and your own) time, however, for ambiguous discussions that lead nowhere. If you're just feeling him out, a letter is a more courteous way to introduce the idea.

Finally, consider advertising. A quiet classified ad in professional journals has been demonstrated to get results. Find out what publications go into the offices of professionals in your area. Many national journals offer a selection of ad packages that allow you to choose which parts of the country your ad will reach. It's usually wasted space and money to advertise for ghostwriting clients outside your own area, for extensive personal contact is generally required.

And what would you think of a want ad in your local newspaper? Nothing flashy—no supermarket-size ads or tacky headlines. But a ghostwriting want ad does get results.

The angle to advertise is professional editorial assistance rather than ghostwriting, which carries a murkier connotation. Try phrasing the ad with a hint of your background ("ten years journalistic experience/former editor of trade journal"), along with a suggestion that the reader write for further information. Have a more detailed letter ready for these contacts.

Don't say too much in the advertisement itself; you're running up your cost without gaining any more in the way of benefit. A reader whose interest is piqued will respond to a short notice as readily as to a longer one. If you spend too much money on a large ad, you may even risk looking like the semilegitimate come-on experts who lure naive authors into paying inflated and ineffective fees to have material readied for publication.

Advertisements can attract clients for two ghostwriting specialties which, though radically different, present some of the fastest prospects for painlessly increasing your income.

Résumés

Some writers have provided themselves with pocket money and evened out the occasional feast-or-famine cycle by running ads aimed at getting assignments writing résumés. It's a service welcomed by anxious job-seekers and well suited to the extroverted writer's talents. The help wanted column is the ideal place to advertise—where better to reach those competing on the job market?

Writing résumés demands two main qualities—the ability to conduct a patient, probing interview (which can discover strengths and goals your client may not know he has), and an unflagging tendency to see the bright side. The actual writing is secondary to the act of "framing," with highlights on the client's best points and shadows on those not so good. Producing a good résumé is an act of salesmanship most akin to writing sunny advertising copy . . . without resorting to stretching the truth too far or outright misrepresentation of your client. (A professional résumé is not, no matter what clients may hope, a work of romantic fiction.) The writing itself requires little more than fitting your discoveries into one of the several accepted formats. (A number of books that lay out these forms are available at libraries.) Most résumés can be prepared, from first introduction to completion, in a couple of hours or less. The minimum charge for such a service is approximately forth dollars in my area; because there is little or no competition in most communities, you may find you can charge what the market will bear. Base your starting fee on two hours' work at your regular hourly rate, then increase it in one-hour increments for more demanding jobs.

(A number of books that lay out these forms are available at libraries.) Most résumés can be prepared, from first introduction to completion, in a couple of hours or less. The minimum charge for such a service is approximately forty dollars in my area; because there is little or no competition in most communities, you may find you can charge what the market will bear. Base your starting fee on two hours' work at your regular hourly rate, then increase it in one-hour increments for more demanding jobs.

Rarely will you need to go out of your way to find résumé jobs. I never have indicated I wanted them, but have been asked to take them on anyway as a favor to clients and business acquaintances. For the limited demands they place on your time, they pay handsomely.

Speechwriting

Speechwriting is an especially needed form of ghosting in nearly every locale. At election time, candidates go through an incredible volume of prepared material in addressing all the groups whose votes they hope to win. Prominent businessmen who serve in some civic capacity may welcome a hand in preparing speeches to meet their obligations. Public officials can be steady clients for written remarks, particularly when called upon to represent the community at some larger regional or national event; I know of several writers who've been engaged to write testimony given at federal hearings on issues of major importance back home.

Writing speeches is likely to be a job that you'll enjoy, even if you can't face a crowd yourself. It demands several skills that every experienced writer possesses—the ability to interview and really listen to answers, and to closely observe the client's personality and verbal style.

You have to ask the right questions of your client to prepare a speech that he'll deliver as if he really means it. Sometimes a lengthy discussion of the topic is necessary before the client himself clarifies his position on it. Your job is to probe, to ask him to carry his own thoughts a little further until he's worked the topic through in his own mind. If your research isn't thorough enough, you may face the speech writer's nightmare: a speaker who, as he's reading his prepared text in public, begins to disagree—at first in tone of voice, finally in extemporaneous comments—with his "official" statements.

Writing to the client's personal style gives authenticity to your work. Watch civic and state officials giving canned speeches supplied by charities, for example, seeking a public announcement on their behalf—you can spot wooden, ill-fitting material just by the speaker's uncomfortable manner. A slow, thoughtful talker is mismatched with an original but high-energy statement. One whose style fairly crackles with vitality becomes impatient with ponderous academic thought.

Besides reflecting the client's opinions and his style, your speech should be one more thing: short. Gauge your speaker's normal, relaxed rate of speech and calculate to fill just a few moments less than the allotted time. (You may want to time his speech to estimate length.) Your client's audience will be grateful; and you'll find that brevity improves the reception of almost any speech that you can write.

The finished speech text looks like a manuscript with particularly generous allotments of white space. It's typed in capital orator, if you have it, or at the least in a clear pica-sized typeface. It is doublespaced or, if your typewriter can manage it, triple. Top, side, and bottom margins are wide to keep a nervous speaker's moist palms away from potentially smeary copy . . . and also to allow easy addition of notes, changes, and extra comments that every speaker is bound to toss in at the last moment.

The pages are clearly numbered, and at the bottom of each page but the last is a cryptic notation, "more." The end should be clearly marked too; in the heat of the moment not all speakers realize when they're done.

Charge for your speechwriting, as you do for all ghostwriting activities, on the basis of your established cost per hour. The objective is not to base the price on how long the speech takes to present, but on how long it takes you to put together. Include your time spent interviewing the client, writing, presenting it to him, and rewriting in response to his comments.

One special precaution applies to ghostwriting any kind of project for political candidates and private parties whose credit you're unsure of. Get at least half, and preferably all, of your fee before you begin the assignment. If you're prepaid half, collect the balance before you let the finished copy leave your hands.

Once given, your speech cannot be repossessed for nonpayment of the bill. Nor can you take back work you've done refining another's memoirs, résumé, journal article, or book manuscript. Individuals are more likely than businesses or other organizations to be bad credit risks, and political candidates are absolutely the worst risks of all. They have a nasty tendency to lose elections from time to time, and unsuccessful candidates quite often fail to meet the bills run up during the heat of the campaign.

Ghosted books and magazine articles offer a second option in addition to hourly fees. For books, the standard collaborator's arrangement is to receive all the advance and 50 percent royalties. However, many of the projects you turn up locally won't be taken on by royalty publishers; for a work that's self-published or printed by a vanity press, an hourly fee system is the only safe way to go.

Magazine articles give you a similar choice: split the payment (if there is one) or charge for your services on an hourly or fee basis. (Scholarly journals in particular pay minimal rates, by the way. If approached by the would-be academic author, you'd be better off quoting your regular rates than agreeing to accept some or all of the payment.)

Never, never agree to do ghostwriting on spec for your client unless it was your idea in the first place. There are absolutely no guarantees that your ghostwritten manuscript will ever be published, no matter how impeccably you've written it or how earthshaking its author sincerely believes it to be. Besides, final control of the manuscript lies with its publicly acknowledged author, not with you. The finished manuscript may be quite different than you'd expected it to be.

Because final control of the written copy rests with your

client, it's doubly important in ghostwriting to have a written agreement stating your fees, the work you contract to do for that amount, and mutually understood grounds for acceptance or rejection by the client. A letter is usually adequate for small to medium-size jobs, since your potential profit and the risks entailed don't justify paying for a lawyer's services. But on any major job—say, several thousand dollars or more—a legally binding standard contract is not a bad idea. Consider your client's evident ability to pay, whether he is hiring you as an individual or on behalf of an agency or business. And the warnings of the sixth sense that usually alerts you to a project that's not quite so simple as it seems.

Cautions aside, ghostwriting can be fun. It introduces you to interesting people and reliably reimburses you for efforts performed in their behalf—a good way to enlarge your freelance income without interfering with projects that carry your name and, incidentally, a high rate of risk.

Like editing and copy editing, ghostwriting helps you master the qualities on which writing is accepted or rejected. All three forms are crash courses in clear communication. You'll use lessons learned here to good effect in every project that bears your by-line.

10

Writing for Voice and Visuals: A-V Markets

Hearing your words aloud is thrilling business. It adds a new dimension to writing. As a playwright's work doesn't come alive until it reaches the stage, your own words— projected by a trained voice, sure and dramatic—can teach you much about your craft. Gone are sly allusions and canny quips, the stuff with which writing can so easily be loaded; gone are long, luscious, breathtaking phrases and clauses that create a reading rhythm but catch painfully in the throat; gone, indeed, are sentences just like this one.

Though we writers may lament it, hearing and seeing (and not reading alone) are the way all too many memorable messages capture their audience today. More than at any time since creeping literacy replaced storytelling around a campfire, we're faced with a population that takes in information through its ears and eyes with no printed intermediary.

Does this mean a shrinking market for freelance writers? You should know better than that by now! The audio-visual media—slide/tape shows, filmstrips, movies, radio and television broadcasting—present a whole new world of opportunities for you to sample or specialize in.

Audio-visual writing can contribute meaningfully to your income goal. If you haven't explored this field yet, you may be surprised at just how much it can provide; A-V work has accounted for roughly one-third of my own income for the past two years. Different applications of your craft carry different earning potential: scriptwriting for movies or slide shows, for example, generally pays a most satisfying hourly rate, while writing for TV and radio usually starts out lower but holds more room for growth once you've gotten a good start in the field.

These audio-visual opportunities are an exciting challenge to those of us who start out more accustomed to (and comfortable with) putting words on paper.

The drama of a sixty-second radio commercial or a TV editorial is quite different from the drama of words on paper. Audio-visual writing—for a slide/tape presentation or a half-hour TV script—requires a sense of timing that's either unconscious in most writers or foreign to them.

These assignments give you unprecedented practice in thinking in visual terms—slides to go with your script, perhaps, or sound effects that create an audio "illustration" for a brief regular program on a hometown radio station.

And they offer a chance to see your name in lights. Oh, little bitty lights—a title slide flashed across a movie screen, an author's card filed away in a film reference library. Their audience may recognize you as a kind of celebrity (via radio or television) or as an anonymous craftsman doing mysterious things to put images onto a filmstrip. But these jobs carry more benefit than ego-stroking; there's the special sort of pride you can feel for work that communicates clearly and directly to the audience it's meant for. An audio-visual project successfully completed means you've investigated and mastered territory that only a small percentage of writers across the country have ever explored.

Have you offered your half-baked first drafts of a magazine article to your spouse or friend, then closely observed his every twitch and swallow while he read it . . . eager for some visible sign of honest amusement or amazement? Here's your chance to see an audience react free of any need to please you. When you're long-winded, they fidget. When you're terrific, they laugh or murmur or snap open pocketbooks to fish out hankies. If you're boring, you can tell from the nodding heads and snores. It's a delightful change for those of us whose mates are poker faced or too inured to our lines of thought to even feign surprise.

Audio-visual communication seems simple and direct by the time it reaches the audience. It's a bit more complex at your end, requiring a certain amount of familiarity with equipment and techniques writers don't usually encounter. At its core, however, are the same steps you've gone through with every kind of work prepared for printing: gathering and organizing information, putting it into its simplest and most convincing form, then polishing it into a finished product that gracefully conceals all the labor that's led to those smooth words and well-founded conclusions.

Slide/tape shows

Slide/tape productions are one of the most available and enjoyable kinds of A-V assignments I've taken on. I'd prepared scripts several times before launching into freelancing, but had never had the pleasure of seeing them through to completion. Instead, they'd gone into the maw of an advertising agency, which secured 35mm slides to illustrate them, contracted for music and narrators, and pulled together the many pieces into an impressive— sometimes overwhelming—whole.

I got my initiation into full-scale production by a fluke—a client who had thought of a writer first when considering a slide/tape program, rather than looking for someone who could take pictures. While I heartily agreed with his judgment, it did cause me some doubts (as it might you), for I'd had no hands-on experience with planning photography or recording the narrative for a project.

Three methods that got me started are just as available to you: common sense, a trip to the library, and enough humility to ask questions of those more experienced in the field than I was at the time.

Common sense is the most useful of the lot. Chances are that you already know how to illustrate an article; if you daydream when you write, as I do, you've probably produced many a mental movie. You also have a lifetime of experience as a consumer of visual images in movies, on television, and through all the slide shows and filmstrips you have absorbed as a student and captive audience.

All this background is ready to tap when you plan your own project. You know more about the rhythms and techniques of the photo side of A-V than you may now think you do. You surely know enough to hold your own with the specialists you'll engage to handle parts of your project: the professional photographer and your choice of experienced narrators.

A trip to the library or a bookstore can put more technical information at your fingertips. Kodak has an excellent booklet on producing slide shows. Photo magazines (especially the trade journals aimed at professionals, like *Studio Light* and *Technical Photography*) carry articles on slide show production from a visual point of view. The writer's viewpoint is explored more thoroughly in Allan Amenta's article "Audio-Visual Writing: A World Beyond Words" in the June 1977 issue of *Writer's Digest*.

These publications may at first baffle you with their talk of multi-image slide shows, dual projectors, dissolve units, and as many ultrasophisticated techniques as A-V wizards can dream up to make themselves difficult to replace. But for your purposes, worry only about learning the basic slide/tape setup: a slide projector (usually a Kodak Carousel), a cassette tape recorder, and a programmer to advance slides automatically by encoded inaudible impulses. You can even skip the programmer and introduce new slides with an inconspicuous tone recorded along with your narration.

Books and articles can give you a chance to learn A-V language. But for practical translations of the jargon, your best prospect is detailed, candid conversation with the team of freelance specialists who'll help you create the professional slide/tape production you have in mind.

As I've said, a professional photographer is an invaluable member of the team. Try to find someone locally who does commercial, not studio, work. Though they use their cameras like artists, studio photographers seldom get into capturing live action outside of weddings and other formal occasions. Studio photographers are also accustomed to working with color negative film in larger camera formats. (This refers to the size of the film or negative.) The photographer who's right for you uses 35mm cameras, the only practical size for slide shows, and has thoroughly mastered the ins and outs of working with color transparencies. Don't worry if this doesn't mean a lot to you. It will to your photographer, and you can refer back to Chapter 7.

If your community is minuscule, you'll have to work with whatever photographers are available in the area. Just make sure they're used to slide film and candid documentation. A moonlighting newspaper photographer might be your ally, or a college teacher of photography. Or you can solve the problem as handily as I have, and marry a professional photographer to make sure he's nearby when you need him.

The other member of your slide/tape team is a professional narrator experienced with recording on tape, dubbing music and sound effects, and rendering a polished performance of your scripted copy.

Your local favorite radio or television broadcaster is probably the person you need. He has the training and the voice to bring out the best in your script. I've worked with professionals as well as with eager amateurs who had no experience but glorious vocal cords and a willingness to work cheap. In every case I now would choose the pro over a dulcet-toned volunteer, even if the pro talked like a duck.

My favorite narrator doesn't sound like a waterfowl, however . . . more like the voice of Zeus as a young man. An FM radio broadcaster and TV weatherman, his mellow, fluid voice makes even forecasts of midwinter blizzards sound inviting. Besides his ability to make anything seem reasonable (an asset to a weatherman), he has incredible breath control. That proved to be a real asset while I was still getting the hang of writing for A-V, which requires shorter sentences.

Your broadcasting buddy brings another plus to your team besides his performances, however. Most likely he can use his station's studio facilities for recording after hours. He also has access to their extensive library of music already cleared for commercial use. (Never, never just use a popular tune to open and close your production. Songwriters and performers get royalties just as writers do, and you could be in for extra cost and controversy.)

These team members work with you as freelancers themselves. You can choose to pay them personally, passing on their charges in the bill to your client, or you may decide to have them bill clients directly. In either case, your professional interests mesh nicely. They, too, may be approached to produce other A-V projects. After you've worked together once, you're likely to be included in other projects drummed up by your two colleagues.

You needn't worry about a big investment if you begin producing slide/tape programs. Your narrator should have access to recording equipment, his station's or his own. Your photographer always comes equipped. The only piece of equipment you might want yourself is a slide programmer which puts silent impulses on your taped narration. These impulses make a slide projector advance slides automatically during the course of the program without any manual effort or distracting audible beeps or buzzes to signal when a new slide should be shown. The unit can be purchased for about three hundred dollars and hooked into the slide projector I assume you already have; or you can rent it from an audio-visual supply or electronics rental firm.

So you've got the technical side of production down pat. What you need now are clients. Your regular local writing customers may be looking for audio-visual programs to buttress the printed information pieces you've already produced. Or try government and nonprofit agencies with a need to reach the public, or the public relations or personnel managers of local companies. These jobs are found wherever you turn up other commercial writing clients, as we'll discuss in the next chapter. Make your interest in A-V known and go out looking for your first project. After it's completed, others will find their way to you through references and hearsay.

Scriptwriting is similar to gathering information for any article. Talk with your client to establish what message you're working to communicate. Who will its audience be? Will it be shown within a preordained period of time, or must it be timeless to allow for future updating? Will it be used in one easily controlled location, or sent out to borrowers all over the area? (They could be equipped with anything from Model T projectors to sophisticated A-V labs with cushioned chairs for the audience, which increase average attention spans by at least five minutes.)

The answers to these questions make a great deal of difference in the same way that a magazine's special readership profile influences its approach to topics. One of my first slide/tape programs, for example, was for the state emergency radio network. Much of the information was technical in nature and would be fascinating to other radio specialists—but incomprehensible to the general public. Our audience was to include legislators, who fund the network; law enforcement officers who use it but sometimes don't understand how to get the best from it; and finally, the general public, homemakers' clubs, high school classes, and visiting dignitaries.

The director wanted the program to explain the duties of his chief officers. But the program's life-span was to be forever, more or less, and the people holding these positions could change.

It would not be sent out on loan, so one concern, varied equipment, was eliminated. But it would be carried into the field by agency personnel armed with only the machinery they had on hand: one Kodak Carousel projector, a battered tape recorder-programmer they borrowed from the office next door, and the office extension cord. This ruled out some of the more spectacular techniques we could have used—dual projectors and a dissolve unit to eliminate black space between slides, stereo sound and the like.

We resolved the question of the audience's comprehension of radio technology by taking the safest route, making it understandable by virtually anyone who had no background whatsoever. While this benefited the visiting homemakers, it helped no less the lawmen and legislators who might be loath to admit their lack of expertise. We decided that those better versed in radio technology would be able to question the director after the program, since he would be on hand to show it in person.

The problem of musical chairs with staff positions was also easily solved through one of slide/tape shows' most adaptive features. We mentioned the positions, but not names of the individuals, in the narration. We used photographs of the current personnel to illustrate these portions. If titles are shifted and new managers hired, new slides can replace the old; the narration, which is much harder to alter, can stay exactly as it was recorded.

Slide/tape scripts are usually typed in a special format that allows room for notes about illustrations and sound effects. Double- or triple-space the copy, leaving an extra-generous margin on the left side of the page; about three or four inches is usual.

The script is augmented by a photo-shooting "script" called a storyboard. Block out the approximate number of slides in the program; then sketch out (in words, if you're no artist) the general content needed. You can scribble these views back into the margin of the written script for your own reference; present the storyboard to your photographer with a heart-to-heart talk about objectives.

I have never worried too much about music and sound effects, as the narrator I work with is a master at matching them to my scripts. If you're not blessed in the same way, suggestions for sound additions to the narration should be added at the appropriate spots in your script. Be sure to mark them off with parentheses so they don't slip into your flowing prose when it's being read for posterity.

A few hints may help you plan your first program. Length is limited not by the engrossing material you uncover, but by the attention span of an audience usually parked on hard folding chairs or sweaty plastic seating. Fifteen minutes is a good outer limit.

Plan to use lots of slides. For some reason writers become niggardly when allocating slides, perhaps hoping to avoid distraction from their precious scripts. In practice, slides work in just the opposite way. Good illustrations highlight your script, while bad shots or too few shots create boredom over the best of sound tracks. One slide per fifteen seconds is none too many; five or ten seconds each is a better ratio. Of course, if you get into elaborate shows involving two projectors (or more) you'll need more slides than for a straightforward project. Series of slides flashed quickly on the screen create a feeling of motion that is an improvement on the choppy slide-advancing rhythm.

A "good" image for slide show purposes isn't necessarily one you'd choose for your living room wall. It's one that augments the script—tells a little more, or makes an idea clearer, or merely occupies the audience visually while the narrator delivers a phrase that demands more of their attention.

Your first indication that a slide is up to your standards is that it's in absolute focus. While most people edit slides on a light box or by holding them in front of a window (daylight's closer to what they'll really look like), you must go through your slides at least once in a projector to check for sharpness. Slides are tiny; what looks focused when you eyeball it can look like flannel when projected the size of wallpaper across a screen. Out-of-focus slides give viewers headaches, not to mention the trouble they cause the poor fellow trying in vain to focus his projector.

Artistic merits, in slide shows, are secondary to clarity. Simple, uncluttered images are best. Backgrounds should be quiet or harmonious, allowing the subject to dominate the screen. Good color is vital; you've probably seen, as I have, embarrassing sequences of slides that are greenish, half off horizontal, and which decapitate or cripple the subject by awkward positioning of his physique. Throw out every slide that fits this description, even if it's your only picture of a Tasmanian wombat. When you're really in a pinch, you're better off with an artist's rendering, a graph, or some other diversion than a photo that causes gastric distress. (Incidentally, those Martian-green indoor slides that turn up so often are caused by using film color-balanced for daylight in a room lit by fluorescents, which have an entirely different color temperature. Blame them on your photographer; he certainly should have known better.)

I look for one other nicety when editing slides: I want all horizontal views. While some perfectly acceptable slide shows use both horizontal and vertical pictures, they're an unnecessary distraction for viewers. Choosing all horizontals also makes your task easier if the slide show is to be converted to a filmstrip, since filmstrips rely without exception on that format.

Watch out for clients who just want you to write a script to accompany slides already in hand. The slides in hand almost always are of the wrong subjects, have that greenish look, or were recently recovered from a crushed file folder, a drawer into which mimeograph fluid was spilled, or a shoebox unearthed in the storeroom. You find that you're writing around an impossible collection of images. When the script ends up choppy and awkward, you—the writer—will probably be blamed.

You want to produce good programs. One good program leads to another, for nowhere in the country are slide/tape shows not received with interest. As a freelancer, your charges are much more reasonable than the client's other alternative for production, an advertising agency. You may also find that your community has never had anyone making really professional A-V productions. One good effort then raises the standards of all who see it, creating more business for you in the future.

Filmstrips and movie scripts

One good slide/tape production not only leads to another—it also leads to production of filmstrips and scripts for movies or videotapes.

Filmstrips are what you turned by hand through a viewer back in sixth grade . . . but how they've changed! Today they're an accepted educational tool and sometimes come complete with sound tracks and automatic advancement from frame to frame.

The difference between filmstrips and slide/tape programs depends on their degree of sophistication. At filmstrips' best, the only real difference is that one strip of film replaces a cumbersome tray of slides. At their simpler levels, you may have to reduce your narration considerably or even distill it into subtitles that appear on each frame. No matter what your aim, you can obtain service from professional processors to convert your program to filmstrip form; ask your audio-visual equipment dealer for names and addresses, or consult a commercial or technical photographer who's worked with such a company in the past.

Movies aren't limited to Hollywood extravaganzas foisted on the hinterlands. Your chances of writing that kind of script are not good. Consider instead the thousands of industrial and educational films produced across the country every year, for clients ranging from tourism groups to manufacturers of lawnmowers and microwave ovens.

Every state has at least several companies in business to produce 16mm movies or videotapes, the new TV-based technology taking over the industrial and educational fields. Your telephone directory can guide you to local specialists. They often hire freelance scriptwriters, since their main business lies on the photography end of film-making. Your previous scripts for slide/tape programs are sound samples to back up your query, since they demonstrate you've mastered the mating of visual and audible communication.

You may also be approached by commercial clients who want to put together their own film or video packages, hiring a photographer to shoot the movie, a writer to do the script, and a production company to complete the other chores. Here, your local experience in slide/tape is invaluable, since scriptwriting is a rare accomplishment outside metropolises.

Remember my advice about scripting first and photographing later—rather than wrapping your words around existing images. If fitting slides to narration is awkward (and it is), scripting a film already shot is even worse. Visual transitions obvious to the photographer—based on color, composition, motion—can be downright impossible to tie together logically with words. Some of the most rough-edged, uncomfortable films you've seen have undoubtedly been created when a scriptwriter was called in at the very last minute to try to save a visually appealing project.

The solution is to try very hard to become part of the film-making team before the last minute, while all is still in the planning stages. On occasion you may find yourself called in just under the wire, as sometimes happens with film-makers not particularly accustomed to providing their own scripts. Push for the right to have the film re-edited if you find yourself written into an impossible corner. You may not get it, camera-wielders being the jealous artists they are; but at least you've tried your best to insure a smooth finished product.

Film scripting is much like writing for slide/tape programs, with a couple of exceptions. Films inevitably have much bigger budgets than slide shows. A rule of thumb used in the trade is the budget for the whole production starts at a thousand dollars per finished minute, and increasing costs are rapidly making that rule an antique. Film scripting should earn you more than writing for slide/tape programs, because of the bigger budgets, greater length and complexity of movies.

More than with slide/tape shows, payment methods vary

for film scripting. You may be paid at an hourly rate or a flat fee based on your estimated number of hours. Or you may be offered a flat percentage (usually ten) of the total budget. Because of the considerable cost of making films, you'll probably be better off with the percentage. The one exception is if you're expected to do an endless number of rewrites; try to build some clause into your contract to cover these extraordinary demands with an additional hourly charge.

Though they vary, most 16mm movies and videotapes are about twenty-eight minutes long. The promotional nature of these movies should alert you that their length has everything to do with standard blocks of TV programming time. Their sponsors fervently hope that television stations will use them to fill non-network hours after 2 a.m., or odd minutes on Sunday afternoon after an abrupt end to a football game, or during those dark moments when network trouble or local station error interrupts the regular broadcast of a prime time hit show. Shorter films, ten to fifteen minutes, are sometimes offered to movie theaters for much the same purposes.

Think visually as you compose your film or video script—even more than you do when you're writing slide shows. Film visuals show action rather than static images. When you're stuck for a while watching the silhouette of a mountain or a package of the sponsor's product, you can use camera motion (close-ups or slow pans across the subject) to fake some energy, though these techniques grow old amazingly soon. And don't expect a cameraman to interpret your verbal script with lots of lively activities. If film shots suggest themselves, build them into the copy (within parentheses to alert the producer). Funny things catch photographers' eyes. Take nothing for granted.

If scriptwriting appeals to you, your markets needn't be limited by clients close to home.

Hundreds of professional A-V production companies are scattered across the country. Many of them are listed in *Writer's Market*, and the names of others can be found by digging through educational and informational movies and filmstrips at local schools and libraries.

These companies purchase scripts and, sometimes, concepts for projects from freelance writers. While a good query letter on a particular topic is never entirely wasted, a strong résumé heavy with local A-V experience is a better way to approach these houses. Include a list of shows you've produced and clients who sponsored them, along with part of a sample script and perhaps a few illustrations.

Querying a producer on a show you have already planned out is usually a futile effort unless you know the work he specializes in and his needs for coming months. Write for a catalog and writers' specifications. Only then can you map out a theme that might catch his eye and fit into his plans. While your own idea may not quite fit, it serves as a good demonstration of your adeptness at thinking in A-V terms.

Allan Amenta's *Writer's Digest* article (June 1977) mentioned earlier is perhaps your best source of information on selling to A-V companies. Other useful suggestions are listed in *Writer's Market* and *Photographer's Market*. It's definitely worth your effort to investigate these markets, for scriptwriting—successfully completed—pays better than a comparable number of words for publication. The field is as challenging as the magazine industry, and the competition is demonstrably less. Once you've broken in, it can easily become a major source of your freelance support.

Radio and TV

Do you still think of television as a "vast wasteland" and radio as the repetitive Top Forty racket you listen to while driving? Well, think again. Both radio and TV can be good markets wherever you live.

Radio and television don't just offer possibilities to glamorous grinning clones. The facets of broadcasting that require a writer's touch are diverse enough to satisfy the most solitary or gregarious soul. And these are among the special benefits of living beyond the fringe of metropolitan centers. While major stations are less likely to be in the market for a great deal of freelance assistance, the opposite can be true in more remote communities. It's another one of the variations on Catch-22, however: the smaller the station, the better your prospects of providing assistance; but the more likely you are to have to prove it to them.

There's a great deal of written material that goes into

local programming on radio and TV, from commercial breaks to public service programs. Any random hour on radio, for example, includes commercials (both prerecorded and read from a script by the announcer on duty), news copy, public service announcements for worthy local causes, and even a handful of quips that, while they might make you groan, probably came from a costly jokebook or comedy service.

Television has its news, commercials, and public service spots, too, along with local programs, editorials, and the little station-break announcements that cause agonizing mental cramps to those who write them day after day after day with an eye to originality.

Newswriting isn't likely to fit into your freelance plans, since it's usually either a full-time job or no job at all—as many radio station announcers just rip copy off the wire service Teletype and read it over the air.

Commercial and public service announcement copy is probably staff-written but may still be open to you, either by writing on contract for the station or for advertisers themselves. Prewritten quippery could be lucrative, but only if you have the peculiar turn of mind that can produce one-time hilarity in volume.

But there are more opportunities. Consider these:

■ Regular programs of five or ten minutes (or more) once or several times a week on topics of special interest to you and listeners—the outdoors, hunting and fishing, cooking, consumerism, travel.

■ News programs aimed at special-interest groups to which you have a pipeline—minorities, senior citizens, residents of outlying communities, farmers.

■ Editorials promoting the station's viewpoint. (These are very often ghostwritten.)

■ Series of public information segments around which advertising can be sold in special campaigns—back-to-school tips, Christmas safety, local history anecdotes, outstanding area personalities, or whatever appeals to you and the ad manager of the station.

■ Interview or talk shows that require more background or preparation than station announcers are interested in investing.

Freelancers have one big paradox in their favor when

proposing these kinds of projects. It's the media's age-old quandary: Local programming draws local listeners and local interest, not to mention local advertisers—but costs far more to produce and air than canned programs created elsewhere. Small stations have neither the staff nor the time to do as much original community broadcasting as they'd like. As with a gap in newspaper staff coverage, these weak spots in radio or television programs present an entrée to creative freelancers.

Like the other media, radio and television exist—at the very bottom line—to make a profit for their owners. The profits come from the sale of advertising. Any idea you propose, therefore, stands a good chance of being accepted if it will appeal to listeners or viewers whose attention, in turn, will cause advertisers to brighten.

The classics in my part of the country are hunting and fishing programs. One well-known full-time outdoors writer, though he had no previous experience in radio, produces five-minute broadcasts run during drive time on local stations; their sponsorship by outdoors firms is almost guaranteed.

You may be able to adapt your own writing specialty to the same practical considerations, especially on radio. Consider topics that interest not only you, but their potential audiences and sponsors. If you write regularly about cooking, for example, how about a program on gourmet masterpieces? Grocers or retailers of kitchen equipment might be interested in supporting you. If you're well informed on travel, how about travel agencies, airlines, and hotels?

Another approach is also possible for news in the public interest, even that which has no automatic moneygrubbing associations. Radio and television stations are licensed by the government and need to demonstrate, at renewal time, that they are serving the public interest. Civic-minded programming can help them satisfy this requirement and also lend that local touch to the program schedule that means so much to faithful listeners.

Senior citizens' news falls into this category around here. So does a talk show concentrating on Indian issues and guests. Programs related to local charities and worthy causes can also provide good material for your freelance program—and help build up a public service record for the station that sponsors you.

Use your hourly rate as a bench mark for remuneration for your broadcast efforts. You may have to start off at a lower total income if your goal is to have your program aired by more than one station (as outdoor programs often are); if station management is doubtful about your program's drawing power among its listeners, you may also want to start at an amount less than your ideal hourly income. But if this is the case, be sure that your fee goes up as the program's success (in terms of attracting listeners and advertisers) is demonstrated. Like everyone else, broadcasters seldom give raises in payment based solely on merit or gratitude. If you don't ask, you'll probably make beginner's wages as long as you pursue the project.

Everyone benefits from local freelance programming: you, of course, but also the station, the advertisers, and the listeners. The station can sell your sponsorship at a premium because you reach a selective, interested audience. The advertiser not only reaches customers with his message; he also gains a bit of philosophical fallout for taking an interest in supporting sportsmanship or gastronomic excellence or whatever you've cooked up.

Producing your own radio programming may smack of stardom to you. (Actually, it's something less than that, but you can count on at least a tinge of notoriety in your community.) There are other freelance assignments associated with radio, however, which might be equally or more lucrative in the long run.

Writing commercials can be financially rewarding and often downright fun. Packing a substantial message into a tiny bit of time with thirty well-chosen words is a challenge that reminds me of crossword puzzles or party word games. Humor is welcome in advertising, and you can be as creative as possible to help distinguish your message from the audio clutter around it.

You have two avenues to freelance copywriting of commercial messages. One is to approach the advertising managers of local radio. Their own copywriters are traditionally overworked, and they may welcome an opportunity to shift some of their workload onto capable freelancers.

The drawback in freelancing for stations is the payment. Station copywriters are not only worked to a frazzle, they're also underpaid, as a rule. While a freelancer should always expect more than the going hourly salary for similar services (remember all the money you save clients?), the top limit is apt to be fairly inflexible with station management.

But you can go straight to the source of ad messages, the advertiser himself. A business that books time on radio or television is a good possibility for freelance commercial copywriting. Unless it's a major national franchise with a big ad budget or uses canned co-op commercials provided by the lines it sells, it's likely to rely on copywriters at the stations to come up with motivating nuggets of ad persuasion. Retailers in the small-to-medium range probably can't afford ad agency services for their commericals; yet they're bound to be dissatisfied with the sameness that even a dedicated station copywriter gives to the messages he writes for the advertiser's account . . . and his competitors'.

The advertiser, moreover, is less likely to blink and stammer when you mention your hourly rate. Advertising, even on smaller radio and TV stations, is extremely expensive—a major entry in their annual budgets. To spend that sum without presenting a fresh, clear message that brings in customers is folly. So clients are inclined to substantially reward someone who can make their investment in airtime pay off.

Commercials proven to bring in customers allow you to virtually write your own ticket with local advertisers. So does a flair for the inevitable occasions that elicit advertising with little content but lots of good will—Thanksgiving, Christmas, Easter, the Fourth of July. At all these holidays ad salesmen urge their customers to wish the public well with the verbal equivalents of gooey greeting cards. Yet all the yammering about joy, warmth, patriotism, and motherhood becomes deadly dull over a day's time, sort of like audible wallpaper. Put a flick of originality into those messages—to make the client stand out just a little from the competition—and your holiday shopping or vacation money is assured.

Not only businesses may be interested in your talent for writing radio messages. Nonprofit organizations (those that raise funds for disease research and charitable work, for example), government agencies, service clubs promoting public projects—all need the same kind of skill you provide for commercial clients.

Public service announcements are run at no charge by radio and TV stations for the same benevolent but pragmatic reasons that interest them in your program suggestions: as evidence of their commitment to the public good to offer at license time, as well as to actually serve their listeners.

As with your commercial copywriting, you'll probably submit PSAs double-spaced with extra-wide margins for production notes. You'll seldom, as a freelancer, go ahead and record or film the announcements that are to be issued to stations. That chore is generally carried out by the station's staff (for small organizations, at no charge) or by ad agencies (for the biggies who can afford full campaigns over large geographic areas).

At smaller stations in areas like mine, typed public service announcements are entirely acceptable; they're read over the air by the staff announcers. Direct them to each station's public service director, usually an individual with myriad additional chores who simply opens the mail, screens PSA requests, and inserts them into a logbook for announcers' use. The screening in my area is relatively perfunctory; the critical test is whether the request is for charitable purposes or has a visible profit motive, which is a universal no-no. (Those who want to profit from ads are supposed to pay for them.)

Finally, there is the unique subject of disc jockey quippery. Not many people have the knack of knocking out topical one- or two-liners that can be marketed to radio personalities. If you have this rare gift, you can apply it for moderately good rewards to writing on-air material, either for the nationally distributed humor services like Robert Orben, or by marketing your own material to disc jockeys in your part of the world.

Drop in at a station and talk your proposal over with an announcer whose work you admire. He'll probably be able to show you samples of the publications he or the station subscribes to. If your own samples sound good to him, he may agree to pay you a set fee for a set number of jokes and comments on a regular basis.

You won't get rich by providing sharp-edged comments to one announcer; but there's no reason that good material be limited to one. You're free to market the same work to others—provided they're in noncompetitive markets, usually at least 250 miles apart. Work through individuals, not stations, when selling on-the-air material. Disc jockeys are a notoriously nomadic lot; the good ones work hard on their ratings, and fresh humorous material is one weapon they can use in building up their followings and bettering their prospects for the next move.

Television offers many of the same kinds of opportunities you find in radio. But the differences in the two mean that the possibilities for a freelance writer are both better and worse.

Better, that is, if you can convince station mangement to engage you to work on the larger, more expensive, and more committed scale required by TV's programming procedure, advertising rates, and special demands as both a visual and audible medium.

Worse . . . if your local stations are closed to all but full-timers, or if you're not ready to put in the time necessary to do good TV work, or if your personality and inclinations clearly rule you out as television material.

The rule holds true again: The smaller the station, the better the opportunities. Large urban operations may welcome occasional freelance copywriting assistance but little more. Smaller TV stations, however, respond to the same needs that propel radio management—more local programming, better ratings, demonstrable interest among high-ticket viewers who inspire advertisers when gathered around one time slot.

Writing commercials or "continuity" is no one's idea of the glamorous television business . . . not, at least, at a smaller operation where the job is one step above receptionist. In the very smallest settings, the job may not be even a full-time assignment. In others, those who currently hold the copywriter's title are anxious to tackle other station assignments to broaden their experience, head into more inspiring positions, or simply avoid the inevitable ruts that face those who think in terms of minutes and fractions thereof.

For all these reasons and because good copywriters are

scarce in smaller markets, the field presents a freelance or part-time writing opportunity. As with radio copywriting, television work comes in two categories: employment by the station, where you come free with the advertising contracts, and freelance employment among advertisers. The latter pays better and, oddly enough, is often easier to come by.

The TV copywriter has a double challenge. He or she has to create not only a memorable message in capsule form, but a visual accompaniment that catches the eye while the ear is being seduced. Experience in working with audio-visual projects is invaluable background for this work. (The reverse is true too: experienced copywriters are in a good position to go into audio-visual production.)

If copywriting is at the bottom of the TV creative heap, producing or even hosting a regular program is near the top. You may have a shot at it if you've compiled an impressive background and reputation as a writer in a consumer-oriented field, or if you find an opportunity to research and write for an on-air personality or locally originated project.

My background in the news media and my freelance availability brought me into television several years ago as the producer of a weekly news analysis program called "North Dakota This Week." Broadcast by our statewide public television network, my panel of print journalists gather for coffee-cup conversation about stories they've covered that week . . . discussions that have sometimes added measurably to the renditions of the news available to readers.

Did I have experience in control rooms or with video cameras? No, but that bars neither me nor you from broadcast production. Like so many hidden freelance opportunities, it requires the skills of a generalist, not a hard-technology expert.

As producer of my public-affairs program, I do all the "soft" work leading up to our tapings. I keep on top of my subject matter, compile research, stay in touch with journalists who may become panelists when their stories reach statewide proportions. Each week I line up four of them to tape in our studio in Fargo. I book travel, negotiate topics, and prepare a script for the moderator that sounds as close to his own casual style as my detailed machinations can make it.

Lack of background in video production hasn't handicapped me as a freelance producer, nor would it you—in fact, my director claims it's an asset because I'm not inclined to second-guess him.

Television production won't bring you fame. The better you do your job, the more spontaneous, natural, *non-produced* your finished program will appear to viewers. But it does bring you the excitement of working in broadcasting, the satisfaction of mastering a medium most writers regard with distrust, and the financial return that you as a freelancer require.

To find your own production jobs, talk with a station manager or program director about his or her plans, needs, and programming daydreams. Your experience as a writer (especially as a veteran of some type of A-V) recommends you, as well as your knowledge of your subject matter and your willingness to consider the station's priorities.

In commercial television, pre-selling your idea to potential advertisers is the most convincing evidence you can bring with you. In either public or commercial television, your proposal for filling viewers' needs, coupled with practical knowledge of how to make your scheme work, make you a candidate worthy of serious and enthusiastic consideration.

The more assignments you've successfully tackled in the whole A-V field—slide/tape, movie scripting, copywriting, or production—the more your future opportunities can be counted on to grow. The audio-visual media need writers...more writers than they can afford to feed full-time.

The skills that you bring to every kind of writing enterprise, the same benefits that make freelancers attractive to magazines and other markets, all heighten your prospects in A-V. Once you've gotten your feet wet, you'll find you enjoy the splash—of writing for voice and visuals.

11

Bread and Butter Writing

Your career as a freelance writer has all the elements of good drama: an unusual setting, a struggling hero, unexpected joys and sorrows, and the potential for a happy ending.

Now it's time for a word from your sponsor.

All the highs and lows of a writing life can be underwritten by commercial writing in your own neck of the woods.

Scoff. You're entitled. You don't read about such things as annual reports, brochures, publicity campaigns, grant applications in books about Making It as a writer. But those are the financial support beneath some of the brightest writing careers in the country.

Sure, you've never read about them in author's bio-notes on book jackets or in the little italicized comments at the end of a magazine article.

Yet it remains an uncontestable truth that you can smooth your creditors' furrowed brows while launching your freelance livelihood by finding and fulfilling a whole spectrum of unsuspected local assignments. They go under myriad respectable names—public information, public relations, research and information, consumer education. They're all commercial jobs; you're engaged and paid, not by an editor, but by a client who wants what your words can accomplish for his company, his public agency or, as often as not, himself.

Commercial writing. Does it sound like a step down from the lofty books, articles, and media work we've been examining? It's actually a step up in dependable financial support. Commercial jobs, in my experience, are more likely to return your necessary hourly income without argument or compromise. It's a step sideways in technique. The same skill you use to gather and concoct other writing assignments serves you well in working for a commercial master.

A master—is that it? That aspect of commercial work is, I think, the reason it can be a step down in just one category: status. If you've worked in the news business, you know that reporters regard flacks as hack writers (and, privately, as people who make more money than reporters, which is immoral).

That attitude dies hard. And yet many of the newspapers I'm familiar with would be sorely pressed to cover their territories with the thoroughness they value if their flow of public statements from politicians and authorities were cut off; if no more business news releases filtered down to the business editor; if no food distributors or clothing manufacturers or home decorating companies sent recipes, fashion hints, and interior design tips to their women's or lifestyle editors; if information centers sponsored by industry weren't there to fill in the sketchy background on stories of even the slightest technical nature; and if all the sports departments of the world no longer got a steady flow of photos, bios, and news releases from college and high school athletic promoters.

The dignity of any assignment is in the eye of the acceptor. You may never know what commercial reasons led to a magazine sale, but they're there nonetheless. Books are published in the hope they'll make a profit. Outright commercial assignments come with no less practical purposes. The difference is that your clients are up front about what they hope to gain from your work. Layers of editorial and publishers' swathing protect you from that knowledge in many other markets.

If you dig back far enough in the origins of this insidious

attitude, I think you'll find the traditional antipathy between artists and businessmen. You may be an artist, but you're in business, too. (A respectable common ground for you and your business clients.)

The wealth of commercial writing opportunities in good old Bismarck surprised me, as I've told you, when I was taking my first excited steps toward freelancing. Wherever I found an organization that needed to get its message to the public, I had a potential freelance writing client. Their reasons vary—some want to persuade, others aim at pure information, and still others forge a combination of those two motives to promote their projects, their ideals, or their products.

Sometimes, I've found, their reasons are more ambiguous than anything else. While some commercial clients do know exactly what they want written, many more have only a general idea that something needs to be done. Not precisely what it is, or who it's for, you understand—filling in those blanks is going to be up to the writer.

As a freelancer, you're a temporary partner of the client who contracts for your services. You have to work together to find out what his needs really are in the way of written work. Together, you arrive at the best way to fulfill them.

Freelancers from outside your client organizations really are in a better position than staffers to identify and analyze many of these needs. Staff members have been steeped in the traditional dos and don'ts of the company. Their familiarity with how things have always been done can hamper the ability to see problems in a new light. They're bound, by their salaries, to hallow sacred cows that an outsider (benefiting from ignorance) can ignore.

Commercial work varies most from writing for other kinds of publication in who ultimately gets credit for your work. In magazine and book writing it usually reflects on you. In commercial work, your clients bask in the glow of your job successfully done, or carry the burden of factual errors or mistaken approaches that affect their ability to reach their chosen segments of the public. Most commercial publications carry no by-lines. In fact, their creator's identity is only rarely considered; the few readers with a real interest are other potential clients who observe and remember a job that served its purpose well.

But don't let the anonymity of commercial work convince you that it doesn't deserve your better efforts.

Commercial writing does have a mercenary nature, to be sure; your writing is not to satisfy a Muse or a cause, but a straightforward exchange of product for payment. But so is all the work you take on in the course of your freelancing.

The real reason so much commercial writing is mediocre, I think, is that the writers sometimes felt they didn't have to respect it. Much of it is put together carelessly by nonwriters, to be sure. Yet I've seen enough dull, pedestrian commercial prose composed by ostensible professionals to wonder.

The assumption that commercial jobs are something less than magazine or newspaper writing has led some highly competent people to write down to their clients—to turn out work that'd make a beginner blush—work they'd never consider foisting off on an editor but which they think is par for the commercial course. It's all too easy to act out your worst expectations: If commercial writing is a routine mechanical exercise to pay the rent, then it gets written routinely, mechanically, and confirms these low opinions.

If you believe you can toss off a less-than-professional product for a client just because it is, after all, public relations work, you may be quite sure that what you've written won't be something you'll point to with pride. Of course you'll make excuses for it. You should.

Just because commercial work pays better, is readily available, and even appears almost unbidden at the far-flung freelancer's door is no reason to underestimate the quality of challenges you'll meet in pursuing it.

Commercial work is not free money. You'll work for it just as hard as you do for the most gratifying and ego-satisfying publication. If you're prepared to respect the part you play in bringing information to the public on behalf of your clients, you won't regret trying out this application of your craft.

There are two main assignments for which commercial clients may seek you out. One is to write and produce publications of any kind, from brochures, annual reports, and catalog copy to the newsletters and house organs we looked at in chapter 6. The other is to plan and carry out information campaigns through the news media, direct-mail contacts, and other routes you chart to reach the interested public. Related to this area are audio-visual projects, discussed in chapter 10.

Of course, not all clients for commercial writing and production come looking for you. While you're getting started, you'll approach them—in most cases—a time-consuming practice, but one that can't be sidestepped if you're going to use these opportunities to reach your income goal.

Advertising agencies often use presentations to impress and secure new clients. They bring samples of work they've done for customers with whom their quarry will identify, an explanation of the services that they provide, and more than a few fast words about how effective their past efforts have been in reaching donors, increasing sales, or convincing voters.

As a freelancer, you're in a similar position. You have to convince your future client that he needs your services as a writer, that you can provide a full range of help in getting the message into finished form, and that you've already succeeded in achieving these goals for others whom the prospective client respects.

Your presentation needn't be elaborate. A folio of samples is a necessity, along with an edited résumé mentioning past clients or projects. (Be sure that past clients have no objection to being listed. Those who hired you to ghostwrite often do.) Beyond these props, you are your own best evidence that you know how to communicate and can relate well with the person you're calling on. Be pleasant. Be bursting with ideas. And—unless you're encouraged to stay—be brief.

Cold calls are the hardest. You can avoid many of them by choosing prospective clients with an eye to your own personal resources. In which fields or businesses do you already have contacts? Where does your background lie? (My own years with state government provided a natural access to other state agencies I'd already worked with.) What connections can you dredge up—shared memberships in service clubs, in-laws in common, playing racquetball together at the Y? When all else fails, turn to the best recommendation of all: Choose those people whose work you genuinely admire, and offer to become part of their team. Honest respect will get you fifteen minutes of the busiest man's or woman's time.

I've never felt that I was competing with anyone for the jobs I've been hired to do. Many of them didn't exist until I made the right contacts, which suggested to some client that a project should be begun. A freelancer's availability has often been the reason that a new plan was put into action.

Beyond that, freelancers are positioned differently than advertising agencies, for example, which do compete—ferociously—for accounts. Few agencies deign to take on work that adds up to less than four or preferably five digits: their overhead makes small jobs unprofitable. But the same projects can be extremely lucrative for you.

Once you've convinced a client to try you with an assignment, he's unlikely to look up half a dozen more freelancers and listen to their claims before making a decision. The kind of commercial work in which freelancers specialize usually amounts to small change in the corporate budget. While hiring an ad agency represents a commitment of a chunk of money large enough to demand justification and careful comparison, the projects you'll take on are more of a convenience which an executive can easily work into "fees and services."

What kinds of figures are we looking at? I base my own costs, as I've said, on my basic hourly rate. When figuring a bill, I try to include every minute legitimately spent on a project, including discussions with the client, writing and research, travel time, hours spent working with designers or printers or the news media, the whole works. Yet it's a rare brochure for which I charge more than two or three hundred dollars.

The budget of any brochure includes far heftier sums than my own fees. Printing always equals, and usually doubles or triples, the sum I've billed. Graphic designers who charge by the hour or the job can earn at least as much as I do, especially if given free rein with the artistic side of the project; none seems to do much for less than a hundred dollars.

The client would encounter these costs even if he had his file clerk or sister-in-law patch together some information for a brochure he was planning. By contracting your professional services, he's actually protecting a far larger investment. The best-designed, most finely printed brochure will miss its goal if it is poorly planned and written.

Printed communications

Organizations have any number of reasons for producing publications, from the logical functionality of the annual report to ambiguous institutional brochures cranked out because the competition seems to have one.

Done right, each shares the need for a well-chosen slant, fine-honed selectivity in presenting material, and appropriately flavorful writing to attract and hold readers long enough for the message to sink in.

The answer to those communication challenges has to be concise and punchy. Reasearchers have shown that a brochure has three seconds flat to catch the casual reader's interest. If his interest is piqued, you gain another thirty seconds to lure him into reading it more fully. Only the best material clears these two hurdles to get the reader's full attention—and unless he's really fascinated, you have three minutes from that point to get your entire message across.

Are you nervous yet? The same quick hook and sticky lead make good magazine articles successful; but as one writer in a big fat magazine, your role in catching readers can be a little blurry. In a publication you've produced yourself, your central role is unmistakable. If you don't succeed, the brochure gets tossed aside without a second thought.

As a freelancer, you face a fascinating challenge when you take on a one-shot publication project. In an all too finite space you have one chance to convey that all-important message to the reader, who's usually no more than casually interested in paying attention to your performance.

And before you ever get to that prospective reader, you've got weeks of work to do. You need to identify your message and your audience, organize your content, and do the actual writing.

But you also have to come up with an orderly design, with or without the help of the fascinating breed called graphic designers. You have to proceed from idea to concrete type and illustrations . . . find a printer who'll do your work at a reasonable cost . . . resist (in most cases), all his temptations of gold foil on parchment and four-color art and still create a classy product. Finally, you usually have to badger every party involved to meet your deadline, which is always too close for comfort.

When you're done, if you've done well, you'll get your rewards. A brochure or similar publication that you create from start to finish is among the most satisfying pieces of work you can drop into your sample file.

Don't be overwhelmed by the task of working through the production process—working with graphic design, type, and printing. Those are areas where you can call in your own outside experts to carry the ball. Nor are those areas as difficult to understand as you might think; their mystique lies mostly in your unfamiliarity. Look at the brochures and reports you pick up around town every day. If your pickings are like most I've seen, you're probably sure you can do a better job yourself.

I've handled hundreds of brochures and reports for clients ranging from the Mental Health Association to our local junior college, and can attest to how quickly you become acquainted with the basics of laying out designs and badgering printers. As a nonartist, I've occasionally been baffled about how to communicate my ideas for art or express my reactions to that which I've seen. As a nonprinter, I've been befuddled more than once by talk of printing two-up, saddlestitching, die cuts, color keys and separations. I've learned—and you will, too—not to be intimidated by the technical side of production.

Though parts of the process have little to do with your skills as a writer, you've still got the best credentials to oversee it. You've come equipped with the ability to recognize a theme, present it in a manner most likely to reach the readers, and, with any luck, concentrate on it with enough stubbornness to prevent your goals' being lost from sight.

The production of any printed brochure requires a certain amount of experimentation if you haven't been through the process before. Taken a step at a time, there's absolutely nothing mysterious about it—nothing that requires a degree in graphic design, or public relations.

What you must be is observant. Watch what others are

doing in your part of the world. Note which pieces capture your own interest and which leave you cold. When you encounter a real loser, think about how you'd have made it better. (You already do the same when reading magazine articles; just transfer your professional rivalry to these new targets.)

I had a great store of others' printed work on hand when I began—not by design, but because I'd already squirreled it away as a source of potential story ideas and background data. If you haven't already started your own bottom-drawer file of brochures and other printed matter, I'd advise you to start today.

Call it a "swipe file"—but don't be horrified by that hint of larceny. These samples of other work illustrate techniques you can use yourself, in your own way, to improve work you do for clients. Don't waste a second thought on the ethics of so-called copying. There are very few ideas under the sun that haven't appeared in some form before. Every advertising agency I ever visited had its own swipe file of idea-starters stuck away somewhere, collected not only from its own city but from wherever its personnel happened to stray.

Ask yourself three questions when you're considering a piece you really admire: Why was this produced? Who is supposed to read it? Does its style match or contrast with its message?

Any brochure worth the trees that died for it provides answers at a glance through its slant, its choice of material and the graphics and style that flavor it. Slant, selectivity, and presentation. They're what make good printed projects work and poor ones mystify their readers.

The most successful projects, without exception, are those where the writer has a well-organized idea of what his work is to say and who's going to read it. No matter how dazzling the graphics and impressive the printing, fuzzy focus or lack of direction will undercut its effectiveness.

A set of department brochures I revised for our community college, for example, had suffered from an undefined target audience. They were handed out to service clubs and community leaders when the president was called on for a program at the college. They were given to prospective employers of graduates by the placement staff to sum up the educational programs students had completed. And they were also apparently supposed to speak to students' questions about enrollment—which had little or nothing in common with what the local Lions Club wanted to know or the concerns of prospective bosses.

We decided, after a surprisingly lengthy debate, that the material was primarily intended for prospective students. They needed to know what they should have as aptitudes and background, what they could expect to learn in each department's curriculum, and what kinds of jobs they'd be qualified for at graduation. Once this had been determined, the remaining steps—gathering hard information from the teachers, working with a graphic artist on designing covers and layout, and supervising printers and production—were just means to an end.

Another of my favorite projects was an institutional brochure for Pride Industries, a workshop preparing mentally retarded adults for outside employment. Pride needed a piece that would be everything to everyone: information to be used in drumming up community support, in reaching parents of prospective trainees, in finding jobs for graduates, and in approaching potential donors the financially pinched facility desperately needed.

We chose to address the community (instead of the smaller, more specific groups). The folder's simple, inviting graphics carried a clear description of how trainees reach the level of employability on the open job market. Large, uncluttered photos of men and women in training backed up the copy's claims. Only one small panel carried a message referring to the need for financial support. A separate flier with more information on fund-raising was inserted only in those copies that went to possible givers. By resisting the temptation to tell too much, we greatly increased the folder's impact and its chances of being read by those who picked it up.

Ever wonder why you see so many architect's sketches of new buildings on brochures that fund-raisers give you? I think it's because the client was seeing his project from his own point of view inside the institution, and not from the waiting-to-be-courted position of the mildly interested outsider who reads it. That new building may be Nirvana to those housed in the old cramped, musty quarters. Outsiders, though, care only that the program is doing well, that the community needs what it provides, and that their support can help it fill that need even better.

Brochure copy and illustrations call for all your writerly judgment and precision. The standard brochure, an 8½-by-11-inch sheet folded to fit into a No. 10 envelope, allows space for only a few hundred words unless you cram them into microscopic type.

There's just room for the essential, appealing facts. Don't bemoan all the good stuff you have to leave out. Any piece you write is only one link in the communication between your client and his public; you'll live to write more on another occasion.

I usually have a rough layout in mind when I approach a graphic artist to help design a project. That's not because I'm an expert at graphics, but because I love color and felt-tip markers and have a childlike passion for messing around on paper. Giving your artist some idea of the direction you want to take is a good idea, to be sure; but if I weren't so fond of my Marvy Markers, I might concede that providing too much can limit his own approach to the project.

Finding your graphic artist is as important and elemental a pursuit as picking the narrator and photographer you work with on audio-visual projects. I suggest you try to find a seasoned artist working as a freelancer. Some might be set up already as you are; others may have retired to raise families or progressed up someone's corporate ladder past the point of doing artwork themselves.

If your community college has an applied art department, as ours does, you will find a coterie of trained professionals on its faculty willing to do freelance work. Creative art departments may also harbor some excellent designers; but be sure your new team member has a background in preparing artwork for printing. Many artists and art instructors do not, since graphic design shares the same kind of suspicious status in the art world that commercial writing does in your own.

Don't be sidetracked, as I was at first, into using art students to do your design. I've learned the hard way that even the best students lack the experience required to produce a really top-notch layout and design. You're better off, too, working with someone already experienced in carrying out freelance assignments. Your hands are full enough with writing copy and supervising production without also teaching a newcomer the ins and outs of conducting a freelance business.

Alternately, you might want to learn the basics of layout and graphic design yourself. That local college art department may have an evening course designed for those whose vocational fields are other than art. Just be sure it's not a basic art course; though those classes can be fun, tips on oil paints and landscapes are ill-adapted to graphic design.

There are several very good books explaining the basics of graphic art production and printing stocked at the local library. After you've become fluent in the jargon of the trade, you'll find you're capable of communicating with printers and coming up with rough layouts that can be transformed into finished art at reasonable cost.

After you have the copy typeset you and your artist can produce the finished master version of your brochure ready to be printed, called a paste-up, yourselves. You may also choose to have this mechanical work done by the printer's own art department, which usually performs it at a most reasonable charge.

Both you and your art partner should have a say, along with the client, about the paper on which it's to be printed, the colors of ink, and the special effects selected to dress it up. You'll want to decide beforehand and then call several printers for price quotations. (You may be surprised how dramatically those quotes can differ for the same job.)

Once the project is in the printer's hands, you sit back and wait for the next development. Such as delivery two weeks later than promised. Such as having the inside printed upside down (or worse!). But in most cases your real surprise will be what a polished, good-looking piece of information you've succeeded in producing.

Of course, not all commercial publications allow you as much latitude as brochures. Annual reports, for instance, closely follow a prescribed format. You can translate business jargon into English or brighten it with striking illustrations. But an annual report is still what you have to end up with; vary it too much, and you've created something else altogether.

Other commercial jobs offer much warmer receptions to creative copy and design. A catalog aimed at consumers can be a pure joy to conceive. With the enormous expansion of direct-mail and retail or wholesale catalog selling across the country, your chances of becoming involved in such a project are better today than ever before.

You find catalog work by following leads to businesses who need printed inventories of their stock—gift shops or department stores, of course, but also wholesale distributors of plumber's pipe, suppliers to do-it-yourself mechanics, and manufacturers (smaller book publishers, perhaps?) looking for a conduit to businesses. Those who've issued catalogs in the past are the best initial prospects. Printers may also have leads on businesses considering new publications, since the first step is looking for bids on printing cost.

Catalog work is the best exercise you can give your store of adjectives. Writing descriptions is a circumscribed process, limited by length, similarity of products, and legal rules on false advertising. If you say it's warm and cuddly, it had better be just that; if it's plumber's pipe you're pitching, your claims and measurements had better be exactly on the mark.

Catalog work pays either by the hour or by the printed page. If you find you have a facility for striking, succinct descriptions of hubcaps or fine china, you'll find the per-page payment more rewarding, as hourly rates are rarely on par with the figure you use for a bench mark.

Producing any kind of commercial publication freshens your thinking, and fresh thinking is a necessity for the freelance writer. Too, my commercial endeavors have filled me in on a dozen subjects that I'd been curious about or never dreamed of; all this is fodder for more traditional kinds of writing.

The danger is that commercial work may be too seductive—that it'll capture more and more of your time, cutting down on the writerly work you began freelancing to accomplish. But finding yourself struggling to apportion your time between too many fascinating projects is good trouble. You'll never be bored again.

12

PR Prospects

As a commercial writer on the loose, sooner or later you'll be approached to take on a media campaign. It's a tribute to the news media's impact that every special-interest group in town—government, business, charity, religion—is eager to harness them to carry their message to the reading or listening public.

There's no special trick to producing the mundane, monotonous news release—a page or two of double-spaced copy liberally larded with mentions of your client's product or project. It works . . . not well, but well enough to satisfy most media groupies and allow you to collect your fee.

But working with the news media can be much more rewarding, both for you as a writer and for your client. No matter who the media are in your part of the world—a rip-and-read radio station and a county seat news weekly, or several competing TV stations, a daily newspaper and a host of eager radio AMs and FMs—you can serve them as well as your client with a good, professional media program.

You can use your skills and savvy to bring people out for a nursing home's ice cream social and to air a politician's rebuttal. You can help the public learn more about screening clinics for diabetes or free immunizations against the flu; you can aid a business in presenting its story to the public or help consumers use their products more wisely.

Performing these public-spirited functions can be an excellent source of income for the freelancer with one eye on his income goal. These jobs are readily obtainable, they work into your weekly writing schedule without major adjustments, and they pay well for the generally enjoyable duties they entail.

Freelance writers can be the very best choice for handling media campaigns . . . and the right prefreelancing background is a great help. Years spent in journalism (newspaper, television, radio, or wire service) or corporate or governmental public relations are optimum. That experience gives you automatic familiarity with the means by which news is made.

If you lack that familiarity, you need a crash course from those who have it. The *Public Relations Handbook*, a weighty anthology, can provide some insight; another good book is *Professional Guide to Publicity* by Richard Weiner. The Public Relations Society of America has an excellent series of booklets on every aspect of publicity campaigns.

Talk to successful staff publicity people. Meet with news directors and a city editor or two to learn exactly what they'd like to see. The purpose of your reading and questioning should be to demythologize the news media. If you share too much of the public's awe of headlines, you won't be able to effectively feed your client's information into them.

Learning how to work with the news media is a fascinating educational pursuit and, if you've got reporting experience under your belt, you already know how many other news releases yours will have to compete with for a limited amount of space. Standing between you and that public are the reporters and editors who decide what, finally, is news in your community on any given day. To get your message to the public you'll have to convince these astute observers that it's interesting and worthy of being used to fill their precious space or time as a legitimate story.

You also, incidentally, empathize with the skepticism with which news releases are greeted by news editors. Since releases are sponsored and produced by a client,

Once you've established yourself as someone who can deal with the media, you have three ways to charge clients for your services. One is by straight time billing for all your assistance, based on your established hourly fee. Another is to agree on a flat rate for the job, based again on your fee and the hours involved, but computed as one sum. (This is especially helpful when dealing with clients who, unaccustomed to dealing with freelancers, gape at the mention of an hourly rate as substantial as yours.)

The third method is to receive a retainer and remain available to handle the client's media work as the need arises. Because it guarantees the receipt of a check of a certain size each month, some writers and most public relations agencies prefer it.

I don't. It seems to me the retainer system is an unnecessary security blanket that encourages a lot of wasted time on my own part and money on the client's. While payment is supposed to average out with services performed over a period of months, I've found that the issue of that check creates a desire in the client to get his money's worth—right now, whether media contacts are appropriate or not. At the other extreme, you might go for months with few demands placed on you and then be called to take on an unexpected and time-consuming project. The client, who's been helping support you during quiet times, justifiably expects you to drop whatever else you're working on and come to his aid. With freelance deadlines and workloads as unpredictable as they are, you cannot count on being at his beck and call.

I prefer to take on each job as a discrete unit, wrap it up nicely, and present an equitable bill. I believe this is fairest to my clients. It also allows me to keep my independence. Last-minute callers are forced to be realistic about my other commitments. In the long run, I seem to come out at least as well financially as those who cling to the security of retainers.

they're immediately put to the test of public interest versus the client's private agenda.

Yet news releases and those who write them perform a valuable service at all kinds of papers and stations, from the very smallest to the largest. The smallest may use their offerings to fill space that otherwise would have to be taken up by the product of expensive staff time. The largest—those with sizable reporting staffs—can afford the luxury of checking out or, at least, rewriting your releases.

What do they have in common? In every case, they depend on you and your counterparts to keep them in touch with what's going on in the community. Without news releases of employee promotions, new branches opening, and new lines added, most business editors (a traditionally overworked breed) would have only the thinnest columns in their Saturday business pages. Without nonprofit charitable groups' releases on recognizing or treating diseases and handicaps, many women's or lifestyle editors would find their sections sparse on Sunday.

And without the kind of continuing, pointed communication with the public provided by a steady stream of news releases, the editors of every department would be more isolated than they care to be from coming events, community concerns and, yes, even ambitious politicians' thinking.

So you certainly needn't feel like a mendicant wheedling favors from the news media when you're involved with news releases and press conferences. The function the writer fills is an important and persuasive one; the better you fill it, the more you learn about communication yourself.

News releases come with as many motives as there are clients waiting for your services, or trying to get along without a writer's help. Usually you can count on their belonging to three distinct, but overlapping, groups.

The promotional: These are the workhorses of the news release world. They're probably the kind you think of first—announcing to the public that a car wash, rummage sale, open house, or arts-and-crafts show is coming up on a certain date at a certain place and time. These stories cause the widespread public confusion between news and advertising, since in a sense they really are "free advertising." (Editors wince at those ill-fated words.) But they're also legitimate information for media who pride themselves on informing the public. Investigative reporters are often chagrined at how members of the public value these promotional stories more highly, in many cases, than their thorough, insightful articles, which give a well-rounded picture of an issue . . . but don't do a thing to get folks out for the benefit auction.

The informational: This second type of release embraces the gamut of information offered the public, from straight stories of employees' promotions or attendance at banking school to elaborate human-interest features on advances in the treatment of cystic fibrosis.

These stories can be difficult to recognize when they reach the news columns. They may be helpful pieces on how to use a particular mustard in preparing wonderful picnic foods, or travel stories that mention the pluses of vacationing in RVs . . . a certain model, by the way.

They're the staple of business and women's sections on many smaller newspapers, though routinely laundered of their obvious brand-name connections. But never mind; a certain number will mention that company's mustard, and anything that gets the customer thinking "mustard" will be of ultimate benefit to the firm which commissioned the release.

United Funds across the country use this principle in creating "hard" news—that they've reached a certain percentage of goal, week after week, until the moment they hit the top (and prompt an editor-assigned photograph on the front page of the newspaper's local section). So do ethnic associations, helping build a public sensitivity to the pain caused by the more subtle forms of prejudice.

The argumentative: Public figures' statements to the press generally start out as news releases. When an up-and-coming local politician gets his name in the paper again and again, commenting on his opponents' doings or sayings, you can be sure he has initiated it.

During the legislative season, many apparently spontaneous controversies begin as press releases issued by someone ready to fight. The replies, too, come in by mail. Reporters are sensitive to these challenges and rebuttals that use them as a medium; but since such exchanges are often of public interest (if only because crowds always gather for a good fight), they generally continue to accommodate the ever-more-public figures.

Candidacies begin with news releases and carefully planned news conferences. So do "waves of public support," often originating at a typewriter of the association that endorses the candidate's position.

These pieces, of all the types of news releases, are most apt to be mistaken for "real" news . . . and reporters' acceptance is heightened by the urgency they convey. When the media pick up on these released statements and pursue them on their own, they're demonstrating the thin line between public relations and straightforward news.

All of these releases provide both direct and indirect access to newspapers for you and your client. First, your story may be used as you prepared it. But it can also produce the best kind of repercussions: By creating media interest in your client, it might initiate thorough and ongoing coverage of his programs or industry.

One little news release cast adrift on the sea of information can have only a limited impact, unless its message is momentous, like the adoption of a new homestead act or a decrease in local taxes. In most cases, it will carry only superficial information to the public.

The secret of a good media campaign is repetition and goal setting. By planning not one, but a year's worth of news releases and other contacts with the news media, you can help create a much deeper understanding of the message you're trying to communicate to the public.

That's the reasoning behind the old adage "I don't care what they say about me, as long as they spell my name right." But since most of your clients will be looking for genuine understanding of their goals, rather than voter recognition in the polling booth, you'll be aiming for more than mere reiteration of a name.

You may also want to consider how exposure you get through the mass media can be built upon through other avenues. Look to newsletters, upcoming programs, and face-to-face contacts with the client's own constituency (whether members of a nonprofit group or a store's customers), where this information can be discussed in greater depth and detail.

But before you can build on anything, you have to master the techniques of reaching the right people in the newspaper, television, and radio news worlds.

In war, you're counseled to know your enemy. In the competitive arena of public relations, you'd do well to know your friends. Knowing the reporters and editors who will receive your client's releases can save you a lot of time and unsatisfied curiosity about whether or not a story you've written will suit their needs and, thus, be used.

The three most valuable contacts on your daily newspaper staff are the city editor, the business editor, and the women's editor (or "lifestyle," or "family," or whatever euphemism is used locally).

The city editor is your gateway to local and state news of general interest, the great bulk of the newspaper. This person is both influential and extremely busy. He oversees the staff of general-assignment reporters who may be assigned to your subject area, and makes the decisions about whether to cover specific events and controversies.

Since the city editor always has a tight schedule, you may want to ask him if you should talk to one of his reporters. You can spend much more time with the reporter, as a rule. You should be able to develop an ongoing interest in your subject area by helping him master the basics, providing background information and story leads. But the editor is the one who ultimately decides whether a story makes it or not; so meet him first.

The business editor, on all but a few major newspapers, is a harried individual who relies heavily on businesses themselves for news tips. This may change in the future, as editors recognize the wealth of vital information and juicy story ideas awaiting them in the business community. But in the meantime, the business sections of all too many papers (and business segments on TV) depend on news releases issued by those the stories mention.

After talking with your business editor, you may find this is a fertile field for stories about trends, personalities, and other topics in your client's area. Chances are the editor will be glad to receive something unusual to enliven his section. On many smaller dailies, including our local paper, business news is too often confined to announcing which real estate salesmen have changed firms, which door-to-door salesmen have won sales awards this month, and who's been hired or retired at local banks.

The women's editors of this country are the unsung heroines of hundreds of good causes. Their section seems to have a deeper commitment to public service topics than any other department of the average newspaper (just as the woman who hosts the afternoon talk show on your local TV station is more interested in charitable works than anyone else on the staff).

Women's departments or their renamed counterparts tend to be the best targets for coverage of health-related stories, consumer articles, benefit events, and education topics. Since they usually have a specific number of pages to fill in every edition—and often are understaffed—the editors are generally receptive to longer, detailed stories that can readily be edited to fit a given news hole. They can also be counted on to do the original follow-up stories that mean so much to public awareness of your client's goals.

How do you find out who these people are, much less what they want of you? You read (or watch) their work closely. And then you stop in to introduce yourself and ask their advice.

Personally meeting your news media contacts is the most worthwhile way you can begin any project. It lets you explain why your message is important and of interest to their audience. It lets them see a face to attach to your name, and inspires a little extra interest when they get your articles in the mail. And it allows them to easily ascertain whom to call for further information on any of the stories you send them. It's the beginning of an easy alliance that can help you get your information across more clearly and prevent editorial misunderstandings from creeping in.

When I was arts editor of the newspaper where I got my start, I depended heavily on organizations to send in news of what they were up to. With a good share of two states within my working territory, I could no sooner know all that was going on than could a sports editor get by without all those proud coaches who call in scores after they've won the game.

One woman, who cared deeply about the local symphony orchestra, set an example of the ideal public relations chairman. She made an appointment for coffee or lunch once—only once—per symphony season. At that time she'd give me all the background information she had on the upcoming concerts and guest artists, and we'd talk over features that might be developed around them. We'd talk about symphony concerns—how the fund-raising was going, whether the women's auxiliary was planning an active year, the rapidly increasing cost of sheet music. And after we'd said goodbye, we wouldn't see each other for another year, though we'd talk by phone and she'd send updated information by mail.

What Evelyn did was offer me a tiny initiation into her world and its concerns. Our discussions paid off for me in dozens of ways, from ideas for stories to a much better understanding of the symphony. Best of all, our contacts created trust. When I had a question about the symphony, I knew I could count on Evelyn for an honest, informed answer.

I've tried to create the same kind of trust myself in some cases, and—because I've got my fingers in too many pies from time to time—counsel my clients to pay the personal visits themselves. Those chats contribute more to your success in placing stories than could any amount of advice about how many words, how big a margin to leave, or other mechanical tricks of the trade.

Nevertheless, there are a few rules about form that can make your releases look more professional.

The basics include double-spacing on white nonerasable paper with a deep top margin and generous room left on the other three sides of each sheet. In an upper corner, offer a name and telephone number to be called for further information. If the moment of release is crucial, note the right day and time. But be forewarned that news desks tend to be too busy to worry about filing and saving releases; involved instructions on timing any but the most earthshaking announcements cause great editorial pain. To be safe, don't mail your release too early (if timing is a problem), and just note "for immediate release" at the top.

The guideline on length is the shorter, the better. But don't adhere to this logic so closely that meaning is lost to brevity. It's more important to convey your point than to be short at all costs. If you run longer than one page, make sure the critical information (the who, what, where, when, and how) is in your first one or two paragraphs—insurance against chop-chop editing.

As long as you're going to the trouble of writing a news release, try to make it do the best possible job for you. If an event is going to be held by the Boy Scouts to benefit some charity, tell what that charity is and why the Boy Scouts are behind it. Ice cream socials in the abstract are less than compelling; an ice cream social to buy lifesaving equipment for a rest home might garner a good many more readers' attention and support.

On the other hand, if your release is a less timely, more substantial one—aimed at explaining how to recognize a disease, use a product, or choose a vacation destination, for example—you can allow yourself a bit more luxury in length. Two or three double-spaced pages is usable for most publications. Go longer than a thousand words, however, and they'll run into space problems. The ideal length is probably around 500 to 600 words.

Sometimes this just isn't enough to do justice to the scope of information you feel the public needs. Consider dividing the topic into several subtopics, trimming each installment to a versatile, compact size. You'll want to advise editors that the stories in the series are closely related, and may be most effective if used in consecutive editions. Sometimes they'll accommodate you and sometimes they won't, depending on their own pressures. But if your information really is of public interest, you'll usually be pleased with how they choose to use it.

What about photographs? They can sometimes be a convenience to the publication you've approached. But most naive publicity photos are a total waste of time and money. It's up to you to know your medium's policies and needs.

What kind of action? Study the photos taken by the newspaper's own staff. Guest speakers who visit local institutions, committees arguing over proposals, well-dressed visitors getting down on the floor to play with kiddies in a nursery ward—all sound less than compelling, but stand a far greater chance of being run than the traditional shot of two people shaking hands and staring at the camera.

Your subjects will be stiff in front of the camera during

your first shots. Remedy that, and get natural-looking photos, by taking a whole roll of film or even more. After the first few foreboding clicks, they'll become used to the camera and stop making self-conscious jokes about breaking it.

Before you spend a great deal of money on shooting, however, take the precaution of calling the city editor and asking if he might be interested in seeing some photos. Given the track record of publicity shots, the best you can expect him to offer is weak encouragement. If he says anything but "Absolutely not!" you're in business.

If you have reason to believe a newspaper will use your publicity photos, deliver them as quickly after the event as is humanly possible. Photos from a convention that ended three days ago, though weekly papers or trade magazines may still want them, are as welcome as dead fish on a daily's doorstep.

Straightforward head shots of a person who's a principal in your article are appreciated and frequently used, especially if the individual is a prominent member of your community or a visiting personality.

With consumer- and product-related stories, photos are definitely useful to the editors. But check with them before you take any shots or hire a photographer. Many newspapers have firm policies about publicity stills. As a rule, smaller papers tend to be more receptive; the more care the paper invests in its staff photography, the less likely it is to accept yours.

Certain photo ideas which sound brilliant to your client elicit nothing but laughs from the news media. Be wary of the prototypical check-passing picture. You know the kind—the head of a charity accepting a check from the head of a donor group, both flashing gleaming smiles at the camera. There is scarcely a newspaper left in the world that will use those pictures. Speakers shaking hands with the president of the ladies' group who sponsored them are equally deadly.

Appetizing, original photos, on the other hand, are almost always welcomed by editors. Though not every one will be used, because of space considerations and all the little decisions that go into making up newspaper pages lickety-split, the occasions on which they do appear make them worth the effort. Stories with good illustrations invariably get better play—and are noticed more often by the average reader—than those that compete without them.

A photo that may get favorable consideration is simple, and looks as if the subjects didn't know the photographer was present. It involves people acting and reacting with each other, and should be self-explanatory enough that a long typed caption (called a cutline) isn't needed to make sense of it.

Making the television or radio news is a bit different than getting into a newspaper. Often the same news release is sent to all local media. While it may get used all around—especially if it's very timely or newsworthy—its chances are often better in the electronic media if retailored to suit the needs of those who'll read it aloud.

News stories for TV and radio should be shorter than those meant for newspapers. And they should avoid locutions that, though perfectly reasonable when used in print, sound awkward aloud. Run people's titles before their names—"noted author Norman Mailer"—rather than as clauses set off by commas—"Norman Mailer, noted author." Include phonetic pronunciation of difficult names. If you want to make your package look especially professional, consider typing it in the Orator typeface, which uses all capitals for easy readability.

Know a little about your local radio and TV stations before you send them your releases. Most of all, learn whether they have their own news departments or if their news broadcasts are of the rip-and-read variety. If the latter is the case, they're unlikely to use anything you send them. Save a stamp and forego the temptation.

If you're sending photos to the newspaper, you might also want to consider providing them to TV stations for use with your release. Save your black-and-white prints, however. Though they're the standard for newspaper reproduction, there's not one thing a color TV program can do with them. Provide color 35mm transparencies (slides)—not color prints.

And, be careful whom you send your photos to. Your local radio news director will be happy to joke confidingly about the number of lovely, expensive photographs he receives with news releases every week. No matter how terrific they are, photos just don't work on radio.

Two other aspects of dealing with radio and television may enter into your media planning. They are the news conference and the public service announcement.

In some parts of the country, scheduling a news conference is the standard way of getting TV and radio coverage and, to a smaller extent, attracting newspapers. This naturally applies only to the most important stories you wish to get before the public and those that are very timely—visiting authorities, fund drive kickoffs, discussions of an important local issue.

Elsewhere, the news conference is used only for items of cataclysmic proportions. Talk to some of your TV friends to find out the traditions in your area.

If you learn that news conferences are commonplace, you'll be able to use them as a shortcut to good coverage. Best of all, they reach the electronic media, who are much harder to attract than newspaper reporters in other circumstances.

Choose your time and place carefully. Because of TV deadlines (and those of afternoon newspapers), morning is often best. Remember that many smaller TV news staffs don't come to work until 9 a.m. or later, as is also the case with smaller morning papers whose push comes in late afternoon. Ten in the morning is generally an ideal time. Days earlier in the week are also more effective choices. Mondays are usually slow days in the news business, while Fridays tend to be very busy. Only skeleton crews work weekends.

Select a location that's easy to find and offers these important features: a simple, plain background for your speaker, and lots of electrical outlets for video and radio equipment.

Prepare a written statement and, if necessary, written background information to give to reporters as they come in. Though your speaker may repeat this material verbally, a written reference can be a real help.

Allow about five minutes for an initial statement and then open your conference to questions. If it's slow going, you might want a staff person on hand to ask a few starters.

Above all, convey your central message as clearly as you possibly can. Try to keep press conferences uncomplicated.

The setting lends itself to striking single statements rather than involved technical data.

The other special electronic-media technique you can use is the public service announcement. If you're promoting an event open to the public, the free publicity of a PSA can equal or surpass a small paid ad campaign.

Unlike newspapers, radio and TV stations are licensed by the federal government; and with this licensing comes the obligation to serve the public's interest. For smaller stations that can't afford a great deal of original public service programming, this often takes the form of frequent PSAs, which are in essence unpaid mini-ads.

A good public service announcement should be short—no more than fifteen or twenty seconds when read aloud. It should be as clear and direct as you can make it, because it's rarely supported by any kind of visuals (especially on radio!). Double-space it on plain white paper, using Orator type if you have it handy.

When a radio or television station has used your public service announcements, it's simple courtesy for a member of your organization to write them a letter of thanks. It not only shows your appreciation; it also gives them concrete proof that they're meeting the community's needs when relicensing time rolls around.

Saying thanks, in fact, is a good policy to follow in all your dealings with news staffs.

Too often people engaged in pursuing what they consider good causes forget that the news media have no real obligation to cover their stories. The media's obligation is to the public who reads or watches their news, not to those who want to reach that public through their good graces.

Of course they should be serving the community, and of course you've done them a favor in bringing a worthwhile subject to their attention.

But remember to say thank you.

The news media get all kinds of responses when people disapprove of what they've done, but rarely earn more than a resounding silence when they've done a good job that benefits their audience as well as special-interest groups.

Say thank you. Call it or write it. You'll find it does more for a continued pleasant working relationship than all the free lunches your client's budget can hold.

13

Great Grant Writing

Another kind of commercial writing stands distinct from all the others. It's writing grant applications and reports. Though the general public never notices them, they're a fact of life (indeed, lifeblood itself) for many agencies of government, nonprofit charitable and educational institutions, and even individuals looking to better themselves under someone else's philanthropic support.

Grants have an intimidating reputation.

Do they make you think of Rockefeller's foundation, and Ford's? Of endless piles of bureaucratic forms and certifications? Do you imagine foundations paying writers to spend months ensconced in comfortable isolation "for art's sake"? Do you fancy piles of money there for the asking? Or, conversely, such fierce national-level competition that they might well be labeled "elite only"?

Make friends with the grant-writing process, as well as those wonderful people who hand out the money. It might be one of the best things you do for the sake of your geographically underprivileged writing career. No matter where you live, there are foundations and other potential grant-makers whose purposes and contacts with groups they fund hold promise for your salable skills.

A handful of grants is distributed each year to fund

artistic works in progress. Among these, grants to writers are few and far between. If your work borders on Bellow or is well received in national poetry circles, you might investigate further, most notably into the National Endowment for the Arts.

On the other hand, if your aspirations (*like mine*) are more on the order of craft than Art, your chances of getting a grant yourself are not at all strong. But your chances of working on grant applications (as a writer who can prepare a readable, persuasive proposal for the funding agency's consideration) are very good indeed.

I have seen dozens of grant proposals that were drafted in Bismarck then sent winging their ways all over the country. Most of them had two things in common: They were shots in the dark whose prospects were as poor as the results they achieved. And they were the dullest piles of pages ever. Deadly dull. If I were the foundation director who had to plow through those wordy, stilted, self-consciously erudite packets of pontification, even I—who greet the postman's arrival as I do Santa Claus's—would get an unlisted mailbox.

Do you see a mission here? A writer who can bring to grant proposals good will and clarity of communication is like a breath of mountain air. If you choose to hire out your skills in the grants field, you'll find you can accumulate any number of grateful customers—grateful, because they hate writing dull, ineffective proposals as much as you'd hate reading them, and "customers" because the financial stakes are high enough that they can well afford to pay a writer to increase the odds of success.

Who prepares grant proposals? They might be nonprofit charitable groups or professional associations looking for outside financial support. Or government agencies designing pilot projects in cooperation with local groups. Or community-based committees organized to find a way to fill some special local need.

The grant-seekers could be requesting support for a shelter for battered women . . . planning a series of informational meetings on public policy . . . trying to convince someone to buy the local YMCA a few dozen volleyballs to keep troubled youngsters off the streets . . . or asking for equipment to better treat hospital patients. Imagine the most exotic scheme to solve a social ill, and the most mundane, fundamental local need possible: Chances are that grant-seeking groups in your own area have equalled the wildest and most basic and every conceivable degree in between.

Over twenty-six thousand incorporated foundations exist around the nation, funded by families or corporations or a mixed bag of special interests. Though the majority are headquartered in New York and along the eastern seaboard (with offices, no doubt, right next to the editors to whom you've been writing), almost every state has anywhere from a few dozen to a few hundred located within its borders. North Dakota, of course, is the exception. At last count there were approximately five. . . but every one of them was active in supporting projects that fit its definitions of good causes.

As a writer, you may be contacted to help a grant-seeking organization put its case in order. Your role is to clarify the reasons they believe their project is necessary; sort out specifics of how they plan to go about filling this need; develop a plan to evaluate whether the potential project has done its job for the sake of the grantor, and then—after all this groundwork—write a succinct, persuasive grant proposal for your client to present to the foundation it believes will be interested.

Grant writing has a lot in common with the garden-variety editorial query. You'll feel right at home. You'll do initial research to determine where the most salable story lies, then dig a little more to learn how to go about getting it. Finally you wrap it up into a sales letter that falls onto a desk crowded with other queries, before an editor or foundation administrator whose needs and prejudices often can (but sometimes cannot) be foretold by studying past history and stated market requirements.

The best grant proposals are no more than ten pages long, typed double-spaced in what you already know as manuscript form. Granting groups usually require this information:

■ An introduction of about one page which sums up the proposal in an attractive way and gives an accurate boiled-down version of all the material that will follow. Often this is the only part of the proposal automatically read; it has to be good, or the idea truly revolutionary, for the screening committee to want to read further.

■ A summary of who your organization represents and what its purposes are. The group's track record is important; any past successes in comparable projects should be highlighted.

■ A rationale for why the project is needed. If it proposes a shelter for battered wives, is this a widespread problem? Do you have figures? Are there figures now available on battered spouses seeking help? Why was your project's approach selected as the right way to go?

■ A précis of how the project will work. The granting agency doesn't need or want a thoroughly detailed rundown of every move you've planned; all that's really wanted is an overview of how you'll go about using their money and how you'll take the story to the public.

■ A plan to evaluate how the project is working. If you're looking for sponsorship for public meetings, will you pass out evaluation sheets? (Though limited in usefulness, these are the classic cliché of evaluation and rank approximately better than nothing.) Will you follow up existing data? What's really wanted is some indication that the organization applying for the grant plans to assess whether their approach has been effective, rather than taking the money and running.

■ The budget. While you won't be responsible for developing it, urge your group to include not only what they want the foundation's money for, but also what they plan to get from other sources. Government agencies gave birth to the terminology of "hard matching" and "soft matching;" the former means money or tangibles purchased, while the latter includes the blue sky of grant administration—volunteers' time, the use of a corner of somebody's office, a telephone, some Xeroxed copies of the grant proposal. Harder is always better when it comes to matching grant money.

You can put this material together in two ways. The traditional method is to break out separate categories under roman numerals in familiar outline form. The more readable style is to put it all together in narrative. If you choose the outline format, try to keep your total package under a dozen pages. More length is not an improvement from the viewpoint of the granting agency, the reader that counts most in these cases.

If you lean toward the narrative—the typical writer's slant, I suspect—try to get your message across in the same space as a long magazine query. Two pages of single-spaced, readable data will gladden the hearts of some unseen screening committee. Five pages is the outer limit.

The tone you want is the same friendly, straightforward confidence-inspiring one you use in writing unknown editors. Don't be a supersalesman; but don't go too far in the opposite direction and employ the verbal weapons of academia to sound serious and unassailable. You'll end up sounding serious, all right; total boredom is not to be taken lightly.

Your organization may know its most likely funding sources. But if its ideas are still ambiguous, you can add to your proposal's chances by reminding them of a truism in the grant-writing field: The closer to home, the better.

Not only foundations should be considered for the funding proposals you'll help develop. Well-heeled area corporations and state organizations are equally likely to be interested in helping you out, as are some government agencies.

The best question to ask in identifying a funding source is not "Who has the most money?" but "Who can get the most out of this project?"—in public approval as well as actual progress toward goals it supports. Those nearby clearly have more to gain from positive local impact.

I've written grant proposals aimed at national medical foundations, as well as community foundations, university departments that give cooperative education grants, and state organizations, including the Bankers Association and the Farmers Union. I can assure you that local sources, no matter what their structure, are much easier to sell on a grant project. They believe in the betterment of the local (or state) community and benefit from being identified with public-interest issues.

Their self-interest is similar to that of the editors who screen your queries. While you've set out to fascinate the editor, he has to keep his own constituency in mind, whether it's potential readers and advertisers or the public with whom an organization's future good will lies.

Your own self-interest lies, of course, in the commercial side of grant writing. While you might get satisfaction from helping good causes, you need to safeguard your own source of support—and that has a lot of bearing on how you set up your payment.

Some grant writers build their own fee into the budget requested in the grant, so that the applying organization can better afford them. This appeals to your client. It means you have minimal impact on their regular budget, which is already tight or they wouldn't be looking elsewhere for money. The grant writer sometimes feels this gambling approach gives him or her the justification for a larger fee.

The danger is obvious. If your grant proposal is rejected, you may not get a cent for your labor. And the proposal can go down the drain for reasons that have absolutely nothing to do with your role, from an ill-conceived project to simple lack of money to pass around among too many deserving applicants.

Unless you can afford to gamble, require your own payment be a transaction apart from the grant itself. The organization should have enough faith in its own proposal to invest in your services. The cost of professional writing help is insignificant next to what they hope to gain.

There are ways, however, that your services can be built into a grant to help its sponsor make sure the project succeeds.

Most grant projects have a publicity budget, both to reach the public whose needs the grant is intended to serve and to make sure the sponsor gets the credit he expects. Good publicity depends on written communication, from press information plans to published materials for the people the project hopes to reach.

Some grants also rely on outside administration, assuming that the sponsoring group's staff can't take on the extra work. A freelance writer is in an unusually good position to help them make contacts, plan meetings, and take care of details. Unlike most people in the work force, you're free to take on short-term obligations that have a definite termination date.

Finally, you can be on hand to write the second most important document of the whole grant-seeking, grant-administration cycle—the final report.

The foundation or company that gives the money does attach a few strings to it. Of primary importance is that the grantor be informed of what happened to their cash. A financial statement is mandatory, of course. But that final report can be much more (and much more stimulating to write)—a candid, informative tale of the project in action. Such a report is a courtesy to the granting agency, like a long thank-you letter; in addition, it's superb future grant insurance for your client. Chances are they'll want support again some day for another project. A strong, honest final report leaves an impression of confidence, competence, and good will. It's commensurate with the good investment your project really did prove to be. (Calling a dud a dud, by the way—in better-chosen terms—doesn't hurt your standing as much as you might think. Everyone knows some grant projects don't work out in history-making splendor. Admitting it, but explaining the reasons behind the weak points, inspires future trust in all but producers of real fiascos.)

Each kind of commercial writing has its own rewards. Working with brochures and their printed brethren sharpens your precision with words and sensitizes you to graphics and printing quality. Reaching the public through the news media prompts you to appreciate how news is made, how messages are made memorable, and how the public actually fishes its information out of the flood of words around us every day. Grant writing puts worthy petitioners together with worthy donors—a service that enables you to do good works and incidentally generate more assignments for your well-honed writer's craft.

The variety of commercial assignments available to you is ultimately limited only by your own ambition and spirit of adventure.

You can take on enough of these handy, handsome jobs to underwrite your basic expenses while you invest the rest of your hours in projects like books or magazine sales that have a deferred payoff. You can have fun and reap the rewards of commercial work and still find—and face—new challenges.

Writers Out Loud: Working
With Students and Strangers

Writers are nearly as famous for talking about their work as they are for doing it. Procrastination, you may call it. But it also goes by more reputable names: public speaking, consulting, teaching, and convention planning.

These varieties of "writing out loud" are all a good way to pry your fingers loose from your typewriter and rub shoulders with other creatures in the world outside your office.

Freelancers in more remote parts of the world (like North Dakota) actually get two-way benefits from taking their case directly to other human beings. It's like a silver lining within a silver cloud. You get offers to speak when people learn of your interesting, oddball vocation. These earn you notoriety and bank notes. And when people hear you talk about your line of work they have a way of coming up with matters of prime interest to your ears—story ideas in pursuit of an author, consulting and writing assignments. Your credibility is heightened when you call on those in your audience later as a writer in search of local leads.

You never know when you'll discover your fear of public speaking has evaporated and you've turned into a ham. I was an unlikely candidate for hamhood. My first public speaking engagements, high school speech contests in which my English teacher forcibly enrolled me to improve my world-class timidity, were less than auspicious. I was once disqualified, not for my content, but for my "incapacitating German accent." (You must understand I am a third-generation Norwegian complete with "uff da.")

I was sent forth to address high school journalism classes all too often during my newspaper years, either because of my presumed rapport with bored teenagers or because I was such a junior staffer that I never dreamed of turning the boss down cold. I won't say I wasn't spellbinding; but I did grow accustomed to inspiring only two questions in my audiences: "Why wasn't our volleyball score in the paper last weekend?" and "Have you really met Ann Landers?"

So you can imagine how surprised I was when, as a freelancer, I discovered a wondrous penchant for carrying on in front of audiences. A small but significant part of my income has stemmed from talks to various groups. Not only have I visited cities throughout the five-state area of the Great Plains; I've been paid in cash as well as with the opportunity to speak before captive audiences.

The lecture circuit is a fine old author's tradition. From Mark Twain to Mark Lane, from Brownmiller to Bombeck, ladies and gentlemen of letters have capitalized on their books' success in an atmosphere that's a pleasant break from royalty statements, rejection slips, and bouts with an unfeeling typewriter.

You needn't be a best-selling author to delve into public speaking. What you do need is a tendency to warm up in front of an audience and some topic to warm to—whether it's the one you write about as an expert, or some other field in which you have a degree of authority.

I would have sworn I wasn't expert enough on any popular topic to become a speaker. I'd overlooked the one big subject you and I have in common, and which interests audiences for reasons both obvious and unaccountable:

■ I talk about communicating through the written word.

■ How to become a professional writer.

■ How to work with magazines, newspapers, and the electronic media, whether as a writer or an individual seeking for their attention.

■ How to survive as a freelancer in a place where they said it couldn't be done.

You may not want to speak on freelance writing until you've tried and succeeded at meeting its demands. A year of practical experience and the achievements it'll encompass adds authority to your comments that the early months leave lacking. If your background lies in journalism or public relations or advertising, however, you may find—as I did—that you can ply the speaker's trade much sooner based on the expertise that salaried employment has given you.

What audiences might want to hear you? Students with a vocational interest in writing. Groups that harbor would-be writers—retired teachers' associations, penwomen's clubs, historical societies. Businesspeople who can benefit from better communication skills. Political action groups, as well as those formed around a public issue, gravitate toward how-to sessions on the media.

It's sometimes hard for me to figure out how the average man in the street becomes so curious about our craft. But nonwriting friends remind me that what we do for a living is something of an arcane art to those unfamiliar with what we take for granted. You may find, as I have, that you have a ready market for your talks on convention programs, service clubs' agendas, professional improvement work-shops of all kinds, and your nearby college's educational outreach program.

I stumbled into these potential markets when a state health department staffer asked me to fill one slot on a regional workshop—"How to work with the news media." I arrived half an hour early to size up my audience and was treated to an eye-opening program on sperms and tubes and hormones: I'd been booked as the only nontechnical speaker on an agenda for family-planning workers.

It was an inspiring experience, one I reproduced in four other states in as many subsequent months as a member of the workshop's traveling team. In every city I was intrigued to learn that my topic, the news media, was as unapproachable to my listeners as their field was to the public. I learned that the simple act of calling an editor to suggest a story on their interesting, controversial programs was completely foreign to most in my audiences, who nevertheless could not imagine why they weren't getting the coverage their work with teenagers certainly deserved.

Get to know a reporter or editor! (I had 'em taking notes.) Take in a couple of news releases every year without fail. (They looked dubious.) Hire a professional writer to handle your news-making needs. (Light bulbs flashed above their heads.) Don't stand in awe of the news media—they need you as much as you need them. (Applause! I modestly retired to enjoy my stardom.)

Since then I've talked to community action groups, senior citizens, outreach workers, publicity chairmen for several different alliances, state committees needing publicity and encouragement, and candidates for office who above all needed to know how to get their positions before the public.

Public speaking carries many benefits—new contacts, a chance to clarify your own thinking on important topics, the refreshment of a novel experience. And it also pays. While you can't count on earning a major portion of your annual income from public speaking, you can expect it to pay for the time you invest in it. That includes not only the minutes that fly when you're in front of the audience with your mouth open, but the time spent preparing the speech, traveling to give it, and following up by answering questions and fielding comments from your listeners.

My fees have ranged from twenty-five dollars for an engagement that took half an hour away from my writing schedule to a hundred or more for a local half-day workshop, and considerably more when extra preparation or travel time have been involved.

But I've done the same talks before countless other audiences for little or nothing, and some of those groups undoubtedly had budgets at least as healthy as those of sponsors who paid me well. Which has led me to formulate Hanson's Law of Reimbursement: Unless you ask for an honorarium, you probably won't get one. Unless you try to increase it, you'll be paid the minimum. If you do ask, they'll come up with it if they want to hear you badly enough; if they don't, cross one program chairman off your list. You can always use the time writing, after all.

How do you get started? If your background doesn't now include some speaking experience, you probably start for free. First public speaking encounters can quickly determine whether you enjoy contact with an audience or lose several days' good work time dreading it. (If the latter turns out to be true, drop the idea after a few experimental attempts. The rewards for local public speaking are not so enormous that they should threaten your writing schedule and peace of mind.)

Everyone who's stood on the business side of the podium has his or her own method for organizing a talk and conquering stage fright (which never goes away entirely, but has a way of returning at the oddest times).

Since I've spoken on the same topics several times, I have notes on file from which I work for each new engagement. I retype them, inserting a few comments directed specifically toward the current audience and sometimes rearranging them to include fresh thoughts added by a previous audience's questions. I also try to find a couple of current examples (when my subject is the news media) to give more immediacy to my basically timeless themes.

My notes (typed on five-by-seven-inch file cards, three or four for an hour's talk) would mean nothing to anyone but me. You'd see single words, names underlined with wavy lines, exclamation points, question marks, handwritten additions between the lines. I go through these hieroglyphics several times before getting up to put them to use—not to plan every word I'll say, but to have a firm idea of how each topic leads into the next. Otherwise it's easy for me to get lost on a tangent with no graceful way to find my way back to my conclusion.

A sense of direction helps, too, when you interrupt your planned talk to field questions from the audience. They're an invitation to losing your place. The outline helps me keep to the point at hand; offbeat questions get postponed until a more appropriate spot in the talk.

I always ask for questions and answers . . . and seldom get them when I want them. That could be a peculiarity of Great Plains audiences, who are super-polite; it could also be because nothing blanks out your mind like the necessity of asking something intelligent without warning. At any rate, questions are a valuable way to make real contact with the audience, and deserve special attention. When I can, I plant a starter query or comment with someone in the audience—one of the sponsors, perhaps, or someone who's come up to talk with me beforehand. One question can prime the pump and produce a virtual torrent. If not, thank the audience and sit down.

One of the great advantages of living in rural areas is that word of your availability as a speaker gets around very quickly. If you've educated or charmed one audience, that message will spread to others looking for a new face for their programs.

Alternately, you can advertise your service with a letter or simple brochure. Get quotes from those to whom you've already spoken, with their names; their comments count for more than all your own claims.

Check your local chamber of commerce to see if a speaker's bureau has been set up. It provides a list of men and women willing to talk about a wide variety of professional and personal topics, some for a fee; it's circulated to service and professional groups and provided to convention planners. If no formal speaker's bureau exists in your community, talk with the chamber staffer who works with convention groups. His personal suggestions influence many others looking for help in putting their programs together.

I never expect to make the professional lecture circuit. Maybe you will, when your best seller gives you a national audience for your expertise. The rewards there can be excellent.

But the regional speaking engagements I've booked have more than satisfied me. For an hour out of my day, I can often earn the equivalent of a good sale to a minor magazine or half a local brochure, whichever's greater. When you add in the publicity I've received for my writing business and the fun I've had in meeting these new groups, speeches are one of the finest little extras I've encountered as a writer.

Consulting

Being asked for your advice is a heady experience. That in a nutshell is what consulting work consists of—giving advice, and being paid for it.

For a writer, consulting usually means ghostwriting. It can also, however, be the purchase of a few hours of your time by a client who can't afford (or won't pay for) your primary services: critiquing a public information program, for example, and giving reasons why it has failed to get the expected reaction from the news media; or finding ways to retailor government information programs so that listeners can actually understand them.

I've included consulting in this chapter because most of my pure consulting jobs have grown out of speeches I've made before professional groups. Grown out of them? Sometimes they've almost duplicated what I told the group for a far more modest fee. Nevertheless, I've apparently touched a chord here and there, and I'm more than happy to offer the analysis (and often, reassurance) they desire.

Not all freelancers, however, will find the way to consulting opens for them so easily. My background in the news media and government has provided me with something of specific usefulness to share with clients, as well as a way to measure the effectiveness of what they've done in the past. If your own work experience is short on these tangible skills, consulting may not be the best possibility for you to pursue until you've built up background expertise. An attempt to bluff your way through is all too apparent to the client who's agreed to pay for your assistance, and may sour him on other projects you might propose in the future.

Putting your experience to work as an information consultant requires three distinct steps: talking to your client to find out his real message and the audience he hopes to reach; studying what he's doing now, as well as his past efforts, and matching them with evidence of success or failure; and developing a report to the client on your findings and suggestions for future directions. While the report is usually given in person, a written version helps satisfy him and reinforces your conclusions.

The difference between consulting and actually accomplishing commercial writing tasks is the contrast between teaching and doing. In most cases your role as a consultant is to offer an ideal course of action, tempered by the limitations of which you're aware.

Your role, as a locally based freelancer, can lead in either of two directions: Applying a program that's worked elsewhere to the area which you know firsthand, or translating a client's knowledge of the local market into effective ways to communicate with his special segment of the public.

For this reason, you have two target groups of clients. One is the organization or company from outside your area that's well staffed on its own, but unfamiliar with your own community. These are the people to whom your knowledge of local interests, prejudices, and history is most valuable.

The other is quite different. It includes smaller local groups or businesses with "homemade" publications and relations with the news media. While they may not want an outsider to take over these functions (for prideful or fiduciary reasons), they welcome the professional expertise you can bring to their planning.

Personal contacts are the easiest way to turn up consulting jobs, but the first move is usually up to your client. The same people whom you approach as potential commercial clients may instead turn out to be sources of your first consulting contracts. Your reputation and credentials as a proven freelance writer are your best references . . . presented to top advantage when you're invited to expound on them from the speaker's podium.

Normally you will charge more than your basic hourly rate for consulting services, since you're offering highly distilled information rather than personally putting it to work. Try to find other consultants locally (perhaps in management) to get an idea of the going rate. Talk about fees with the client before you begin; you may find he has a figure in mind that is higher than you expected, for consultants command substantial sums in every field. I accept these jobs for nothing less than a hundred dollars, increasing the figure based on the amount of time spent in researching and preparing a report.

Teaching

The third kind of face-to-face opportunity is teaching. Perhaps education is the world you're trying to leave behind by turning to freelancing. Or maybe you've never considered yourself equipped to help others learn an intangible art like writing. In either case, the economics of freelancing can be reason to reconsider and look into what opportunities might be awaiting you.

Teaching noncredit or evening classes makes use of your experience in the most generous way—sharing it with others to help them avoid some of your own costly mistakes and to help them polish latent talent into salable writing. It's also a change from days alone at the typewriter, and it helps pay the rent.

In the back of your mind, do you admit to a low-grade resistance to teaching others to become your local writing competition? I know I do; writers are insecure creatures, especially when we're not used to others typing away on our turf.

Yet I wouldn't let such doubts keep you away from such an interesting adventure. You suffer from overconfidence if you believe one night class under your leadership will equip enrollees with ammunition to take your own hard-won assignments. And more writers (even some conscientiously trained by yours truly) don't really seem to hurt the market for freelancers. Oddly enough, I've watched new writers make it better for all of us here in Bismarck, familiarizing more contacts with freelancers and (in the case of inept ones) making the professionals look all the better in comparison. Writing compatriots stimulate your own thinking, keep you on your toes . . . and give you someone to commiserate with when all's not well on the writing front.

The give-and-take between you and your students can help you see your vocation from a fresh, excited viewpoint. Enthusiasm that's slowly seeped out of your daily grind suddenly returns with a rush. You appreciate your life as a freelancer when you share it with eager disciples.

Convention Planning

Making your living as a freelancer is a matter of flexibility. If you're really good at staying flexible, if you like people (but perhaps need a push now and then to get reinvolved with the world outside your office), and if you're in the market for a boost to your income that interferes very little with your writing routine, how about considering occasional bouts of convention planning and promotion?

Unlike other options I've explored as a freelancer in the boonies, convention planning is only partly dependent on time at the typewriter. Research, diplomacy, and a flair for communicating with the public are the main requirements— writing is only a fraction of the assignment.

Why, then, include it in a book for freelance writers?

I've found that putting together a public hearing or workshop from time to time is an ideal way to reinvolve myself with the human race. I can see the signs that I need to work with people again: I begin to enjoy hearing the telephone ring in the middle of a chapter, or I encourage the UPS deliveryman to share complaints about his route, or I'm tempted to discuss metaphysics with the door-to-door religion peddlers who are usually the bane of the at-home worker's existence.

Jobs planning meetings and seminars are real plums among your freelance pickings, paying well and making relatively modest demands on your work week. And you, a freelance writer, are exactly what the planners are looking for. You can easily accommodate a temporary assignment and, unlike others who may also be available at the moment, possess continuing connections with the working world.

Jobs as meeting planners are among those bonuses I promised you for working as a writer where you're least expected. In metropolitan areas, staging conventions and meetings may be handled by staff members who concentrate in those areas, or turned over to firms that specialize in putting gatherings together. In smaller, more remote communities like mine, the opposite is the case. Staffs are spread thinner, and there are few or no full-timers plying this highly specialized field. Conventions and meetings come up infrequently enough to gain a lot of attention among their sponsors—and to inspire a mild but real sense of panic in the overworked, overextended men and women responsible for seeing them carried out.

Your skills and freelance work schedule make you an ideal candidate for these undertakings when they do come up. The meeting's sponsors are looking for someone with professional credits who's plugged into local promotional and professional circles. Yet most with these qualifications are already employed full-time, and a juicy six-month job still isn't sweet enough to entice an employee into leaving a permanent position. You'll probably find when you apply for these positions that your own credentials are easily the best of the field of unemployed or underqualified applicants, while your freelance style of doing business is exactly what the doctors (or the plumbers, or the social workers, or the ad hoc planning committees) ordered.

I wouldn't have become such an avid supporter of meeting planner jobs, I think, if I hadn't agreed to try one during a weak moment.

The time was early 1977, remembered by feminists and their opposites as International Women's Year. A national conference on women's issues was to be held later in Houston; to prepare for it, all fifty states were charged with holding their own conferences to discuss major concerns and elect delegates to the big convention.

Those were the first days of my freelancing, and friends still tended to worry that I was really unemployed. One who was a member of the planning committee asked if I'd like to take on the part-time executive director's position to publicize, organize, and generally nail down the meeting.

Did I jump at the chance? Of course not. I was a writer, not a trail boss. But those weeks of waiting for editorial acceptances had already begun to stretch a little longer than anticipated, so the salary was distinctly appealing. Most of the duties, besides, tallied neatly with work I knew I could handle: writing brochures and press kits, news releases, federal reports, and the like. Of course I could book a few rooms and order coffee and work with a committee of twenty-six fine, outstanding women, most of whom lived some hundreds of miles away and were unlikely to be around often.

Famous last words. But through the ensuing brouhaha— inevitable with any sizable, strong-willed steering committee—I learned enough about pulling a program together to savor future opportunities in the field. The meeting did get off the ground in four months' time and was quite a success, one of the larger voluntary nonpolitical meetings held here in recent years. It has led to other statewide meeting assignments on topics as far afield as revisions in our state commitment code for the mentally ill and how to handle the daily stresses of farm life.

I've taken on a series of meetings a couple of times a year ever since. They've enabled me to meet all kinds of people from stress-ridden farmers to the head of the state hospital for the mentally ill to perfectly amazing women activists who've gone on to national prominence. Those projects have helped me set up some ground rules that apply to any meeting:

Identify the committee members or leaders of the sponsoring group who are likeliest to do what they say they will. Do not, under any circumstances, ask the rest to help with matters that will affect the smooth flow of the meeting you're planning. Let the procrastinators be in charge of subgroups that are clearly identified as their personal area of action; then develop contingency plans in case they do fail to remember to come.

Have the chain of command spelled out for you before you accept the assignment. Then stick to it, ignoring all enticements to take shortcuts and alternate solutions after the decisions have been discussed and made.

Watch for signs of serious internal dissension among the sponsors. If they're arguing or show signs of getting a good row going, the benefits of the assignment won't be enough to prevent you from wondering why you were born.

Have fun with the job. Taking it too seriously is foolish, for it's only a moment in time (and without a by-line, at that). The potential for real enjoyment is very high in planning meetings, making new friends, solving day-to-day problems with common sense, and being paid to have your mind opened to new concerns and issues.

Successfully planned meetings lead to other kinds of assignments as well, especially those more closely related to your writing expertise: public information campaigns, newsletters and publications, even speechwriting or ghosting for the nonverbal experts who "star" in your show. I guarantee you'll come away from the experience with at least a fat handful of new story ideas, even the introduction into a new field. And don't forget your salary as the meeting's planner.

Tracking down these assignments is not just a matter of knocking on doors and showing your samples. There's a less tangible element involved: You have to be ready to stand up when they call out for volunteers. The wider your network of friends and acquaintances and the more who know of your freelancing, the better your chances of pouncing upon opportunities when they first come into sight.

Some opportunities simply turn up in the want ads.

These are sponsored by the unfortunate souls who don't know anybody dependable free to take their part-time, short-term project. Don't be afraid of applying for these, even if they are blind ads. If you find you're not interested after learning more, you can always say no. And if the sponsors' original plans aren't to your liking, you may be able to negotiate changes that suit you better. More than any other position the sponsors will ever advertise, these jobs are flexible and open to negotiations on services to be provided and salary to be extracted in return.

Another spot to make your predilection for planning known is at your chamber of commerce. Even in smaller communities like mine they are busy establishing convention and visitors' bureaus to attract and serve those planning major gatherings of all kinds. Their motives are clear—conventioneers spend (according to the national average) about a hundred dollars apiece for every day they're in town. The more convention-planning services available locally, including your own ready assistance, the more appealing your chamber's delegation can make their city sound.

The manager of Bismarck's convention bureau has been a stalwart ally for turning up leads on meeting-related assignments. She fields questions regularly about who's available here to handle a whole bundle of meeting-planning tasks, and often has referred coming conventioneers to me.

Your commercial writing clients are also sources of information on meeting-planning jobs. They may be interested in your service themselves if you let them know of your interest, for public relations personnel of business and government are often the contact points for sales meetings, professional seminars, and conventions.

Ask a few critical questions of anyone who proposes to hire you before you accept any of these planning positions.

Can you work in your own office? The right answer is yes. Otherwise, the job can easily eat up much more of your writing time than it should require. If it doesn't fit in with your writing schedule, it's probably not worth whatever it pays.

Will you be reimbursed for basic expenses like telephone, supplies, and mail costs? In almost any legitimate case the answer will be yes, but be sure to get these points cleared up before you spend any money out of your own budget.

Is there a clerical support staff? Don't agree to become a glorified secretary. A lot of paper must pass through the mail to bring the average meeting or workshop to life.

What is the chain of command? Get it laid out clearly, then go over it again. Try to have it in writing, just in case.

What functions will volunteer planning committee members play? Who gets the final say on conflicting plans? Again, get answers down clearly—then circulate a copy among the committee to insure that everyone understands.

Some of these questions may seem unnecessarily mechanical. But they're going to come up in one form or another in the course of planning any gathering. Since your position is a novel one for most groups, there is no fund of tradition to fall back on. Safeguarding yourself with a job description and a very clear body of instructions will prevent the kind of nervous eruptions of temper or dissatisfaction that undermine even the best-laid plans.

Planning meetings of many kinds can be a refreshing break in your writing program. It enlarges your professional contacts enormously, both among local sponsors and the visiting city managers who attend the gathering you've pulled together. One job leads to another; one or two meetings well planned and well received may elicit more offers than you can easily manage, and you'll have the luxury of picking and choosing the most interesting.

Face-to-face assignments present you with variety, satisfaction, and a chance to recharge your creative batteries. Whether you speak to a convention or help plan it, teach a class or advise clients one by one as a consultant, you get to share your professional insights and gain new perspective on your own field through the eyes of others.

You get paid for it.

It can be fun.

And it's the ideal antidote to writer's cramp.

Epilogue

As I write this, winter's coming on strong in North Dakota. I've never savored more the advantage that writing bestows on my daily routine.

This is the perfect season for freelance writing. While others are out at 7:30 scraping ice from car windows and battling every hurdle nature blows before them, I'm in front of the draft-free fireplace. The dog curls up behind my chair and just rolls over when I head to the kitchen for coffee, to the front porch for mail, or to the living room for my daily luncheon installment of "Days of Our Lives."

From my desk, I can hear the mailman crunching up the driveway bearing my ration of rejections, checks, correspondence from clients and editors, maybe a long-anticipated acceptance. I still count his visit a high point of the day, but I don't have time to wait at the window for his arrival anymore.

Editorial and commercial assignments are both in full swing here in winter. Everyone gets very serious about saying what they think they need to say and making sure others hear it. The farmers have time on their hands to listen.

You couldn't ask a better time to be a freelancer. Except maybe summer.

Freelancing is a real joy during the North Dakota summer. That's the time for traveling, camera and notebook in hand, to gather a winter's worth of stories, photos, and leads—a time all too short, but sweeter for it. While the farmers are out sowing, spraying, and looking anxiously at the sky, so am I. Few assignments go to market in the summer, but a pleasant sense of urgency underlies the gathering and nurture of fresh ideas. Leisurely interviews, lazy travel. All this somehow is harder, scarcer when the summer ends.

Fall might be the best, though—a great time to freelance on the prairie. I wake up to geese honking southward just before dawn. Dime store displays of pulpy tablets and pencil boxes still remind me of going back to school to write the Great American Essay: "What I Did During My Summer Vacation." I do that too: wrap up a summer's worth of experiences that had all of leisure's virtues but portend well for sales. Fall's time to enjoy the harvest.

Spring sows new beginnings, new enthusiasms. Those are what keep freelance writing fun, more than all the late mornings and by-lines and words that sound just right to your own ear. When you come down to the magic ingredient that makes writing possible in your own hometown, it's the little green growing things that prevent boredom, keep thoughts fresh, and augur well that you'll be writing—and making a living at it—in years to come.

Across the country, my counterparts work to the same comfortable rhythms. Someone's sitting on Martha's Vineyard in July, typing in surges to the lapping of the surf. Another takes notes on nature while the family fishes on a cold Canadian lake. When the leaves turn in Vermont, a writer's already thinking of stories to bring to market next spring, while a Detroit writer's summing up the auto crop for the year to come. Mardi Gras's assignment time for a team in New Orleans. A Georgian watches peach trees bloom from her office. A Nebraska writer takes time out in August to drive a grain truck from field to elevator.

Our work knows seasons, but few daily bounds. The hours from breakfast to the evening news aren't set aside from the real fabric of my life. Freelancing has reattached my days and spun the edges of career and avocation into one long skein.

I work roughly four and a half days a week from nine to five. Some days are longer; I experiment with different hours for writing and for detail work from time to time, and always hope to find a new corner to chuck all phone calls. Some days—especially summer days—are shorter and farther between.

Calling these hours in my office "work" is merely a salute to conformity. They don't feel like work. They often don't look like work, either, since you find me doing much the same after my hours are up. I enjoy what I do that much. (I'd always hoped to be able to say that, without adding one single "but . . ." Another goal realized.)

I don't observe a strict schedule of "writing" and "regular life." When the thought strikes, I write it down, whether my neighbors are watching "Three's Company" or my mother is setting up the holiday feast. My work spills over into national holidays, Saturday mornings, and family trips to the badlands. I don't mind. Writing is part of my life, like reading or baking pies. It's welcome wherever it fits.

Writing is addictive—not only for the hours spent pursuing elusive thoughts, but for its new beginnings. Infinite beginnings. Next year always holds a degree of mystery, a tantalizing aura of what is possible. As a freelancer, I can sample the best of all career worlds: the security of developing a skill that's scarce and valued by the settled world; the dynamic ability to make things happen in my life rather than flowing along with some anonymous current; and the adventure of not knowing exactly what comes next. If it were a book, you'd read long past midnight. But freelancing isn't fiction, and it doesn't have to have an end.

Nor need there be limits—of geography, of income, of what one can accomplish.

I don't need New York City or any other megalopolis to be a successful writer. I've learned that; I'm a writer here. If I don't need to leave to write, I don't need New York at all. I suspect I share that realization with thousands of writers all over the country, as well as thousands more down in the concrete hollows of New York itself, who're there only to seek the opportunities they've always heard bear fruit only around the Big Apple.

About the income mentioned in the title of this book: You

can believe it. It is well within your reach. It's a reasonable goal, surely not the highest amount one could make writing from wherever you happen to live. My gross income has been in that range since the first year I began freelancing here in Bismarck. Had I accepted every assignment I've been offered, I could pump the figure substantially higher.

That twenty thousand dollars represents, to me, a different kind of superlative. It's not the most I could possibly make. Nor is it the least I could expect if I assigned my time to projects with the longest odds and highest risks of failure. Instead, it's a comfortable compromise. It allows me to live the life I want to lead, and still maintain that balanced writing diet—a good proportion of work for income to work more nearly for love. It keeps my options open. It underwrites experiments. It prevents freelancing from becoming its own kind of rut, the dread routine that knocked me loose from the salaried world in the first place.

Being able to stay afloat as a freelance writer isn't a fluke. No, it's the surprise result of an experiment in writing that worried me as much as it worries you right now. When I began I really did not know whether I could do as well on my own as I had done for sundry others. Could I last more than six months where so many writers prudently fear to tread?

I can do it. You can do it. They could do it, too, if they overcame their brainwashed fear of the unknown and set out to chart untested, exciting waters.

Learn what your part of the country is waiting to offer you. Make the best of what you've got. Don't ignore the half-hidden opportunities that aren't quite what you'd always envisioned. Stretch your visions—stretch them as wide as your horizon.

Geography gives you back every opportunity you thought it denied you:

Markets for your writing. Research sources and story ideas. Lucrative assignments that bring out your best, and the chance to try new techniques and new approaches.

You don't have to hit the trail to the metropolis to gain those options. All you need to do is open the door to the many ways you can use your address to your advantage. Lean on your geographic strong points. Shore up the weak ones; New York isn't perfect either.

Freelancing is not a low-energy occupation. You have to go after it—want it badly enough to make some adjustments in what you expect and where you expect to find it.

But I think the life you'll get to lead is worth every adjustment. I want to confirm your suspicions about freelancing in the country.

You *can* make a living as a freelance writer wherever you live right now, whatever you may have thought a week ago, whichever routes you choose to follow. If you want the freelance writing life strongly enough, you'll manage to make it happen right on the spot that you call home. It is real work. It is a real challenge. And it's everything you'd want it to be . . . the best way I can imagine to make a living.

Index

Accountant, 30, 53
Advance (book), 148-149, 153-154, 165
Advertising: authors, 160; copyediting, 180; editing, 172; ghostwriters, 184; lectures, 250; meeting planning jobs, 256-257; (in) newspapers, 116; radio and TV programs (sponsors), 204, 206; regional magazines, 111-112; stringers, 123; travel writing subjects, 90-91; Yellow Pages, 41
Advertising agencies, 25-26, 215, 219
Agents, literary, 151-152, 156
Artists, commercial. See Graphic design(ers)
Audio-visual, 190-210; equipment, 193, 195-196; filmstrips, 190, 198-199; income from, 190-191, 199-200, 205-206; jargon, 193-194; narration, 194; photography for, 193, 197, 200; radio, 190-191, 202-207; scriptwriting, 190-191, 195, 197-202; slide/tape programs, 190, 191-199; television, 190-191, 201-210
Authorities, for magazine stories, 86-87; as book authors, 159; as lecturers, 246
Autobiographies (ghosting), 181-182
Background, technical for writers, 74; for producing media campaigns, 225; for consulting, 251
Bargaining, 65-66, 248
Books: advantages of writ-

ing, 143-145; checklist
for publishers, 164-165;
illustrations for, 129; national publishers,
145-152, 165; outlook for
publication, 145; pre-
mium (sponsored), 161-
165; query and sample
chapter,150-151; regional
publishers, 152-156, 165;
researching markets,
147-148; rewards of
writing, 165-167; self-
publishing, 156-161, 164-
165; subsidiary rights,
149-150; topics, most sa-
lable, 146; vanity press,
156
Brochure(s), 56, 136, 214,
216-223
Cameras, 133, 135-139, 193
Catalogs, 214, 223
Clients, commercial, 22-
23, 25-27; best bets for,
27-28; consulting, 250-
252; freelancers, advan-
tages of, 55-56, 215;
grants, 239-240; how to
research, 27; meeting
planning, 254-255; needs
of, 219-220; retainers,
226; working for,
211-215
Columns, newspaper,
114-120
Commercials, radio and
television, writing of,
203, 205-206, 208
Commercial writing, 68;
annual reports, 222;
benefits of, 211-215;
brochures, 216-223; cata-
logs, 223; consulting,
250-252; freelancers' ad-
vantage in, 213-214;
grants, 238-244; media
campaigns, 224-237; use
of photos, 135-136
Consulting: for national
firms, 124-125; for local
and regional clients,
245, 250-252
Contacts, 28, 32, 172, 215-
216
Contracts, writers', for
books, 149, 163-164; for
ghostwriting, 188-189
Copy editing, 168, 178-181
Copywriting. See Televi-
sion, Radio
Correspondents, newspa-
per. See Stringer
Deductions, tax, 50-54, 67
Editing, freelance, 168-178;
Also see Copy editing,
Ghostwriting
Editors, 168-169; advan-
tages of using freelan-
cers, 55-56; book (work-
ing with), 166-167; catching the interest of, 24,
24, 84-85; copy editors,
166-167, 168, 178-181;
freelance, 168-178;
ghostwriters as, 181-189;
hiring a, 182; how to
meet, 76-79; in person,
25; media campaigns,
working with, 225, 227-
228, 230-231, 234-235;
newspaper, 114-122;
photo, 127-133, 135, 138;
skills needed by,
173-174; sources of in-

formation, as, 23, 25; trade publications, 123-124

Entertainment, business expenses for, 50-51

Experience, needed by freelancers, 33-34

Exposure (photographic), 138-139

Fees, billable, 60-61; flat, 64-65; setting hourly, 62-64; *Also see* Rates, hourly; Income

Fiction, 145-146, 153

Film (photographic), 132, 136, 139-140, 198

Filmstrips, 190, 198, 199

Financial reserve: investments as source of, 29; limiting need for, 30; moonlighting as source of, 30; requirement for, 29

Flexibility, need for, 14-15, 55

Focus (camera), 138-139

Foundations, charitable, 238, 240, 242, 244

Freelancers, full-time: 7, 14-16; advantages of, 55-59; disadvantages of, 31; emotional reserves of, 31; female, 39; routine, daily, 260-261; *Also see* Income and specific topics

Fringe benefits, 55, 60-61

Fund-raising, 162

Furniture, office, 41-42

Ghostwriting, 181-189, 203, 215, 250

Government, grants from,
238, 242; news (as stringer), 125-126; working for, 61

Grants, writing of, 238-244

Graphic design(ers), 44; books, 159; brochures, 216, 217, 221; cost of, 44; do-it-yourself, 222; finding, 221-222

Guidebooks, city/regional, 158

History: books, 153-154, 158-159; magazine stories, 89-93; photographs, 134

Home office, 38-40

How-to books, 146, 158-159; illustrations for, 135

Humor, books, 146, 154-155; newspaper columns, 119-120

Ideas: magazine stories, 84-86; newspaper column, 115-116; running dry of, 10

Illustrations. *See* Photographs

Income, freelancers', 9, 14-15, 61-65, 261-262; audio-visual, 190-191, 200-201; books, 163, 169, 171; commercial assignments, 212, 216; consulting, 252; editing, 171-172, 180-181; ghostwriting, 187-189; grants, 243; media campaigns, 226; national magazines, 100-103; public speaking, 248-249; radio and television, 205, 206; regional magazines, 106-107

Inspiration, stories, 89, 95-96; books, 146

Interviews, 47-48, 87

Lenses (camera), 137-138

Letterheads. See Stationery

Library(ians), 23-24, 86, 148, 174, 192

Light meters, 139

Lobbying, 125-126

Locale, how to research, 22; in book publishing, 171-172, 178; national perception of, 24; personal experiences in, 94-95; as stringer from, 120-126

Magazines, national, 6, 15, 16; payment by, 100-103; relative profitability of writing for, 68, 69-71; topics, easiest to sell, 89-100; topics, hardest to sell, 71, 79-81; topics, location neutral, 81-84

Magazines, regional: advantages of writing for, 35-36, 104-106; definition of, 107; illustrations for, 108-111; rates paid by, 106-107; sponsorship and audience of, 111-112; working with freelancers, 107-108

Mail. See Postage

Market listings, 81-84;

Markets, regional, 6, 18; scouting out, 24-25; Also see specific subjects

Media campaigns, 214-215, 224-237; charging for, 226; contacts within media, 230-232; news releases; photographs in, 233-235; public service announcements, 237; radio and television coverage, 235-237; subject for lectures, as, 246-248

Meetings, planning of, 243, 245, 253-258

Moonlighting, 26, 30, 38

Movies. See Scriptwriting; Audio-visual

Narrators, audio-visual, 194-195, 197, 199

Negotiating. See Bargaining

News conferences, 227, 236-237

Newsletters. See Editing, freelance

News media. See Newspapers, Radio, Television, Media campaigns

Newspapers: approach to stories, 85; dependence on news releases, 227-228, 230-231, 235; as experience for freelancing, 33-34; gaps (in coverage), 115-116; as markets, 104, 106, 107, 113-122; payment by, 114-122; prejudice against commercial work, 212; publicity for authors, 160; releases for, 224-225, 227-230; stringers for, 120-122; syndication, 118; working with freelancers, 122

News releases, 224-

225, 227-237

Nonfiction, in books, 146, 147-148. *Also see* Magazines, national and Magazines, regional

Office, 38; furnishing of, 41-42; home, 39-40, 50; rented, 39-40

Office supplies, 42-45

Outdoors: books, 146, 157-159; radio and television programs, 203, 204-205; stories, 93-94, 128-129

Overhead, business: accountant, 53; advertising, 41; answering service, 49-50; entertainment and travel, 50-51; equipment, 42-43, 195; office, 40-42; supplies, 43-45; telephone, 40-41, 47-50

Pay-on-publication markets, 100-102

Personal experience, books, 146; stories, 94-95

Photographer(s): amateur, 132-133; becoming a, 133, 136-142; equipment freaks, 136; husband-wife teams, 142; studio, 131-132; working with, 132-133, 193, 197

Photographer's Market, 130, 202

Photographs, 127-142; fees for, 130-131; income from, 127-130; media campaigns, in, 233-235; newsletters, 172; quality of, 132, 138-140, 233-235; regional magazines,

110-111; releases, model, 134-135; rights to sell, 129-130; uses of, 133-134

Postage, 45-46, 87-88

Presentations, sales, 215

Printers, 27, 159, 173-175, 217-218, 222-223

Processing, photographic, 139-140, 198-199

Producer, television, 209-210

Production. *See* Graphic design, Printers, Television

Production companies, audio-visual, 201-202

Programs, radio and television. *See* Radio, Television

Public information services, 211

Public relations: agencies, 25-26, 34; assignments, 211; media campaigns, 224-237; *Also see* Commercial writing

Public service announcements, 203, 207, 237

Publishers, national, book, 145-152, 165

Publishers, regional, book, 145, 152-156, 165

Queries, 11, 71-72, 82-83, 135; to agents, 151-152; for audio-visual jobs, 201-202; for books, 150; grants, 241

Radio, 190-191, 202-208, 230, 235-237

Rates, hourly, 62-63, 101-103, 107; books, sponsored, 161-165; commercial work, 216; consulting, 252; media campaigns, 225, 227; writing for less than, 106-107

Records, keeping 50, 52-53

Releases, model, 134-135

Religious, books, 146; stories, 95-96

Research: Local sources for, 85-87; by mail, 87-88; *Also see* specific subjects

Résumés, 183, 185-186

Retainers, 226

Rights: editor's, 177-178; photographic, 129-130; subsidiary, 149

Royalties, book, 144, 148-149, 164

Rural books, 146; stories, 96-97

Salesmanship, 13

Sample copies, 81-82

Savings, 29; *Also see* Finances, reserve

Scriptwriting, 190-191, 195, 197-202

Secretary, 40; avoiding need for, 43; part-time, 50

Self-discipline, 11-12

Self-publishing (book), 145, 156-161

Single-lens reflex camera. *See* Cameras

Slide projectors, 193, 195, 196

Slides, photographic, 132, 191-194, 197-198

Slide/tape programs, 192-199

Slush pile, 71-72

Speaking, public, 245-250

Speeches, writing, 186-188, 249-250

Sponsored books, 145, 161-164, 165

Stationery, 43-45, 75

Stock photo agencies, 129-130

Stringers: for commercial firms, 124-126; for magazines, 123-124; for newspapers, 120-122; payment of, 125

Syndication, newspaper, 114-119

Tape recorders, 193, 196

Teaching, 245, 247, 252-253

Telephone, 40-41; best use of, 47-48; communicating with editors via, 76, 78; interviews, 88; rates, 47-48

Telephone answering services, 49-50

Television, 201-211, 230, 235-237

Trade magazines, 97-100, 123-124, 128-129

Transparencies, photo. *See* Slides, photographic

Travel, books, 146, 153, 158; magazines, 89-93, 115, 128-129; radio and television, 203

Travel expenses, 50-52, 88

Travel writers, 89-93

Typewriters, 38-39, 42-43

Vanity press, 156

Other Writer's Digest Books

General Writing Books
Beginning Writer's Answer Book, 264 pp. $9.95
Law and the Writer, 240 pp. $9.95
Make Every Word Count, 256 pp. (cloth) $10.95; (paper) $6.95
Treasury of Tips for Writers (paper), 174 pp. $6.95
Writer's Resource Guide, 488 pp. $12.95

Magazine/News Writing
Craft of Interviewing, 244 pp. $9.95
Magazine Writing: The Inside Angle, 256 pp. $10.95
Newsthinking: The Secret of Great Newswriting, 204 pp. $11.95
1001 Article Ideas, 270 pp. $10.95
Stalking the Feature Story, 310 pp. $9.95
Writing and Selling Non-Fiction, 317 pp. $10.95

Fiction Writing
Creating Short Fiction, 228 pp. $11.95
Fiction Writer's Market, 504 pp. $15.95
Handbook of Short Story Writing (paper), 238 pp. $6.95
How to Write Best-Selling Fiction, 300 pp. $13.95
How to Write Short Stories that Sell, 212 pp. $9.95
Secrets of Successful Fiction, 119 pp. $8.95
Writing the Novel: From Plot to Print, 197 pp. $10.95

Category Writing Books
Cartoonist's and Gag Writer's Handbook (paper), 157 pp. $9.95
Children's Picture Book: How to Write It, How to Sell It, 224 pp. $16.95
Guide to Greeting Card Writing, 256 pp. $10.95
Guide to Writing History, 258 pp. $9.95
How to Write and Sell Your Personal Experiences, 226 pp. $10.95
Mystery Writer's Handbook, 273 pp. $9.95
The Poet and the Poem, 399 pp. $11.95
Poet's Handbook, 224 pp. $10.95
Travel Writer's Handbook, 274 pp. $11.95
TV Scriptwriter's Handbook, 322 pp. $11.95
Writing and Selling Science Fiction, 191 pp. $8.95
Writing for Children & Teenagers, 269 pp. $9.95

The Writing Business
Complete Handbook for Freelance Writers, 400 pp. $14.95
How to Be a Successful Housewife/Writer, 254 pp. $10.95
Jobs For Writers, 281 pp. $11.95
Profitable Part-time/Full-time Freelancing, 195 pp. $10.95
Writer's Market, 917 pp. $15.95

To order directly from the publisher, include $1.25 postage and handling for 1 book and 50¢ for each additional book. Allow 30 days for delivery. Prices subject to change without notice.

For a current catalog of books for writers or information on *Writer's Digest* magazine, *Writer's Yearbook*, Writer's Digest School correspondence courses or manuscript criticism, write to: **Writer's Digest Books, 9933 Alliance Rd., Cincinnati OH 45242.**